FOUR CORNERS

WORLD BIKE RIDE

4 teams of 4 cyclists riding to England
from Bolivia, Hong Kong, Zimbabwe and Australia

BY
MIRANDA SPITTELER

The Oxford Illustrated Press

To Mum and Dad
a token of thanks
for the gift of life

The Oxford Illustrated Press

ISBN 0 946609 86 1

Published by:
The Oxford Illustrated Press Limited, Haynes Publishing Group, Sparkford, Nr Yeovil, Somerset BA22 7JJ, England.

Haynes Publications Inc., 861 Lawrence Drive, Newbury Park, California 91320, USA.

Printed in England by:
J. H. Haynes & Co Limited, Sparkford, Nr Yeovil, Somerset.

British Library Cataloguing in Publication Data
Spitteler, Miranda
Four corners world bike ride : 4 teams of 4 cyclists riding to England from Bolivia, Hong Kong, Zimbabwe, Australia
1. Long distance cycling
I. Title
796.6
ISBN 0-946609-86-1

Library of Congress Catalog Card Number 89-84453

Contents

Acknowledgements

With Four Corners I witnessed so much giving by so many that whatever I write here will be grossly inadequate. Though each individual was working towards the aims of the charity Intermediate Technology, I am extremely glad of the opportunity to express my heart-felt thanks to all those involved for the inspiration that their efforts provided.

First, it should be remembered that it was Andy Hansen who started the ball rolling with his idea of cycling round the world for Intermediate Technology. However, I am also personally indebted to many others for their support during Four Corners and in writing the book. Of these, my deepest thanks must go to Dick Crane. He is someone who demonstrates through his own activities that the impossible can sometimes be possible, and in doing so, encourages others to reach their own potential too. In the period of unwinding after the event, he would greet various comments of mine with an emphatic 'that should go in the book' — a book which I had never planned to do. The last thing I thought I was capable of or even wanted to do was write a book, and without his faith and enduring powers of persuasion it would not have been done.

My thanks also go to the World Bike Riders for the use of their diaries. The colourful accounts of their experiences were often written in the most difficult of circumstances, when they were in a varying state of exhaustion at the end of each day. Their dedication to the ideals of Intermediate Technology led them to undertake the mammoth task of not just pedalling thousands of miles, but also the enormous workload of spreading the word about I.T. Their effort was the inspiring force which got so many others on their bikes raising money for I.T. My thanks to them also for their very helpful criticism of the book, especially Jo Doran, Sebastian Best, and Norman Carr.

I would like to express appreciation for the enduring love and affection of my closest friends. Especially Helen and Alisdair Liddle for being there whenever I needed them and to Freddie and Robbie Coles-Riley for their frankness, honesty and words of wisdom which I so valued during Four Corners and whilst writing the book. Also my thanks to Helen Alexander and to Manina Weldon, both of whom read parts of the manuscript and gave essential feedback at its earliest stages.

I would also want Brian Hansen, Hallam Murray and Nick Crane to know how important their unstinting moral support was, both during and following the event. They gave more than just their time and energy and became regarded as mentors and friends by myself and many of the riders.

Certainly I would like to thank Jane Marshall the Editor at Oxford Illustrated Press, whose job of dealing with a first-time author was no mean task and who brought greater coherence to the book.

Finally, and most importantly on behalf of all involved, I should like to thank the staff of Intermediate Technology in the UK and those the riders met out in the field. Without the motivation provided by the aims of that organisation Four Corners would simply not have happened. Special thanks to their Press Officer, Steve Bonnist, who played a particularly important role in firing all the riders with the enthusiasm about I.T. which they carried with them along their routes. I am also personally grateful to him for finding the time to read and re-read the manuscript despite his mountainous task of ensuring the general public continue to hear about the work of Intermediate Technology.

Four Corners brought some of the best people together, behind the scenes here in London, with the UK events and throughout the world, linking them in an incredible energy of goodwill and I count myself amongst the very fortunate to have been in the privileged position of being part of something so special.

Introduction by Steve Bonnist, I.T.

The ruling passion, be it what it will
The ruling passion conquers reason still.

Alexander Pope, Moral Essays, III 153

The story of Four Corners is rooted in passions. Everyone concerned with it was driven by passion, whether it was for something they individually wanted to achieve for themselves, Intermediate Technology, or people in developing countries. These desires, these ruling passions, were the engine of Four Corners, and without them nothing would have been achieved at all.

But passions also have a way of creating chaos, even if they are directed at roughly the same end. They over-ride objectivity, trample reason, and stifle practicality. The means become vested with more power than the ends. They can tangle and strangle, and threaten the object of desire.

It is, looking back on the tumultuous two-and-a-half-year life of Four Corners, a miracle that it survived the stresses and strains it — and all those connected with it — underwent. Some say it should have been strangled at birth; some say it could and should have aimed higher, others lower. Whatever people's feelings, Four Corners was, in the end, a triumph over diversity and adversity. 'All's well that ends well.'

To understand Intermediate Technology's involvement with Four Corners, it is necessary to go back a few years, to the winter of 1982. Although commanding a great deal of respect overseas, the charity was little known in Britain itself. Most of its funding came from the British Government's Overseas Development Administration, trusts, foundations, other charities (such as Christian Aid and Oxfam), large corporate or individual donors, and earnings from consultancies undertaken overseas for organisations such as the World Bank or the UN agencies. Very little came from the British public itself, which is not surprising, as the charity had few resources with which to publicise its work. The Fund-raising Office consisted of a fund-raiser and a secretary, and the Information Office had two officers and a secretary, whose main work was more concerned with answering enquiries and briefing and debriefing visitors from overseas. There was no Press Office, no Development Education Officer, and no money in the budget for normal charitable fund-raising endeavours such as advertising, direct mail appeals, or organising street collections.

One quiet Christmas holiday night, as I sat watching the dire fare on television, my 'phone rang. It was Winifred Dalby, our Fund-raiser, wanting to know if I could come in the next day and meet two lads from Cumbria who wanted to raise £5,000 for us by running a marathon 'or something'. That was a lot of money to us in those days! So, the next day I trudged into our old Covent Garden, London offices, fully expecting to hear that these two brothers, Richard and Adrian Crane, planned to run around Basingstoke in scuba-diving gear or race around Trafalgar Square dressed only in nappies on New Year's Day. Over a cup of tea, I found out that their idea was even more bizarre: they planned to run the 2,000-mile length of the Himalayas in 100 days — alone.

To make a long story short (read their book on the adventure, *Running the Himalayas*, to get the full impact!), these two left just a few weeks later for training in Nepal, and by June, they had hit the headlines all over the world. Their 101-day run from Darjeeling, India, through Nepal, and over to Rawalpindi in Pakistan on the roughest racetrack in the world — the Himalayas — was the stuff of legend. These 'eccentric, mad Englishmen' achieved real fame, appearing on television and radio for weeks thereafter. Everywhere they went, they spoke about Intermediate Technology and its work, appealing for money. Eventually, £80,000 was raised, which is no mean feat in itself, as I.T. had spent no money on advertising or street collections. We depended mostly on the media to mention our name and address as our main 'mechanism' for raising money. The response was all the sweeter because people had to really *want* to send in their donation. There were no collecting tins rattling under their noses and no pre-addressed, freepost envelopes at the ready to make giving easy.

Although I.T. spent very little money directly on Running the Himalayas, the success of the Venture (as we began to call such events) did cost the charity time and effort, particularly by letting me pursue the thing day and night for six months with the media. This was my first real contact with the media in the six years I had worked at I.T. and I approached the job with a great deal of trepidation, quailing at the idea of phoning *The Times* or the BBC. By the end of it, though, I was playing the BBC against ITV to ensure that both had television crews covering the finish in Rawalpindi.

After R.T.H., Richard Crane went on to hit the headlines by winning the Quadrathon — billed as 'the World's Toughest Race'. Once again, there was that grinning, handsome beast sporting an Intermediate Technology T-Shirt pictured in all the papers under the massive headline, 'Superman'. He then won the Krypton Factor Celebrity Special on ITV, receiving a cheque for £1,000 to be donated towards our work. There was more — much, much more — and for the first time my colleagues and I began to meet people who actually recognised the name of the organisation we worked for.

All of this coverage generated literally millions of pounds-worth of free coverage for the charity, once hardly known except in rather select circles. This was all very exciting, but I was soon back in my usual job of Information Officer, answering the rather larger load of enquiries, giving lectures to classes of Third World Studies, and briefing visitors from Sudan or Thailand.

Then began the trickle that later grew into a flood. Yachtsman Chris Smith approached us with the idea that we rename his boat 'Race Against Poverty' for the duration of the 1984 Observer Singlehanded Transatlantic Race. The BBC, pleased with the two Radio 4 documentaries made about 'Running the Himalayas', agreed to make another about Chris' effort. The Radio 4 'Today' programme agreed to broadcast live two to three times a week during his crossing, and Chris generated lots of local coverage on TV and radio. Three days into the race, his boat hit a submerged container and cracked in two, sending him home to port. But we did get that documentary (as Chris recorded his disappointment on a Walkman on his sad journey home) and £8,000 in donations.

There were good lessons in this nearly disastrous Venture. For one, it had never occurred to any of us that Chris might not make it across the Atlantic! We simply assumed that, once the publicity was arranged, it would all happen, just like 'Running the Himalayas'. We did not think about the risk to Chris or the charity's name if something went wrong. Our only concern was that he might not win his class, as expected! 'Race Against Poverty', then, taught us to try to be more careful and to think through the possibilities in advance, to 'look before you leap!'. It is a lesson easily forgotten, though, in the face of enthusiasm, and one which few proposers of Ventures have patience with, or understanding of, when they themselves are so confident of the success of their quest.

Meanwhile, Intermediate Technology as a whole was undergoing a massive change itself, growing from what was once a tiny group of enthusiastic volunteers to an organisation of over 100 enthusiastic professionals. The demands for our assistance were increasing dramatically, but at the same time, we were having to approach our work in a different, more in-depth way to achieve the sort of successes we and our overseas collaborators were aiming for. We were finding that developing or adapting technology hardware was the easy part of our job. The hard part was more subtle in nature, requiring longer, more sensitive investigations into what people really want and need and whether the skills, resources, customs and environment really could support any changes in the way things are produced. 'Development' is a much more complex process than most people realise, and consequently more boring to explain in the hopes of enlisting support. We were just managing to maintain our overseas projects support, but we were not generating enough income to the charity to cover new developments, publish new books for people in the field (invaluable to them, but they always lose money for us), or run our free technical enquiry service. We needed to expand the means to bring in money, but didn't have the money to do so. Ventures, then, remained a key way of bringing in money.

At Christmas of 1984, Richard Crane and his cousin Nick Crane took off to Kenya and Tanzania, for their zany, front-page winning Venture, 'Bicycles Up Kilimanjaro', which raised eyebrows, smiles and £30,000. Intrepid mountaineer Martin Moran raised another £30,000 by becoming the first person to climb all 277 Scottish peaks over 3,000 feet (collectively known as 'Munros') in the dead of winter. Both Ventures resulted in books (*Bicycles Up Kilimanjaro, Munros In Winter*), and masses of publicity for the charity.

These singular feats by singular people required a great deal of personal day-to-day effort on my part to achieve their aim: to give the charity a low-cost introduction to the public. While we could not hope to raise millions this way, we could engender interest and perhaps enlist more people to go out and raise funds and create more publicity for us, to extend our own meagre resources further.

Then, as a result of the successful coverage given to the Kilimanjaro Venture in the *Sunday Times*, the paper approached us to become the main beneficiary of the National Fun Run in September, 1985. This is the largest mass running event in Britain, with 33,000 people jogging through Hyde Park. As of this writing, we received more donations than any other charity before or since from the day — £33,000 — no doubt due to the much higher profile gained by our other Ventures.

Suddenly, we were inundated with ideas from people wanting to raise money for us by undertaking all sorts of serious and not-so-serious activities: we had sponsored Morris dancers dancing across the Severn Bridge; raft races down the Tyne in Newcastle; 15 canoeists paddling down to London from Lancashire, while Brian Wilson canoed all the way round Scotland (read his book *Blazing Paddles* for the account of this adventure), two 19 year old lads running from John O'Groats to Lands End, a 20 year old girl riding her horse from Lands End to John O'Groats and Life Ride UK's Bike Ride. By the summer of '86, we had dozens of mini-ventures on various roads, paths and ponds around the world, with a few larger exercises looming, one of which was Four Corners.

Four Corners

When Andy Hansen first proposed a 'Round The World Bike Ride' to Intermediate Technology in August of 1985, the massive success of Band Aid in raising funds for Ethiopia was still reverberating through the minds of the public, media and charities. Band Aid had both positive and negative facets to it: on one hand, it raised an enormous amount of money towards relief, rehabilitation and long-term development in Sudan and Ethiopia. Geldof himself had gone to particular lengths to stress the need for the type of change necessary to ensure that such famines do not strike again. On the other hand, however, the media very often projected a negative and patronising image of Africa, reinforcing prejudices about the abilities and even the will of Africans to work themselves out of poverty. There was also the worry about what could ever follow such an event; wouldn't everything be judged in its light? In Intermediate-Technology-Speak, would 'Small' Ventures ever be 'Beautiful' again?

The Four Corners proposal changed dramatically when Miranda Spitteler came up with the brilliant idea of changing the plan to bring teams of four cyclists from the four corners of the earth back to London. This would provide a real focus for the Venture, which is part of what the media needs, to make a Venture into an event that people want to follow. It is a principle we learned the hard way: with 'Running the Himalayas' the Cranes provideds a start — Darjeeling — and a goal — Rawalpindi. Their last Venture, 'Journey to the Centre of the Earth', was constrained by the need to keep their goal secret: the Cranes did not want anyone to know that they would be aiming for the furthest point on the planet from any open sea, because it happened to be in China near the Russian border. They did not want to be arrested, entering a sensitive military zone! Thus, the 'Will they make it, bet they won't' principle could not and did not work, at least in publicity terms. (Most of the publicity happened after the event and very little money was raised from the Venture.)

With Four Corners hoping to attract masses of sponsored people on their bicycles, they needed advance publicity of the 'Will they make it' type. Miranda's innovation could help provide that, but it would not be enough, I thought, because of the time factor. The four teams would be covering a lot of ground through a lot of countries, but the public and the media simply cannot maintain their interest in an expedition over such a long period of time (one team would be on the road for nearly a year). It needed something at the end to provide razzle dazzle, attract the sponsors and the media, and therefore public support and participation.

The Finale, then, became the most vital aspect for Miranda and her team to plan and get funding for, if Four Corners was to succeed. If a vision of what the media would see and report could be prepared, we thought that the sponsors needed to fund the operation would be eager to come forward. After all, commercial sponsorship of charity events is not really about philanthropy; it is about image projection and advertising. Sponsors want to be able to visualise where their banners will be hung and if and how often the TV and press cameras will be able to see them. Their calculation is really based *not* on how many people are present at the event itself, but the potential number of people who will be able to see or hear about their association with such a 'warm and caring event'.

Four Corners, despite strenuous efforts on their part, never really found the funds it needed to achieve its real potential because it never really found the vision of the Finale until the last few months — by which time it was too late. Potential major sponsors would indicate their interest, then fade. And without major sponsors, Four Corners could not bring in people with experience in mounting mass-participation events on a full-time basis. For months on end they had to rely on a dedicated, passionate covey of volunteers. This was frustrating for all concerned, especially Miranda, upon whose shoulders the whole project rested. But it was also frustrating for Intermediate Technology.

The charity had several reservations about the project, mostly centring around risk. One problem concerned its legal liability if anything went wrong, even though we had helped set up Four Corners as a separate, legal entity to protect us from just such an eventuality. We worried about the risk to the charity's name if the project collapsed or if there was a 'disaster' for whatever reason, and we were publicly associated with it. We also worried that 4C would engulf us: if no sponsorship turned up, we might be morally obliged to devote more and more of our staff time to it, diverting us from our real work overseas; if it *did* receive major sponsorship, the project could swamp us as well, requiring supplies of printed information, posters, stickers and other paraphernalia which were not budgeted for, as well as for the entire staff and all our overseas collaborators to pull out the stops to help keep the media happy. Either way, some staff felt that the whole thing was far too risky, particularly to our overseas commitments, which we are always hard pressed to fulfill.

On the other hand, it must be said that there were many of us in I.T. that desperately wanted Four Corners to succeed. People who work for charities do not do it for the money, they do it because they have a dream, a desire, a passion. To see that vision, a reality requires support from others, morally and financially. Four Corners offered us the chance to put over our message about what can be done and achieved in a less patronising, more positive way. It could be a 'crusade' to counter the negative images that the Ethiopian famine produced in the public's mind. It could bring in desperately needed funds, too, to expand our programmes and to support others working on long-term, sustainable development. And deep down inside, some of us felt it would give us legitimacy. No-one in charities likes to admit it, but there is competition between us. I.T., despite its outstanding record overseas, has always been overshadowed by the large agencies. Some of us wanted to show them and the world that we, too, can and should be up there on a plinth with Oxfam and Save The Children. Institutional hubris then, was another factor in the relationship with Four Corners.

I.T., it must be admitted, was not an ideal partner for Four Corners. In fact, it could be said that, if Bob Geldof himself had come to us with his idea for Live Aid, we would have balked, as we simply do not have the resources to back up such events.

When Four Corners came to us at the very beginning, they said they would find the money, equipment and staff to run the project and would not divert charity funds or staff time and would only seek our advice as necessary. Obviously, with such an enormous project we had to be involved at decision-making level and as such this meant that we would have to do far more than just offer advice. However, at the outset, Dennis Stevenson, our Chairman, said that we could not back the venture 'Until we see the whites of the sponsors' eyes'. There were a number of occasions where this seemed to be the case and what we should have said was we needed to see a signed contract which represented the cash backing needed for the venture.

It has to be remembered that Four Corners wasn't the only fund-raising venture that was happening at the time. Other events were also demanding more and more of our time and energy than the press and ventures office — myself, a secretary and Richard Crane (by then seconded to us by British Petroleum) — could effectively handle. Nevertheless, the charity, given these changing circumstances, did what it reasonably could for Four Corners.

The continuing bind of overworked, yet enthusiastic volunteers wanting and needing more and more from the charity, and overworked I.T. staff finding it difficult to deliver, was a source of friction between the two. When sponsorship funds failed to materialise, this friction occasionally produced heat. Passionate people from 4C clashed with equally passionate development workers from I.T. The charity's institutional priorities — which meant trying to guarantee the long-term success of projects and programmes overseas — collided with 4C's short-term priorities. Arguments arose about how much the event should be publicised, with Four Corners taking the stance that, without massive publicity, they could not attract commercial sponsorship or tens of thousands of sponsored 'bums on saddles', and Intermediate Technology worried that inflated claims in the media about what *might* happen ('the World's Biggest Bike Ride Generating Millions!') could be embarassing in the light of the cold, current reality. Optimistic proposals concerning potential markets for merchandising of T-shirts were constantly being poo-pooed by I.T., as there was no sponsorship guarantee of capital to buy the merchandise in the first place or guarantee that 4C could mount a large enough event to attract media attention and therefore the people to buy anything! Four Corners in London, with I.T.'s blessing, arranged for the African Trail team to meet with the Pope, but they declined to do so; I.T. maintained that, as they work through a number of Catholic development organisations, particularly in South America, Africa and India, such a visit would be productive, but the African Trail team felt otherwise, and cancelled at the last moment. Although both were trying to achieve the same end, they had differing opinions about the efficacy of the means.

All this may sound as though Four Corners was doomed from the start. The lack of an expressed vision for the Finale, the lack of sponsorship and therefore the lack of experienced, full-time management, the lack of consistent signals from I.T. and, as you will see from this book, the emergence of conflicting objectives of some of those involved in Four Corners itself — all of these things should have meant total failure.

But, The Four Corners World Bike Ride was not a failure. The riders made it back safely, having pedalled tens of thousands of miles through 42 countries, enduring hardships and pain as well as receiving welcomes and pleasures undreamed of before they began. Millions of people around the world read or heard about the Ride and Intermediate Technology. Thousands participated and raised tens of thousands of pounds to help others not only stand on their own two feet, but to move forward. Intermediate Technology gained many new friends around the world as a result of Four Corners. And the dream still lives that someday, Four Corners may ride again.

Intermediate Technology would like to express its thanks and appreciation to all those who struggled so hard and gave up so much to make Four Corners possible: Miranda; the team of volunteers in London; the riders; those who organised local events; those who took to the road to raise funds in so many countries; the sponsors; the creditors (who showed so much patience); the bands, entertainers, mayors and friends in the media — all these people and many more. Their passion overcame reason in the end to make it happen against all logical odds.

PART ONE

Good Vibrations

May 1985 . . . a filthy grey summer's day and I stepped out of the office where I worked in Covent Garden to attend a meeting that would begin the most important part of my life. A few days earlier I had seen an advertisement in the London listings magazine. 'Cyclists wanted for round the world cycle ride in aid of Intermediate Technology. Need not be experienced.' I felt compelled to pursue it. I'd *never* bought listings magazines, but this one was lying around the office and I was casually flicking through the pages. The words leapt out at me as though they had been printed in bold and yet the advertisement was so small that it would have been easy to have missed it even if I had been looking for that sort of thing — which I hadn't. However it struck a chord with an idea I was musing over at the time — I wanted to cycle across China.

I telephoned Andy Hansen, the chap who had placed the advertisement and we arranged to meet in nearby Neals Yard, an alternative haven for wholefoodies. Neither of us had told the other what we looked like and we could not have appeared more different. It was me that spotted Andy amongst the milieu of lunch time gatherers; he was tall, dark and lean. He was wearing an old black track suit and the fluorescent band and protective cycling helmet that proper and sensible cyclists wear. His palid and malnourished look was made more apparent by a five o'clock shadow.

I felt most inappropriately clad in my pair of very ancient long baggy men's shorts. They were so big that belted in with the turn ups turned down they adapted skirt-like for the office. Ideal for pedalling but not terribly chic. I was also wearing a garish pair of paisley-patterned tights! We were an unlikely pair to say the least.

There was no handshaking or any of that stuff and the two of us sat on the nearest step as he unfolded some ideas about what he wanted to do. 'I thought it would be good to get some people together to cycle round the world, maybe over a couple of years or something,' he said. There was no plan as such but it would constitute the world's biggest bike ride; it was going to need massive planning and sponsors.

Andy had been inspired by Richard Crane and his cousin Nick's 'Bicycles Up Kilimanjaro' expedition. Earlier, with his brother Ados, Richard had run the length of the Himalayas. Both of these exploits had been done to raise money for the Third World charity, Intermediate Technology (I.T.). All this began to ring bells, though I wasn't terribly familiar with what Dick, Nick and Ados or I.T. had done.

Andy had first come across I.T. when he was studying at Bristol University. He explained: 'Well, instead of food aid they work with communities all over the developing world to provide long-term solutions to extreme poverty and famine. More like preventative medicine than cure. It's all about using locally-available skills and locally-available low-cost materials that won't harm the environment or the culture but will enable people to work their own way out of poverty. You know the sort of thing, instead of tractors and combine harvesters which often end up rusting because there aren't the parts or fuel to maintain them locally, they help improve the methods and technology already in use. Let me give you some examples: improved and more efficient ploughs so more food can be grown; locally manufactured water pumps to provide desperately needed water and so on.'

It was 1985 and the publicity over the Ethiopian famine was at its height. There was masses of public support for emergency relief . . . but what was going to happen after the millions of lives had been saved . . . ? Also, the problem wasn't just in Africa and I.T. operated in most areas of the developing world. And wasn't this long-term, I.T. approach just what Bob Geldof had been saying was needed? So why didn't more people know about this charity? I thought it was brilliant and I was pretty certain that if others got to hear about it they would too. This World Bike Ride would have to be unique if it was going to capture the public's imagination and be used as a publicity vehicle for I.T.

It had begun to pour with rain but we barely noticed as ideas streamed out. I wasn't at all sure what I could offer. I was a secretary and not a very good one at that. Still, the odd bit of typing would come in useful. Andy had been unemployed for some time and this was a real case of getting on his bike and doing something! What we needed were people with lots of different skills and resources to join us.

I had just left a job of two years at Worlds End Studios, a small businesses complex offering services such as advertising, film production, accountancy, public relations and much more. This had given me an insight into all the facets that might be needed to make this idea work, I realised I might have some useful contacts. 'My friend Jeremy's in advertising, maybe he could design the logo and his company can come up with a catchy name, and Polly knows someone pretty high up in Operation Raleigh, he can tell us how you organise something like this, and I think my friend Manina knows the European MD for Coca-Cola, this would be ideal for them to sponsor, and James Cane, I'm sure he knows Prince Charles, he can tell us how we should ask for his support in the right way. If these people can't help then maybe they would know who could.'

First things first though. We thought we should get someone involved who knew a little more than we did about bikes! Andy had confessed that he knew very little and I certainly didn't — the first thing that went wrong with my bike and it was down to the menders. In fact the chap that usually mended my bike was just round the corner and that wouldn't be a bad place to start. It would be our first chance to see how someone reacted to the idea. We charged down the road through the pouring rain and gained our first interested recruit — a possible route mechanic. 'Yeah, you find the backing and I'll do it.' This was Glen Thompson, a character with flowing blonde locks, who from a distance looked like Greystoke, Lord of the Apes. I was beginning to like this diversity of characters!

A quick synopsis of our cycling experience showed that neither Andy nor I had done more than the daily jaunt to and from work. The London to Brighton Bike Ride was coming up and since Andy would be otherwise engaged I was to ride this and try recruiting cyclists on the way. We parted and I arrived back at work very late, very wet and announced that I was going to pedal around the world! This raised a quiet smile and a 'Well before you go off and do that, perhaps you'd like to type these letters for me' response from my boss. There was soon to be no more 'lunch' hours; these were valuable times for meetings or typing letters, and for the next two years or more, they simply didn't exist.

Qualifications

How on earth I thought I was capable of riding round the world in aid of Intermediate Technology I don't know. I wasn't a traveller, had barely heard of Intermediate Technology and was only *just* what you might call a cyclist.

Memories of my earliest attempt at cycling brings me out in little red bumps — I borrowed my brother's bike and fell off bang in the middle of a large clump of nettles! It was the height of summer and I was wearing the minimum of clothing, hence when I came a cropper, it had the maximum effect.

I was seventeen and living in Norwich when I acquired my first set of pedals. I'd just left home and was living with Lulu in an old fireman's cottage in the centre of town. Lulu and I were inseparable pals who not only lived together but worked together as waitresses in one of Norwich's most upmarket restaurants. We were the youngest of a team that was half heterosexual and half homosexual. At the end of the evening the two head 'waiteresses', Jimmy and Mark would do a 'Hinge and Bracket' duet in the bar. Being just a stone's throw from the restaurant, customers could bring their brandies back to the cottage after closing time. Having led a very sheltered existence at home, it was a great introduction to life, not to mention an education.

The reason for mentioning all this is that Lulu was very much a part of my early cycling days and returns to Four Corners later. She was also involved in the test run on my first bicycle. It was an ancient red boneshaker and in keeping with its vintage I dressed for the part, wearing a white Edwardian tunic found in a local junk shop. Lulu was bang up to date in the tightest of jeans and rode pillion; her legs too restrained to pedal. The trial run took place on Elm Hill in Norwich, a beautiful cobbled street full of timbered buildings. There was blue sky and sunshine and the place was buzzing with tourists. The best way we found to create a clear path was for me to bunch my skirts up, and both of us to kick up our legs and roll down the hill singing 'Good Vibrations' at the top of our voices.

Sadly, my first bicycle and I parted company when it was stolen and it was only when I came to London some years later that I acquired my second bicycle. I was working as a receptionist for a meagre wage in one of London's 'deluxe' hotels. Bus fares proved far too costly and the obvious solution was to pedal the seven miles a day to and from work. Cycling in London traffic developed the necessary fearlessness for competing for wheel space with London cabbies, red buses and juggernauts and it became my regular form of travel and fitness.

These then were my pedalling credentials — which weren't that dissimilar from Andy's who like myself, was more of a commuter cyclist than anything. However, he was deeply involved in all kinds of sport and so was much fitter than I. Once involved in Four Corners though, I did some catching up on the fitness with all the meetings I found myself having to attend, sometimes clocking up to 40 miles a day.

It was a fair time after I had arrrived in this world before I set foot on foreign soil. Indeed, Intermediate Technology's very own explorer, Dick

Crane, called me 'the traveller who 'ad never bin anywhere'. At that point my most interesting travels had been experienced second hand through my father. He had spent the first 35 years of his life in India and so my five brothers and sisters and I grew up with tales of rogue elephants, man-eating tigers and the odd python wrapping itself round his neck. In fact, India was so much in his blood, that when we lived in Paignton above the zoo, our dinner table was in such a position, that mealtimes could be spent taking pot shots at the giraffes and peacocks. Not literally I hasten to add — especially since he always claimed to get them bang between the eyes!

Later, in Norwich, Lulu and I discovered that as well as having other similarities in our family backgrounds, our dads had lived almost side by side in India. In fact, they were members of the same Colonial Club at the same time. The fact that they hadn't bumped into one another was no doubt due to the club rule that those of mixed blood, whatever status they held, were not allowed into the same area of the club as those who were 'True Brits' — and though my Dad is as British as can be, some of his ancestors were Indian.

My father was the Chief of Police of the Madurai District in Southern India and had been in charge of Ghandi's security when he was in the area. As such, when I mentioned the 'small is beautiful' approach, he was familiar with this philosophy already. However, this was not reflected in the view he held that the best donation that could be made to the Third World was a massive batch of condoms! Whilst undeniably, population control is a very important element of development, it doesn't get to the heart of the matter in the way that I.T.'s approach does.

I was 18 when I first took off overseas for a week in Greece. The day before I left, Sue, my eldest sister rang to say she had booked a flight and would join me out there. I later heard that this was the work of my mother worrying about her youngest being taken off into the white slave trade (she really did!). Suzy returned to London but for me the week extended into a 3½ month stay. My Greek experiences involved fighting off a Greek shipping tycoon during a journey in a tiny mirror-lined lift in Athens; a spy appearing in my room one afternoon with his head bleeding and bandaged, and my first proposal of marriage!

Apart from some uneventful backpacking in France, my next jaunt was a week's crewing on a yacht down the south coast of Spain with Sylvia, a deaf, retired school teacher at the helm and two squabbling business men. Since the week began with me bolted up in a brothel in Malaga (the only available room in town), I was grateful when we made it to Gibraltar in one piece.

If these things could happen to me on my minor travels, then a World Bike Ride had lots of potential for the unexpected.

Andy's record on this front would be far more useful. Born on the 9th of October 1962 he shared the same birthday as John Lennon and Bob Geldof and like them he too had a desire to 'change the world'. Andy's parents worked in the German Diplomatic service and soon after their son was born they moved to Sierra Leone. Here he spent his first few years being 'stung, bitten and gored' by the indigenous fauna — building up his resilience for 'events' of later life. At five, he became a football enthusiast in Rio de Janero and another five years on he found himself in Mozambique, from where he went to boarding school in Swaziland alongside Nelson Mandela's children. Here his interest in football was replaced by a passion for politics, which was kindled further by a stay in Malawi and then Namibia. Eventually, he went to live in the 'clean streets' of Germany and shortly afterwards went to school and University in Britain, where he studied philosophy and politics. After graduating in 1984 there were a series of jobs as a porter, salesman and even as Father Christmas at Harrods. This was followed by a spell as a volunteer at Friends of the Earth which is when we met...

These then were the two people who had the gall to play a major role in organising the world's most ambitious sponsored cycle ride that would take in some of the world's most arduous terrain, would encounter every climatic variation and pass through countless different races, cultures and religions...

The Inspiration

The day after my meeting with Andy, I went straight round to Intermediate Technology to get more information about them. They had a little shop in King Street off the Covent Garden Piazza and I got as much literature as I could lay my hands on. I also spoke to Winifred Dalby from Fund-raising and asked if they had any jobs since I thought the best way to learn about I.T. was from within. 'Oh, and by the way, I shall be pedalling around the world in aid of I.T. with this chap Andy, is there anyone we can talk to about that?' After the Cranes' antics, Winifred must have had stacks of people coming in offering to do all sorts of wild fund-raising ideas. 'Oh you're going to do a world bike ride for us, well I'd better put you in touch with Debbie Hill, she's cycling from London to Athens solo.'

Debbie worked in Cranks, the wholefood restaurant in the Covent Garden Piazza and so we had a few meetings over Cranks' salads. The more I learnt about I.T. the more fired by enthusiasm I was, especially when I found that whenever I explained my plans to anyone, I also had to explain the charity. Then it seemed all the more obvious that they needed something to give their work a major focus; something which would demonstrate the concept of Intermediate Technology. It is this which eventually made Four Corners so unique amongst other fund-raising expeditions: it was never a case of deciding to do a bike ride and then the charity being an afterthought, I.T. was the heart and inspiration of the whole thing, the reason for setting it up in the first place. Indeed, the expedition would be designed specifically to fit the charity.

In coming into contact with I.T., I was much reminded of the film 'Ghandi' which I had seen a couple of years previously, for I.T. wholeheartedly embraced the Ghandian philosophy of the 'village economy'. One of the images of that film that impressed me most strongly is the aerial view of the Salt Tax March as it gained momentum on its way to the coast. It looked wonderful, as it started out with just a few people and gradually built up to thousands as more and more people filed in from tracks and roads to join in. When I leant across and whispered to my friend, Liane, 'Wouldn't it be wonderful if it could happen today right across the world!', she dismissed it with 'Don't be so potty Miranda!'.

Later, after I met Andy, the major charity event that was happening was Live Aid, the 'global jukebox' that was broadcast by satellite to millions around the world. On the 25th July 1985 I was with friends who didn't possess a television. Even though we were not watching or listening to it, Live Aid dominated the conversation the whole evening. Like most, I had done my own bit of fund-raising for it, choosing a sponsored fast. In a climate where people are becoming more and more materialistic and self-centred, Live Aid provided a breath of fresh air in restoring faith in human nature. More than anything it created awareness of the need for long-term help in the Third World and Bob Geldof showed that ordinary folk like us could do something about it. The timing for something like Four Corners seemed ripe.

Soon after this I was to meet for the first time, Dick Crane, who was now seconded from BP to work full-time at I.T. on fund-raising projects. Andy had already met him and seemed in awe of him. Not knowing what he looked like, but knowing that he was a mountain-climbing cyclist and geologist, I imagined him to be a bearded, well-girthed bloke who brewed his own beer. I was not aware that amongst Dick's many accolades he had won the award for the Fittest Person in the World, so he was obviously in much better shape than the odd picture I had painted. He was a lot younger too, clean shaven and sporting a surprising little pig tail.

We also met in Neals Yard and I took him to lunch and used up all my luncheon vouchers for that week. This time I was wearing tartan tights and Dick commented 'You've had your legs tattooed haven't ya?' He was really enthusiastic and encouraging: 'It's sort of natural that this should be the next big thing for I.T.,' he said. 'And Andy, 'e's like the cycling one of you two then is 'e?' I wholeheartedly agreed and smiled to myself at the memory of the aches and pains from the London to Brighton ride. However, this made the two of us a balanced partnership: Andy the cyclist and me the secretary. I went away carrying with me some of his infectious enthusiasm and Cumbrian accent, and reported back to Andy that we had had a 'dead good meeting' and everything was 'brilliant eh?'.

Learning more about what Dick, Nick and Ados had achieved for I.T.; that they had raised at that time over a £100,000, and what they went through physically to achieve this, gave us inspiration and helped get over those difficult bumps that arose in trying to get Four Corners off the ground.

Andy had spent the last of his dole money on the *Time Out* advertisement, and when after a few days no-one other than me had phoned, he reported that he was going to find himself a job. It was some time before I could get him to meet again.

I know that for Andy as well as for me, we would not have chosen to travel or work together had it not been for the fact that it was for Intermediate Technology. Lacking the confidence to do it alone and thinking that for something as special as this personalities should be put aside, we both persisted, thinking we should just get on with it. He was the one with the brains and the worldly knowledge and on our first meeting, he had said that he wanted a situation where things would happen so fast that he wouldn't have any choice about doing it. As my contribution, I thought that with my energy and determination I could create that situation.

It wasn't until some time later that Andy revealed how he had come upon the idea of doing the World Bike Ride. He had always wanted to do some major world trip, and possibly by bike. One morning while he was unemployed he was watching the Bill Cosby Show. Bill Cosby was giving a lecture to his daughter telling her that if she really wanted to do something then nothing would get in her way. This is when Andy got up and went and placed his advertisement.

Bill Cosby has a lot to answer for.

An Idea Is Born

It wasn't until August 1st that Andy and I were to meet again. In the intervening nine weeks I had stuck up postcards in cafés and bike shops, had been stopping people on their bikes and telling them about the bike ride and generally had spent time just talking to lots of people about the idea. There had been quite a few enquiries and whilst many of these people were to come to later meetings, on this occasion, the first official World Bike Ride meeting, beside ourselves there was only one other: Sheila Ditchfield.

We met at the Royal Festival Theatre foyer, which was to be our 'board room' for some time. Whilst it was ideal because of its central location and the fact that it could accommodate a good number of us, it was a strange meeting place for travellers. There was always lots of activity going on around us and we'd usually find ourselves serenaded by bands playing in the foyer. However, once the main performance of that evening had commenced, we were left in peace and quiet to get on with our business — until the stampede in the interval as people queued up for ice-cream and coffees!

If we really intended to plan something this big, we were going to have to learn to be businesslike right from the start. I noted down everyone's ideas and action from the first meeting, so by the next meeting much to everyone's surprise, I was able to distribute copies of the previous meeting's 'minutes'. Never having attended any business or official meetings I didn't know how these should be done; the heading 'Agenda' was written 'Gender' and no-one pointed this out. None of us had the faintest notion of how to organise our plan at this stage.

As for the concept, it took several meetings to pin this (the first) down: a cycle relay across all continents, taking between 2 to 3 years. There was to be a core team who would complete the whole route with cyclists from the host countries joining along the way. As I was taking charge of the secretarial duties at this time, Andy was in charge of the route. Everyone attending the meeting was sent off to research the countries. One of the main factors for finalising the route would be which way the wind blew around the globe and when there were monsoons! I was allocated the task of researching this.

I had arranged to stay with Lulu for a few days at the beginning of September so I took my homework with me. She was now living in a croft miles from anywhere; the nearest town was Dundee. I borrowed a bike and pedalled off to the library to do my research there. The head winds were useful on this occasion because the bike didn't have any brakes, but I could imagine they would be most unpleasant in desert or mountainous terrain and probably ten times stronger.

So with the concept in place (we thought!), next we had to decide what to call it. There were all sorts of suggestions: Steve Bonnist, I.T.'s Press Officer had come up with 'Famine Busters'; it didn't get taken up, but at least it wasn't as boring as those that did: 'The Global Cycle Expedition', 'The World Bike Riders' each had a short innings before 'The World Cycle Relay' was chosen. None of us were that happy with it but felt too much time was passing and it was now more important to come to a decision.

Both Andy and I had discussed who should take charge of the overall co-ordination of the venture. It couldn't really be either of us since we wanted to ride and there would have to be someone who would be back at base while we were away. For starters we were to work as partners until this person was in place, though I think both of us thought this wouldn't be easy since we were too different in approach.

Meanwhile, I needed educating. I armed myself with a copy of *the* book by I.T.'s founder, Dr. E. F. Schumacher, called *Small is Beautiful*. I wasn't a great reader and I thought a book about economics would be a real effort but it was fascinating and after finishing it I was even more motivated to make our project work. The book wasn't all about the Third World either, but why 'small is beautiful' would be appropriate in a world of high unemployment. 'If we can recover the sense that it is the most natural thing for every person born into this world to use his hands in a productive way and that it is not beyond the wit of man to make this possible, then I think the problem of unemployment will disappear and we shall soon be asking ourselves how we can get all the work done.'

It may sound daft but at the time I hadn't really looked beyond the word 'development' in terms of what it meant for the Third World. To me it represented negative images of shuffling starving people being given food-aid. It was easy to despair of this since this approach was often only a temporary measure until the next time. There had to be a better life for these people than the unimaginable misery and suffering caused by living on the edge of starvation in extreme conditions of poverty; there had to be something that could break the vicious circle of dependency created by hand-outs. In fact, Schumacher's approach is rather beautifully summed up in his book.

> 'Give a man a fish, as the saying goes, and you are helping him a little bit for a very short while; teach him the art of fishing, and he can help himself all his life. On a higher level: supply him with fishing tackle; this will cost you a good deal of money, and the result remains doubtful; but even if fruitful, the man's continuing livelihood will still be dependent upon you for replacements. But teach him to make his own fishing tackle and you have helped him to become not only self supporting, but also self-reliant and independent.'

By the end of August about half a dozen people were attending meetings. The most committed of these were Lorna Barker and Sheila. I had met Lorna at Worlds End Studios when she was working there as a secretary. I had moved on to another job, but she had been pedalling past me one morning on her way to work when I stopped her.

'Hi Lorna, how's your job going?' I asked.

'It's alright, how about you?' came back a none too cheerful reply.

'Well I've got myself involved in a world bike ride in aid of the Third World charity Intermediate Technology, would you be interested in that?' I asked

'Well maybe, but what's Intermediate Technology?'

I invited her along to one of our meetings.

As for Sheila, I met her when she came to view one of the rooms in the flat where I lived. She had arrived from the other side of London by pedal power. Lots of potential there I thought, so I'd asked her 'would you fancy pedalling a bit further than you just have done, like round the world?'. She responded with a very stunned 'I beg your pardon?'.

I went on 'I'm helping to organise this world bike ride in aid of Intermediate Technology and I saw you rode here on a bike and just wondered if you might be interested'.

'What's Intermediate Technology?' she asked.

'It's the charity that the Crane brothers and cousins have been doing all their fundraising for — you know — "Running the Himalayas, Bicycles Up Kilimanjaro"?'

'Oh, I know. Yeah I'd like to know more about it.' (In an article this particular story had been slightly exaggerated and had said that I had told Sheila she could only have the room if she would do the ride — I wasn't quite that desperate!)

Out of these two it was Lorna who aspired to organising the whole event. What it really needed was a professional, someone who would get the necessary support and manage the project from beginning to end. Not one of us qualified for this task.

One of our requirements would be that of legal services. The previous Christmas I had met a barrister at a friend's wedding reception. He had on his client list many sports personalities and also wrote a column for the *Daily Mail*. He seemed an ideal person to help. When I telephoned he was enthusiastic and keen to meet. He said he could offer more than legal services. He was so forthcoming with ideas that I asked him what role he saw himself playing. 'I could act as the Director and give it the professionalism it needs.' He was impressive. At the end of half an hour I came away with a pyramid plan of action. In my notes of the meeting I had said he seemed 'genuine and honourable'! Like quite a number of people who meant well and who promised the earth, we didn't see him again. The pyramid plan, however, was very important in providing us with a good structure to work to and actually got us going in the right direction. Unfortunately we were still without someone to run our show properly, so this is where the search began for a Director and Co-ordinator.

There were other problems with our 'World Cycle Relay'. Potential cyclists were coming along to meetings but were being frightened off by the length of commitment of two to three years (and more including the pre-departure organisation). Whilst the faithful few kept coming, there were different faces every week. We all agreed the time span of the ride would have to be reduced to a maximum of a year — but how?

We had been at it for several weeks now and a great deal of time had been spent on the 'World Cycle Relay' but through our research we found that many others had gone round the world by bike before us and had got very little publicity as a result. Since that was one of our main objectives, we were going to have to create some new world record that would capture the media eye. We couldn't go for the speed record. Nick Sanders had just completed 'Around the World in 80 Days' and there was no way we could possibly compete with that.

I went and had a chat with Penny Little, an Account Executive at Camron Public Relations. I had stopped her on her bike and by coincidence her company dealt with accounts in the sports and cycling field and she spoke to several people on our behalf 'in the know'.

'Haven't you only got one chap involved in this thing?' she asked me.

'Yes at the moment, why?' I replied.

'Well, because, having discussed it with others, one of the ideas that came up was that it should be an all girl world bike ride, this would guarantee coverage!'

In my view this wasn't an option: it would mean dropping Andy who had originated the whole idea and it seemed likely that the media coverage we might attract would be of the kind that would detract from the serious message we were trying to put across. Her advice was that we would have to go back to the drawing board and develop a much stronger concept, something unique, a first ever.

Friday the 13th!

One night, very late after I'd been working, I decided that this question of concept was being dragged out too long and would have to be dealt with. I produced some very poor sketches of the world, and drew on them various route suggestions. Images and ideas went round and round in my head. Finally, at 3 am, I crashed into bed, no further forward, and lay panicking about how I was going to stay awake at work the next day. I was praying for sleep but no amount of sheep counting, awareness of breathing or any other relaxation technique would work. I tried clearing my mind of all ideas, but as fast as I did that, a whole lot of new ones would rush into my brain. It felt strangely out of my control: my heart was racing and head was pounding, creating the strange force which seemed to squeeze the idea out of me. A vision flashed across my consciousness like a hand reaching across the world, the four fingers as routes coming from the Third World. That was it! The thumb at the end would equal a ride which everyone could join in. A ride from the four corners of the earth with the Paris to London Bike Ride at the end! 'This is it! This is it! FOUR CORNERS!'

I leapt out of bed and went back to my desk to scribble it all down. I was so excited. After all the deliberating it had come so easily. It must be the right idea, it was so simple. I began rattling away to myself and pacing up and down in my room. 'Hang on a minute Miranda, how could *you* possibly have the right idea? No, it is right and it fits in so well with the I.T. philosophy of a small world. If people could pedal from four corners back to London then it demonstrates the small world theory perfectly'.

Any one of the four routes would take six months to a maximum of a year and all four could be pedalled at the same time. That would be great for the media too. With four routes there was far more story potential. I was so excited I could hardly contain myself. I desperately wanted to tell someone, but it was 4 in the morning. Lavender Hill Police station would still be open — I could go and tell them! I grabbed the first things that came to hand — which happened to be a fur coat and a pair of red wellingtons — and put them on. It only dawned on me that they might just decide to lock me up if I arrived looking like that as I was on my way out the door, and decided it might be safer to wake up Sheila downstairs instead. She listened sleepy-eyed to the wild-eyed lunatic standing in front of her, humoured me by saying it was a great idea and sent me back to bed.

First thing in the morning I rang Andy to tell him about the new idea. He wasn't too enthralled. Still, I thought I had better give him time to think it over before we all came together for a meeting later that day. At the Festival Theatre foyer Lorna and Sheila thought it was great. Andy still wasn't in favour. 'It will be impossible to organise,' he said.

'No it won't,' I said, 'we will have three or four people on each route and they can be responsible for setting up their own route which should be easier. Also they won't have to take account of such a variety of climates as going round the world would entail. Besides it'll be easier to recruit riders now with less time commitment involved.'

'It's going to be too cold for the Northern route,' he continued.

'There's no reason why all four routes should set off together, they can set off at different times according to the climate and distance they have to cover,' I replied.

'It's going to be too wide spread for the media to cover it' he said.

'Time wise it won't because it's condensed right down this way. Besides there will be much more story line for the media to use plus if there isn't much happening on one route then attention can be switched to another. Besides, it's much better for I.T., with all four routes covering areas that they operate in, then the riders will be able to visit projects and experience first hand what I.T. does,' I responded.

Andy wasn't going to let up and nor was I. I knew that the idea we had been working on had been losing steam and people were falling by the wayside. Reluctantly Andy came round to the idea, 'Oh no! This means all the hard work we have done has been a waste of time!' Maybe had the boot been on the other foot then I would have had the very same response. Andy had done a lot of route research and the idea of having to start again was daunting.

'All the work we have been doing has been necessary for us to realise that the first idea wasn't going to work and it's brought us to a new one which *is* going to work — besides, we'll be able to use some of the research you've done — in fact, I think we've made a major step forward!' (Oh how sickeningly positive! — how unbearable I must have been!)

Andy was magnanimous enough to say 'At least you're always

positive about everything'. A good sign. Perhaps we were beginning to recognise each other's attributes. Our constant challenging of each other could create a very healthy balance in the whole thing. I decided that this meeting should mark much better relations between us and that I would try and make more of an effort on this score. I can't say I was always successful at this. There were to be some very frustrating times ahead.

Anyway, for now it was maps out on the table and new job lists; we all went home with masses of homework to do.

Making it Work

The following Monday evening Lorna came round to my flat bringing her Four Corners files in plastic carrier bags to hand over her responsibilities to me. 'After Saturday, I realised it was actually going to happen and that it would require an awful lot more time and energy than I can give,' she told me. Sheila was there at the time too and said 'Actually Miranda, I'm afraid I've come to the same conclusion too'. I tried to persuade them to stay with the project but they had made up their minds — the first resignations. They were very apologetic and whilst I didn't quite know how Andy and I were going to manage our own work load as well as theirs, I knew that to carry people who were half-hearted would be much more difficult. We really were back to square one as far as people were concerned, though our commitment was even greater.

At this point Rebecca Langton came to the rescue. She had attended an earlier meeting but we hadn't seen her for a number of weeks. Rebecca was unusual. She was an extrovert 19-year-old Sloane Ranger working in a launderette. She had the most extraordinary accent of Fulham origin, which she produced with great force. Though Rebecca didn't stay around for very long, she was an important pair of hands at that time. In fact she also gave us one thing Andy and I could agree on: that Rebecca was a very eccentric character. She and I agreed that Andy was decidedly strange as well. I'm sure they had come to some similar conclusion about me. What an odd trio.

Others would come to meetings and we found ourselves endlessly wasting precious time repeating what it was that we were about and often we couldn't agree on this anyway. I found this extremely frustrating and suggested that we have an introductory meeting with a polished presentation of the whole thing. This way we could recruit riders and volunteers in one fell swoop. Andy said at the time that it was good that people should see this 'dirty laundry'. However the 'dirty laundry' didn't seem to be encouraging people to join us and thus he agreed that we should give the introductory meeting idea a try.

This took place courtesy of Derek Ground of the London Business School at the end of October. It was very well organised with name tabs for all those attending — about 70 in all — which was a great turn-out for what was a very cold and wet evening. Rebecca, with her authoritative voice, chaired this and each of us had titles with Andy as Routes Co-ordinator, Rebecca as Treasurer and me as General Secretary. There were information leaflets on each chair plus a lengthy and intimidating application form which was a bit like an exam. I had produced this so that people would take the whole thing very seriously.

After Andy and I had spoken about the organisation and routes, Dick Crane fired everyone with an inspiring slide presentation on the work of I.T. Afterwards he spoke about his expeditions: Running the Himalayas and Bicycles up Kilimanjaro whilst Peter Murphy described his experiences on the first ever mountain bike crossing of the Sahara which he and Tim Gartside had done together. Their brief had been to do everything they could to put people off the idea — to talk about the pain and hardships — but I think they had far more to do with the amazing enthusiasm that followed, than our amateur presentation. The idea of pedalling from the four corners of the earth really took hold that evening. There was a wonderful feeling that things were really moving. About a week later we got our first article in *Bicycle Magazine*. We also received about 50 application forms with all kinds of offers of help as well as potential cyclists. This was such an exciting landmark for us!

At this stage I wanted to appoint four route leaders; people with immense commitment to the concept of the venture who could then find and select their own teams. I'd been to an expeditionary symposium at the Royal Geographical Society and they had recommended this. Dick Crane too had suggested it: 'What you need is to get your Route Kings in place, one for each route, the rest will follow'.

I thought he was absolutely right and I'm afraid this is a point on which Andy and I disagreed. Andy wanted to get all 16 riders as quickly as possible and since each person was to be asked to put £100 in the central kitty for administrative costs, the money would have been useful too. I didn't think that was as important as getting the right people, but in the event Andy invited all positive applicants round to his flat and asked them to divide themselves into groups according to which route they wanted to do. That was the selection process.

This latest clash between Andy and I didn't help our already strained working relationship; the problem was that we were both strong and very different characters. It was Andy's girlfriend Shaheed who helped us. She told a friend of mine that she had never seen Andy so involved and enthusiastic about something. This was a side of his character that Andy hadn't readily shared with us, but knowing how he really felt made things a lot easier and made it all the more important that we overcame our problems. I thought frankness would be one route to this and told Andy that since we were to work so closely together that we ought to be honest about what we thought each other's best attributes were. This wasn't a terribly good idea and since in order to be assertive, I probably dealt with it in a rather aggressive manner, I don't know why I was so surprised when Andy told me I was a very brusque person!

One example of differing approaches was that Andy thought promoting the ride through CND would be a good idea. I, on the other hand thought we should remain absolutely apolitical and take I.T. to new markets. This image was particularly important if we seriously wanted to attract commercial sponsorship. At meetings it would be crucial that we should have a united approach. We didn't and it became a positive liability. Our partnership was simply not working, but as neither of us were prepared to give up we had to find a way to resolve it.

I felt Andy was more the brains and I more the salesperson and organiser. After much anguish over the whole thing, I confronted it again and this time suggested he take on the vital role of Routes Publicity and Routes Fund-Raising Co-ordinator. This was a huge task and since he was to travel on the African section, I thought his route would be an especially important focus for I.T.'s development activities. I thought I was better suited to continue selling and promoting the idea and that as such, I would not forget who it was that put the advert in *Time Out* in the first place. I would then be free to look for a partner with more professional skills to come to meetings for the wheeling and dealing. He agreed that this would be a good idea. Once we had our own defined responsibilities we got on a lot better and a mutual respect developed. We had unknowingly learned one of the most important lessons in man-management and successful team work — which is that people work best when given clearly defined areas of responsibilities and recognisable goals to work towards. Given these, people of wildly differing personalities, strengths and weaknesses can work together.

The World Bike Riders

Each World Bike Rider, by hook or by crook had to raise £3,000 to cover their subsistence expenses. Whilst some of those in employment could do overtime, it was particularly hard for those who had committed themselves full-time to the venture to raise this sum. Apart from using up the odd nest egg and the selling of worldly goods all sort of ingenious methods were used to get this money together. There was carol singing in Leicester Square with our own World Bike Ride version of 'It's a long way to Tipperary'; an art auction; the sale of strawberry teas at summer fetes and a mass sponsored fast. Four Corners Christmas cards were designed and sold and there was a sponsored bike ride from London to Wales. The most successful of all however was the African Trail team's raffle. Not surprisingly, with such enticement as a Luxury Nile cruise, this raised £2,000.

Others helped as well: Sarah Shaw, a gorgeous enthusiastic volunteer organised two 1940s dances and the Globe Trotters Club had a fundraising Christmas party two years running. On top of that, individuals, families and friends were extremely generous and backed riders to the tune of hundreds of pounds. As a last resort people arranged loans through their bank managers which they would have to pay off over months or, in a few cases over years, on their return.

Whilst most of the World Bike Riders were qualified up to the neck with degrees of one sort or another, this certainly wasn't a prerequisite of their joining. Having left school at 16 with 5 rather bad CSEs, I tended to operate on a more intuitive level and sometimes found this conglomerate of intellect a touch intimidating. Trained brains or not, everybody had a contribution to make. Whilst I was forced to exercise that somewhat out of shape muscle in my head, others found themselves developing completely new practical skills. In fact, though it might not have been realised at the time, an immense amount of individual development was going on all round.

The riders were organised into 4 teams of 4 people; one team for each route which had now been called 'The Americas Route', 'The Asian Highway', 'The African Trail' and 'The Oriental Path'. Each team member was assigned a specific role within their team: Leader, Publicity Officer, Logistics Officer and Route Photographer. These defined roles were to ensure that individual riders knew which tasks they were responsible for carrying out before and during the ride. They were also an attempt to avoid the major area of team dissension over who-should-be-doing-what situations and thus they went some way to safeguard against this.

The members of the teams were as follows:

The Americas Route Team

The Americas team was made up of Jo Doran as Leader, Alex Sfakianos as Logistics Officer, Meryl Channing as Publicity Officer and Thomas Harding as Route Photographer.

Jo Doran

Alex Sfakianos

Meryl Channing

Thomas Harding

Jo Doran telephoned me early in 1986 and we arranged to meet in a café on Lavender Hill. She looked a picture of health, with glowing cheeks and tousles of fair hair around a broad smiling face and very clear green eyes.

'This is a timely meeting since I am in the throes of deciding between two plans' she told me. 'One is to go to Australia for a year. The other is to apply to various development organisations to see if I can find some way to put my engineering skills to practical use in the Third World. In fact I.T. is an organisation I particularly admire' she continued, getting more enthusiastic and enthusing me too. 'I belonged to the Third World First Group at Bristol. That's where I heard about the use of small-scale appropriate technologies as an approach to sustainable development.'

She didn't want to particpate in any half-hearted way. It was either a full-time role or nothing. An ideal candidate. Whilst there was a jolly hockey-sticks air about Jo, the immediate impression was that she was strong (in the words of someone who knew her at the time, 'she's that tough she could eat bricks'), level headed and had immense commitment to the whole concept. I knew that she could bring a great deal to Four Corners as a whole, not just as a rider.

Jo's background was not run of the mill. Her early years were spent in Tittensor (a well kept secret until now!) in Staffordshire and then various parts of Africa until at the age of eight her family returned to England. Here she was sent to boarding school where she was told that her extra curriculum activities like building canoes and doing the Duke of Edinburgh Award Scheme would jeopardise her academic work. Whilst her contemporaries went off to become secretaries or took to the catwalk at Lucy Claytons, Jo went down a completely different path. Her initial months of work experience meant an apprenticeship in a mechanical engineering workshop; an all male environment. 'Nothing will shock me after that!' she told me later.

When she got involved in Four Corners, she was 23 and had left Bristol University the previous year, graduating with a BSC in Mechanical Engineering. She had heard about us through the Operation Raleigh in-house news letter where she was working as a volunteer in their expedition staff selection department. She was also a member of the Territorial Army. I hadn't met any women members before and asked her about this. 'I love outdoor activities so much and running about Salisbury Plain attacking each other and digging trenches is just like having another go at childhood — it's a lot of fun.' Whilst with the T.A. she had done a lot of team work and leadership training which I felt would be very useful indeed.

When Jo met Meryl Channing they immediately hit it off and decided they were going to ride together. She came on board full-time virtually straight away and spent the next couple of weeks living and working with me at Lavender Hill. It seemed obvious that she should handle the task of Riders Co-ordinator, one which she gladly accepted.

Though Jo came to the project five months after it began, she gave most in terms of herself and materially, selling her car and possessions in order to finance working full-time on the project and the trip itself. She was a pillar of strength to Four Corners and certainly to me. She worked relentlessly over the months leading up to her departure. She was far better than me at knowing when to stop and said later that when she stayed with me she just couldn't cope with the pace that I maintained. Whilst she was known to occasionally turn a deep shade of purple at the apparent lack of commitment on the part of the other riders, she managed to maintain sanity at the same time — a remarkable achievement in itself.

There was definitely a bit of an army temperament in Jo which earned her the nick-name of Sergeant Major Joan Higgin-Bottom! This manifested itself in a tendency towards intolerance and was a potential area of weakness in her skills as leader but she had so many other strengths that I felt she would be able to overcome most problems that might arise along the way.

I met **Alex Sfakianos** in January '86. He was 27 years old, a blond fit, Aryan outdoor type with an expedition background. He had ski-toured various parts of Scandinavia and the Atlas Mountains of Morocco and motorbiked across parts of Africa.

Alex was born in Yorkshire. That always bears well with me since I just assume people of that part of the world have a wisdom and natural down-to-earthness that we Southerners lack. He had a precise, quiet manner of speaking that suggested an introvert side to his character but showed a clear commitment to what we were trying to do.

He told of how many years spent in South Africa and seeing other parts of black Africa had developed a strong belief in the Schumacher/ I.T. approach to development. In fact, he and three other friends had already begun plans for a fundraising expedition themselves which would take them on a cycling and climbing expedition across Africa.

Alex soon demonstrated the depth of his commitment by offering his services to Four Corners and putting aside his own plans. He told me 'I felt that any competition would only detract from both our ventures and that this wouldn't be to I.T.'s benefit'. In his application form he had this to say of Four Corners: 'The World Bike Ride is an imposing and dramatic concept and will definitely be newsworthy. Major sponsorship and fundraising could well be the end result of the group efforts. All this channelled into I.T. could make a tremendous difference to a great many people worldwide. I hope that my taking part in it as a rider and a worker will help to make it happen.'

He was keen to get stuck in and I suggested he meet with the Americas Route team. He began helping on the running of the venture, working with Andy Hansen on route planning. Later he worked on equipment sponsorship and became a full-timer, supporting himself with the sale of his precious motorbike and odd bits of courier work.

With just weeks to go before the Americas Route departure, Alex turned up at the monthly general meeting with his right arm in plaster! A pedestrian had stepped out in front of him and in avoiding her he'd broken his arm. This meant he wouldn't be able to train in the Pyrenees with the team and join the others in finding out each other's mountain cycling abilities and ironing out any personality differences. This concerned me, since being so different to Meryl and Jo I felt this training period was important for the team and indeed Meryl and Jo had already expressed some anxiety about their personality differences. But with only 3 weeks to departure, it was decided that the team shouldn't be changed and although not tested in a team situation, Alex would go.

Meryl Channing was at the introductory meeting and I can remember her very clearly. She bounded across to me after the meeting swathed in scarves and jumpers. 'I've been in bed with flu but there was no way I was going to miss this meeting and now that I know what it is all about I'm just so excited — it's all so wonderful!' Shortly after this her application form came back 'I would die a happy person if I could take part in riding from one of the four corners of the earth!'

Meryl was the bubbly personality of Four Corners with a kind of dancing musical aura. She had a very energetic mind, a flair for creative dressing and a great sense of fun. It was hard to believe her 27 years with so much living under her belt already and a good career on the go. She had done a lot of travelling abroad: Israel, Greece, Canada, U.S.A., Sri Lanka, India, Nepal, Burma and China and it just so happened that she had been planning to go to South America. She was very much a traveller and whilst this formed a large part of her motivation for being involved, having seen parts of the Third World, she had a genuine desire to do something useful that might make a difference to the lives of the people there.

At the time, Meryl was working as a researcher with an international telecommunications consultancy but gave all her spare time to the project before working in the office full-time in the few months leading up to her departure. As Publicity Officer for her route there was plenty to keep her busy but she also worked with me on the publicity material and the sponsorship proposal. The latter was just endless grief. In the early stages when we didn't have an office Meryl managed to persuade her bosses to let us use their office and facilities in the evenings. There were weeks of slaving over a word processor, planning, reworking the copy and going over my ghastly spelling mistakes. Often we wouldn't emerge from her office in Wigmore Street in central London until the rest of London was starting its day. We would go home and collapse for a couple of hours before getting up and going off to work ourselves.

Something else we worked on together was merchandise. A memorable meeting was with Katherine Hamnett, designer of the 'FEED THE WORLD' T-shirts for Band Aid. She wrote offering to design our T-shirts. Meryl and I went along to meet her in her 'cave' in Islington. In it Katherine Hamnett was seated at a very large 'rock' table with a male assistant on either side.

'Hi, pull up a rock' she said. 'I've looked through your brochure, I love the pictures of the cyclists with the maps on their backs and hats on, that's really mad'. (Riders had had the routes painted on their backs and had been photographed on their bikes for our sponsorship proposal.)

Meryl had done her homework on the latest trends in cycle gear and discussed various makes, cuts and cloth of skin shorts. Katherine said she would do something in bright colours with messages on, lots of them, all over the gear. She was spilling over with slogans and talking of design, she said 'What is needed is something that will make people think "Can't live without I.T.", when they see it'.

'Is that another slogan?' I asked.

'What's that?', asked Katherine.

'Well, you just said "Can't live without I.T." and I thought that might make another slogan running down the side of the legs of the skin shorts.'

'Great idea' she said and so it went on. Four Corners would also get a mention — down the arms, up the legs, across the chest — and round the back there would be lots of appropriate messages!

Meryl and I shared some fun moments but I'm sure I caused her a good deal of frustration with my wanting to get everything just right. She must have quietly gritted her teeth because she never gave me anything but encouragement and inspiration with all her efforts. Out of all the riders I felt that she was more of a friend than anyone and there were tears when we hugged each other goodbye at the airport.

Thomas Harding at 17 years old, was the youngest of all the riders. His background of living in Hampstead and attending Westminster school was so privileged that I wasn't sure his feet were firmly enough on the ground for him to fit in. Thomas was a bright spark, and though a friend summed him up as 'the most spoilt young man I have ever encountered', he had other qualities that more than made up for that. He described himself as 'inexperienced yet dedicated to being involved with the ideals behind the trip'. He was deeply interested in I.T.'s approach to development and nurtured hopes of working in the Third World at a later date as an Engineer.

He was fit from head to toe as a result of playing masses of different sports. He read and wrote poetry, ran an Amnesty International group at his school, was editor of the school magazine, president of the debating society and had an obsession with teddy bears. On top of all this he was studying for his 'A' levels and as a result not much was seen of him until the weeks before the departure.

When he finally appeared at the office he could hardly contain his excitement and he was absolutely bursting with jolliness. Everyone loved him for it, but occasionally it was a bit too much for some. His voice would go up an octave or two and he would constantly quiz everyone in the office as to what they were doing and what the outcome of each and every phone call was.

On his birthday the other riders decided to entice him with a birthday cake to the dockside where he was ceremoniously dunked. Thomas took this extremely well and it later became something of a rider's birthday tradition.

Of all the riders, I was fascinated to see how the trip would affect Thomas. What an experience to have so young, especially after having had such a sheltered upbringing.

The Asian Highway Team

The Asian Highway team consisted of Nick Walker as leader, Kate Smith (now Walker!) as Publicity Officer, Jane Evans as Logistics Officer and Pete Cogram as Route Photographer.

Nick Walker and **Kate Smith** had been planning a trip by bicycle to Australia from London in aid of the Third World and decided to pool their energies with ours. They came to the project in early 1986. Nick, 27 years old was a landscape architect and Katherine, 25 years old, a nurse.

Nick Walker

Kate Walker

Jane Evans

Pete Cogram

This was very much a vocation for her. When Nick first met Andy Hansen and I, Kate didn't come along with him and I gave him a hard time about whether Kate was doing the trip because he was or if it was her own decision to undertake it. He reassured me it was the latter.

They really did represent the nicest couple you could hope to meet. Nick had a wonderful sense of fun and was a natural joker. When the going was tough and we were working into the small hours this lightened the burden of the work and fatigue. Kate had a very kindly disposition and was equally supportive. One thing which made them rather different from all the others, was their strong belief in Christianity; it was obviously a strong force in their lives and worked for them. Because of their full-time jobs they didn't work full-time on the Four Corners Ride until a few weeks before the departure and since at this time I was working at the I.T. offices I never really got to know them very well.

Not long before they left for their corner, they got married. I should think theirs was just about the most unusual year-long honeymoon that any newly weds could have.

Jane Evans, also 27 was brought on board as the 'Logistics Officer' though in truth this was a shared task with the others since she came to things rather late in the day and fitted the team rather than the remaining role to be filled. Her involvement came about when she bumped into me and heard about Four Corners. This interrupted her life as a freelance editor of technical literature. It was through the latter that she had learnt of Intermediate Technology.

Jane entered into the spirit of Four Corners with such a passion that she won everyone's admiration. Her determination to raise her £3,000 for the trip was quite remarkable since she had little time in which to achieve this. Everything including her duvet was sold. When departure drew near and still she hadn't got all the money together, her sad tale pulled at the heart strings of a friend who immediately wrote out a cheque for £200. She was that sort of person. Having got her directly involved, I felt very responsible for her predicament and tried to persuade some of my richest friends (very, very few in numbers!) to lend their financial support. Unfortunately this wasn't successful and she ended up taking out a huge overdraft.

Pete Cogram, 28 years old and a photographer was very good at his craft. He was also an extremely keen cyclist and really loved talking about bike bits. He became the photographic adviser to the venture and photographer on the Asian Highway.

He was from a very different mould than the other team members, being born and brought up in Peckham and proud of his 'good working class stock' background. He had been bound for a career in the Navy but in his own words 'got fed up with the uniform and the "Hello Sailor" crap' and became a self-taught photographer.

At the very first riders' meeting he had expressed concern about making sure everything was properly organised. He came to work in the office full-time and apart from doing route and photographic stuff his job was to help organise the office. In truth this wasn't the best use of his talents and he let us know it, but all of us were having to do something that we didn't like. I was glad when a secretary joined us and he could be relieved of the tasks.

Pete gave things a great deal of thought and was a deep character. He was also a bit of a loner and this and the fact that he was desperately underweight and always looked pale worried me. In the end I voiced my doubts to Nick and Kate but in an admirable show of loyalty, they supported him.

The African Trail Team

The African Trail is the one in which Andy Hansen was to ride as Publicity Officer and he chose his other team members: Julia Leeward as Leader, the outrageous Willy Taylor as Logistics Officer, Norman Carr and Moira Poulton as Route Photographers.

Andy Hansen

Julia Leeward

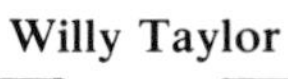

Willy Taylor

Norman Carr

Moira Poulton

Julia Leeward, 31 years old and a biology teacher in a comprehensive school in London's East End was very different to the biology teachers I recall from my school days who were stuffy and conservative. I felt she was the reincarnation of a suffragette. She had a very elegant Edwardian neck and face and a look of intelligence, strength and sensitivity which she lived up to.

When we had Intermediate Technology workshops, Julia's teaching skills were extremely useful in creating lively discussion on development issues. The purpose of workshops was to enable all riders to speak confidently about I.T. when they were out spreading the word, particularly in schools, and she was able to relate what kind of responses and questions we could expect from children.

Willy Taylor, a maths lecturer, was 41 and silver haired with a beard. Both he and Julia had a stylish and relaxed appeal. Willy was so laid back he nearly toppled over. I imagined that he'd get the rest of his team to rickshaw him from his corner of the world! His previous expedition experience had taken him all over Eastern Europe in a double decker bus, and through Europe and Scandinavia in a 1936 Rolls Royce — nothing too strenuous there! Whilst everyone else would turn up to meetings on bicycles, Willy and Julia would arrive in their beaten-up ambulance! In fact his physical appearance was deceptive because both he and Julia took off to the hills at weekends regularly for a bit of rock climbing and other related outdoor, fitness-inducing pursuits.

Willy commanded a good deal of respect and was a friend to everyone. I know this from discussions we had where riders might have aired their grievances with him. He was a peace maker and occasionally he would very tactfully put me in the picture of things that he didn't think I was aware of. He did this without ever betraying any confidences. He would also chair the general meetings, which with so many personalities present was not the easiest of tasks and he did it very fairly.

Both Julia and Willy had to continue their teaching jobs right up until departure. Since this meant they were unable to make any full-time contribution to the project they made a significant financial input to their team funds which made up for the fact that Andy had done most of the organising for them. They also made the team think about team problems that might occur along the way and deal with them in advance.

Andy Hansen was officially Publicity Officer of this team but because he was co-founder of the whole project he was the leading light.

Quite a lot has been said about Andy already, but he was visibly changing as the project progressed. He became more confident and after our initial problems the two of us were far more tolerant of one another and eventually enjoyed a good working relationship. I was quite fond of Andy though we didn't get to know each other outside of the office environment.

He took a class one morning a week in Alexander Technique to guard against stress. He would do it sometimes in the office and at meetings I wondered what on earth was going on at first — all I could see was Andy rubbing his thighs back and forth and visibly growing taller — I thought he had some superhuman powers! In fact it looked very odd because he already had an unusually long back. He also had a fetish about muesli and lived on the stuff. Traces of it were to be found in the drawers of his desk months after his departure in December '86.

Norman Carr joined us when he was 18 and still in the upper sixth form at Sheredes School, Hoddesdon in Hertfordshire where he was studying for Maths, Physics and Chemistry 'A' levels. When he first joined, he cycled to meetings in London from his home in Hertfordshire. He had in fact proposed to I.T. that he do a solo cycle expedition to the North Cape, Norway and they had referred him to our venture.

Norman had fairly long hair and a penchant for Joni Mitchell; he was like a left-over from the 70s, be it a very young one. It is to my detriment that I doubted his full worth to the bike ride at first, and to Andy's credit that he adopted Norman for his route. He would make some very intelligent contributions at meetings as well as contribute his extensive photographic and cycle touring experience and knowledge.

His was not a particularly happy lot in the office having no administrative background and so he, like Thomas, would end up doing the piles of photocopying, doing the books, costing things or couriering artwork and sponsorship proposals around London. Occasionally, teenage insecurity would show itself and he would sit around the office with his feet up on the desk. Like Thomas he had a life enhancing venture ahead of him. He brought out the maternal in me and I unnecessarily had a word in Julia's ear to keep an eye on him and let me know how he fared. Just before he left for Africa, he really tugged at my heart strings when he said, 'I just want to tell you Miranda that I am really proud to be a part of Four Corners and I feel very lucky to be involved'.

This was the only team to have a fifth member; Julia had begun to feel that she would need some female companionship so that when at the end of September '86 **Moira Poulton**, a 24-year-old stage designer, applied, she was accepted. Moira had read about Meryl Channing taking off for South America in her local paper and since she had been pondering the idea of a cycle touring trip (the fastest woman round the coast of Britain or round the world), her application to Four Corners was timely and resolved her dilemma.

I was rather afraid that this last minute addition would mean I would have to re-approach all the sponsors that had provided so much for the 16 riders and was reluctant to divert my attentions from more demanding matters at the time. Consequently when Moira and I met I didn't offer her any hope of support. I did actually get one or two things together and made some necessary links for her, but for the most part she had to get all the equipment and funding herself. Though it was only weeks before the departure of her team that she got involved, she certainly made up for lost time, working round the clock on team publicity and getting lots of coverage for Four Corners from local press. She seemed meticulous about detail and very organised and I rather wished she had come along earlier. A determined woman and not easily put off was the impression she left behind.

The Oriental Path Team

The Oriental Path was made up of Aidan Prior as Leader, Rhoda Morrison as Logistics Officer, Adria Stubbs as Publicity Officer and Sebastian Best as Route Photographer.

Aidan Prior

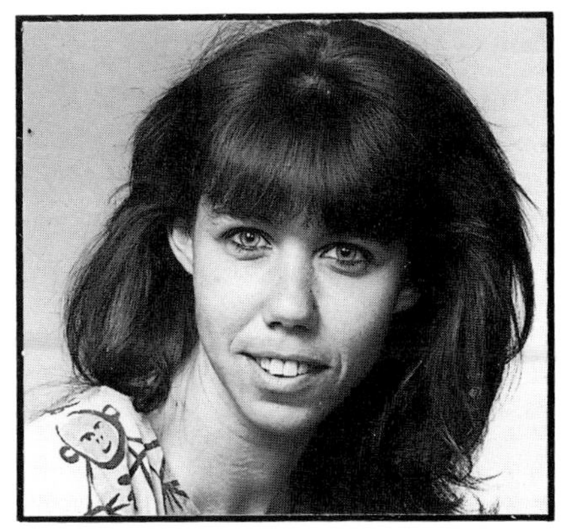

Rhoda Morrison

Adria Stubbs

Sebastian Best

Aidan Prior rang me one morning in the spring of '86. 'Hi, I've seen one of your notices advertising for riders for the world cycle ride. I'd really like to do anything to help Intermediate Technology and I love cycling and travel.' He went on to explain that he'd graduated from the London School of Economics with a Political and Social Geography degree following which he'd gone out to Swaziland to carry out research. 'It was when I was there that I realised Western aid just wasn't working; grand scale agriculture, especially sugar plantations had replaced traditional methods and removed the grazing and land rights of many Swazis. The slump in prices of recent years and soil erosion are a couple more of the detrimental effects of this approach.' It was fascinating listening to him as few of the riders had recently experienced development issues first hand like this.

Aidan was nice and sensitive but a touch serious; not easy to have a laugh with, but then that's probably because the office humour was too blue. He worked in the office for just over 3 months but I was glad for him when he left. There had been a lot of ups and downs within a very condensed space of time which made it highly pressurised. Thus he endured a very difficult time before his departure. On occasions he had been very supportive, for which I was grateful.

The first I saw of **Rhoda Morrison** was on the centrefold pages of a bicycle magazine — racing on a mountain bike. Shortly after this she telephoned me and said she was interested in participating. She came round to a supper at my place with Jo and me. I don't suppose she'll forget the supper. It nearly landed on her head. I cooked pancakes and tossed them in the air or rather into Rhoda's hair. She was completely unperturbed by this.

She came across as very quiet but pretty self-assured. She had worked and biked her way round the world and was taking a couple of years off in London as Computer Operator. She couldn't do much immediately because of work commitments. I spelt out to her the level of contribution of time that would be required if she were to participate. As other teams departed and numbers depleted in the office she would be expected to step in at least in a part-time, if not full-time capacity toward the departure date.

Rhoda, a 23 year old New Zealander, was a true 'Girl Guide'. She'd gained a private pilot's licence at 20, had competed in cross-country running, played hockey in the national team, skied mountains and on water, swam, sailed, snorkelled, dived, fished, kayakked (I'll just stop for a breather . . . !). She broke horses in, rode them at gymkhanas and cross-country events, rounded them up, bred them, led trial rides and built cross-country competition courses, she tramped (that's a N.Z. term!), mountaineered and of course, had done mountain bike racing at international level. Shall we say she was very athletic and a competitive sort of person.

The 'down' side of all this activity was that it took up a lot of time — time which I and other people felt should have been spent helping in the office.

Adria Stubbs, after attending her first Four Corners general meeting, rang me at the office and said 'Hello Miranda. Look — I've decided that I am going to give up my present job and find somewhere to live near Docklands so I can come and work as a secretary at Four Corners'. I explained that I would not be in a position at that stage to pay her any salary but that I would try and help her find some part-time work near to Docklands.

She worked half the week for a local community training organisation, Skillnet (to earn enough money to pay the rent). The rest of the day and evening she spent working with Four Corners. It was an extremely brave move to leave a job as P.A. to a Director of a top P.R. company on a very good salary for a job which she knew would be a sheer slog for no wages. She also gave up a flat in Fulham. Her whole life changed. 'I just feel that to be part of something like this is an opportunity not to be missed.' She arrived at the beginning of June and continued at an increasing pace until February the following year.

Eventually, when a place became free on the Oriental Path, the team invited her to join them. I was very sad to lose her from the office, she was worth her weight in gold, but of all people she deserved to go on the ride. My only reservation was that at 20 years old she was very young, but then the team would have to take that into account. Already a commuter cyclist, she began the most vigorous physical training of any of the riders.

Last but certainly not least of all the World Bike Riders is **Sebastian Best**, a 25-year-old photographer. We met in the interval at a Royal Geographical Symposium on expedition travel. He had already teamed up with a group planning to travel, like Kate and Nick, overland by bike to Australia. He attended the introductory meeting and decided to switch expeditions, attracted by the fact that he would be cycling for others and not just himself.

He was looking for the travel experience and photographic opportunities which he was quite open about: 'the bike ride will offer me lots of new photographic horizons' but he also stated in his c.v., '. . . more importantly, I would like to use my skills for a cause more worthy than corporate publicity and vanity and doing the ride is a step very much in that direction'.

Sebastian you couldn't help but like. He is a pretty straightforward kind of person and had the most disarming chuckle. He appeared to be a member of the Kensington green welly brigade, even turning up at riders' meetings wearing them. He took me along to the opening of a Peace mile in Battersea Park which revealed a side to him that I hadn't realised existed. He was an interesting combination; certainly there was a lot more strength and depth in him than might have at first appeared.

Sebastian contributed a great deal to the photographic department as well as providing the riders' publicity shots. We all had to troop along to a terribly smart studio in Kensington where he worked for a chap who photographed the Royals. I bet the studios had never witnessed a crew like the World Bike Riders before! Everyone laughed about the studio manner Sebastian used to relax and amuse his sitter. He certainly got me laughing when he said: 'Miranda I want you to look into the lens like you're looking into the eyes of someone you're in love with'.

Well there you have them; all the World Bike Riders — and what a variety of characters they were. We all wondered how many of them would actually make it back the following September; some of them would have been away for a whole year. I also thought, though, that whilst leaving the high-speed demands and pressures of the office must have been highly welcomed, how difficult it might be for those who had been at the epicentre of the project from the beginning to leave it all behind. I wondered what expectations many of them had of the project and what would happen to them all; who would come out on top; how all the different personalities would get on with each other; how each would react to any crisis that might occur, to the stresses of living with 3 other people, the physical and mental challenge of cycling thousands of miles through different countries, cultures, climates and terrain.

Asked to Stay Behind

As for myself, I was the rider that wasn't to be.

At the beginning of 1986 I.T. was beginning to take the whole project far more seriously and I was to be told by Mark Sinclair, the Director of Communications, that I was recognised by I.T. as the 'head person' of the ride. I didn't tell the others this at first, convinced that I could find a real 'head person' to take over the role. However, I didn't have long if I was to be joining the Americas Route in September of that year. Shortly after this Steve Bonnist announced 'You do know that you won't be able to go on this ride and that you will have to stay behind and run things from this end'. This was mainly to be for publicity purposes. Mark Sinclair later re-iterated this, saying that a manager would also have to be found, though that seemed impossible without cash to pay wages.

I saw myself as a catalyst in the whole thing, carrying it through until these 'crucial' people could be in place. However, time was running out and it wasn't fair to the other Americas Route team members to hold out to see what happened. They needed to know where they stood and would need to find my replacement. I remember going to do my last bit of route research at the Royal Geographical Society. I was on my way up Expedition Road. It was a beautiful crisp winter's morning in January. There was a clear blue sky. Not a cloud in sight. I'd been told of the heavenly skies in the clear air of the Andes and I couldn't help but imagine what it would be like to be under them, how the air would smell; whether we would turn blue with lack of oxygen; what the people would be like; the colours and the culture; how I would deal with an encounter with a rattle snake or a scorpion(!); how it would feel to touch down in La Paz after all the months of preparation. All these thoughts were going through my head. Suddenly the joy turned to quiet tears; I knew that I wouldn't be there to find out.

For a while I kidded myself that I could join the Oriental Path team as this wouldn't be leaving for another year and allowed me more time to find that 'head person' replacement. A few months later I was listening to some Chinese buskers playing Chinese folk music — they introduced each tune with a tale or myth which the music so clearly depicted. It was beautiful, mesmerising in fact, and transported me to the land they were singing of. But that would be about as close as I would get to it for the time being. I felt myself forcing back tears once again, knowing that I could not go; I had to see the project through to the end; I was needed in London as co-ordinator for all the teams and staff, for publicity purposes, for sponsorship, the organisation of the Paris to London bike ride and the Grand Finale. One person who understood how difficult a decision it was to stay behind was Tim Gartside, an Australian who had done the Sahara crossing with Peter Murphy. He had said to me 'It must feel like being pregnant and not actually having the baby'. Actually, having been so involved in the organisation I think I would have felt like that whether I'd gone or stayed. Some of the riders though weren't so understanding. One asked what there would actually be for me to do while they were away; another couldn't see the point of my staying behind — he thought that I.T. would handle everything; one or two thought I was just being a martyr. One thing I had learned through all this was that it seemed almost impossible to be a decision-maker *and* popular: 'You can't please all the people all the time' was a phrase that constantly came to mind and I wondered how the individual team leaders would fare.

On the Road

With the team members and routes now chosen, we had to move into the second phase of the pre-expedition planning. I had already found us a free office in London's Docklands (courtesy of LDDC) in return for the free publicity they would gain from us using it as the destination of the Paris-to-London Ride. Now, whilst the riders worked to get their £3,000 together and attended first aid, languages and bike maintenance classes, and either carried on with their full-time work or helped in the office, we had to concentrate on the marketing of the overall project.

A basic decision to be made was the name of the ride. 'World Cycle Relay' was no longer accurate. Countless suggestions were put forward, including mine of Four Corners Bike Ride. Four Corners was rejected at first, but later adopted.

The logo was an integral part of projecting the right image. It was important to get right away from the 'cranky' image that bicycles and alternative technology inspired. Also the logo had to work on merchandise which we hoped would be another source of revenue for the charity. The logo needed to be dynamic and optimistic whilst encompassing the ride and charity.

I sent advertising and design companies a brief and asked them if they would donate the services of their art departments free of charge to the project. The best response came from Fiona Gilmore, Marketing Director at Michael Peters and Partners; she set up an in-house competition, offering a weekend in Paris to the winner. It was in March that Steve Bonnist and I attended the presentation of their chosen logo and was introduced to marketing-speak as Fiona explained: 'We feel this one will work best for you. The brush strokes depict optimism and internationalism. The colours suggest dynamism too'. Absolutely! She went on 'The small "c" represents a head, the figure 4 the body and two circles a bike – "4C on a Bike"'. It was perfect and although there were other good entrants this one won the day.

Four Corners World Bike Ride was the chosen name and '4C on a Bike' the chosen logo. Now we had an identity and happily it was one everyone was pleased with.

. . . Aid

Someone I had met earlier on was Philip Rusted, Treasurer of Band Aid and a Senior Partner of an international accountancy firm. Steve Bonnist of I.T. felt it would be helpful if Philip could give an accurate gauge as to the potential of Four Corners, and at a meeting between the three of us he asked Philip to give the venture marks out of 10. After a little thought he answered, '8 at the moment'. What was needed to nudge it up a couple more points he said, was celebrity participation which would help us get publicity and sponsorship.

One of Philip's contacts was Barry Snellgrove, Director of one of the 'World's most successful' sponsorship firms, West Nally. I went to meet him at his Mayfair office. Barry told me that there was to be another mammoth fundraising event later that year called Sport Aid. He couldn't reveal much about the exact concept except that all the major international sports figures were going to come together and compete against each other in aid of famine in Africa. I thought this sounded wonderful. At the end of our meeting when I had told him about Four Corners and I.T., he said he thought we had a better concept than Sport Aid. This was just a little encouraging to a beginner, though hard to believe. Whilst West Nally weren't going to find our sponsorship for us, Barry at least gave me plenty of information and more contacts; it was a useful meeting.

Next I went to visit Dirk Spiers of another sponsorship company, Exposure. Exposure had worked on sponsorship for Band Aid and Live Aid. Dirk showed a boyish enthusiasm for Four Corners: 'They'll close motorways from Paris for this one,' he said. He initially offered to be our adviser on sponsorship but no more than that because he'd burnt out on Live Aid. In fact, he did quite a bit more and gave an enormous amount of time free of charge. He also showed us how to produce sponsorship proposals and got Kodak to donate all the film and processing that we needed. The latter was worth about £5,000 to us.

Obviously a very exciting sponsorship success was Raleigh agreeing to provide all sixteen bicycles for the riders. That alone struck £12,000 off our budget.

Gaining sponsorship was greatly enhanced by the presence of an Honorary Committee. This was made up of various celebrities and dignitaries who lent their names to the Four Corners. The first to join up was Bob Geldof as far back as January '86. The reply to my invitation read, 'It's a wonderful idea and I'd be glad to give my support'. I was so thrilled when this came through the letter box that I kissed his signature 'you wonderful person!'. I rang Andy straight away and he was pretty excited too. This letter was photocopied countless times and was included with requests for support for Four Corners.

Soon after this Cliff Richard wrote back 'all power to you' lending his support as well. As these famous names increased in number it seemed to raise the venture onto a higher platform, giving it more credibility. It also helped in getting round those officious secretaries who always try to fob you off. Now the process was much easier.

'Who's calling?'

'Miranda.'

'Which company are you from?'

'FOUR CORNERS, a venture with the backing of Bob Geldof and Cliff Richard.'

'Please hold the line and I'll put you through.'

Before this, reaching people to whom you needed to speak was a nightmare. In the end I developed my own tactics leaving messages like 'Could you please let him (it inevitably was a him) know that Miranda called?', adding 'oh and if you could just tell him I'm on a different number from the usual, it's . . .'. This way people would return my calls!

One slightly embarrassing moment was when the Managing Director of Young and Rubicam called back. 'Hello Miranda, David here', said this very confident voice at the other end of the phone. 'Ah! David.

Hello . . .er, which David is this?' I had to ask very sheepishly. 'Well I was actually wondering who you were and you had such a lovely name that I had to return your call!' We ended up laughing at his having caught me out. Later he was to allocate various members of staff as consultants throughout the course of the venture.

Many more celebrities and dignitaries became members of the Honorary Committee which was wonderful. **Billy Connolly,** a keen cyclist himself, wrote a lovely enthusiastic postcard saying he would join the riders on the last leg of the ride to London. **Midge Ure** wrote also offering his support. Having Bob Geldof and Midge Ure — the two leading lights of Band Aid — associated with the project was an immediate indication of what Four Corners was all about.

Indeed, this was proved by a response to a letter I wrote to General Accident Assurance. The next day a telephone call came back. 'Our Chairman Mr. Simpson has asked me to let you know that you can stop looking for insurance as General Accident will take care of all your needs.' This was the Publicity Manager, a lovely Scottish gentleman. He continued, 'We weren't able to contribute to Live Aid and helping Four Corners makes us feel that we are still able to do something. We don't want anything in return, just to be able to help out'. The riders' travel insurance was sorted out as well as the company and event insurance — this in itself represented over £10,000 worth of support.

Getting actual cash proved nearly impossible. At one point it looked like it had been cracked. Another Band Aid contact, Hiroshi Kato, had put us in touch with a Japanese fund-raising organisation called Japan Aid. The Chairman, Toshi Hattori was to go direct to Japanese firms for sponsorship. He flew in from Tokyo for meetings and a figure of £300,000 was bandied about as the sum that Mitsubishi were going to come up with. This was the grand total of our international budget, but since we had already secured a good deal of what was needed there would be change to spare for I.T.

Mark Sinclair and Steve Bonnist came to meet our Japanese friends. At the end of the meeting they were making plans to accompany me to Japan to consolidate the deal 'I'll need to get a new suit for this' Mark said excitedly. It was all very serious stuff.

H.R.H. the Prince of Wales is Patron of I.T. and to speed up sponsorship, the Japanese wanted a message of his support for Four Corners. My first letter requesting this had gone out at the end of the previous year asking if he and Princess Diana would be Patrons of the event. I had felt very much on a special mission as I had delivered it to Buckingham Palace in person. I watched the post avidly and a few weeks later an envelope with the Royal seal on it arrived. It was from

H.R.H.'s private secretary, telling me that he would '. . . of course place your letter before Prince Charles'. I rang Andy. We both had our fingers crossed.

As Patron of I.T. the Prince had spoken publicly of his support for their work 'I support it to the hilt . . . People are beginning to realise that the major aid agencies have in many ways got the thing out of balance, and have not introduced enough of the element of helping people on a small scale, which is where it really matters'. (*Sunday Times* article 18.8.1985).

Various hiccups delayed a further response, but finally, in August, a message came back to us:

'The Four Corners World Bike Ride is a global celebration of what should and could be achieved if we collectively use our energy, knowledge and enthusiasm towards ending poverty and hunger. Our future depends on such effort, and I can think of no better way to engage the imagination and commitment of millions worldwide than through this exciting event.'

We were told that Steve Bonnist would be joining us full-time from September. He became super-charged with ideas which he referred to as his 'visions'. 'I've got this vision of wheels racing and Eurythmics playing in the background . . .' Mine was of a concert representing the Four Corners routes. However, in terms of the ultimate it was something a little more elaborate which I relayed to Steve. 'Greenwich Park has got a basin ideal for a concert, it would be wonderful to have a multi-cultural concert. There could be just a few top Western bands with music from the four corners woven in. Thousands of people could gather on the hill looking over this and when the riders make a grand entrance lighted candles can be held high into the late summer's evening twilight . . .' Certainly our various advisors 'in the know' had lead us to believe that if we were to gain the coverage for I.T. that the finale would have to be something of this calibre and that it was quite possible to organise in the space of a few months if we could just get the backing.

Steve's ultimate vision of the Four Corners Grand Finale was to link up with a live Jean Michel Jarre sound and light show that was rumoured to be happening in Docklands at the same time as the riders' return, (oddly enough this happened quite independently in 1988 and was nothing to do with I.T.). Steve's ideas on how to promote Four Corners were not always as I envisaged. 'I made the Cranes stars and now I'm going to make you a star Miranda' he told me. I was a bit of a wimp about this. 'Steve I'd be hopeless, besides there's 16 riders for that very purpose. They're your "stars"' I told him. 'No, the media can only handle one person fronting these things and it's going to be you' he responded. Nick Crane backed him up: 'Miranda, you've got to view this in a very selfless way and do whatever is necessary for the campaign'. That shut me up since that's what I was asking everyone else to do.

This then was the level of potential that was thought to be within our grasp. As for me, I'd come to I.T. telling them I'd like to double their budget which at that stage had been a meagre £2,000,000. I still thought this was possible if we could pin down the financial backing and install strong management, get one or two celebrities from the Honorary Committee involved towards the end and get the media behind us. This was the summer of '86, there was still another 15 months to go, so much could happen in that time.

Ready To Go

Meanwhile Four Corners was nearing its next stage: the imminent departure of the four teams of cyclists. The first to go (with the longest ride) was the Americas Team. A press launch was thought to be vital in creating a focus for the media. It was hoped that this would serve two purposes: encourage major financial backing for the running of the venture and also start the fundraising for I.T.

Another development occurred at this stage. The ride that was to be the Paris-to-London finale for Four Corners was now the Amsterdam-to-London; a suggestion by Dirk Spiers. Since we hadn't met with an overwhelming response to our idea in France this seemed to be a much better option: it was a shorter distance, easier to organise and a great cycling city. I don't know why we hadn't thought of it before.

Anyway, back to the publicity — this was proving unbelievably difficult. After months of long phone conversations and brain-storming sessions with Steve Bonnist, I noticed that little had actually been achieved; it had also become obvious that Steve was already over-stretched with his current work load — at different times I had already lent Helen to work as his assistant, and one of our other volunteers as a photographic librarian from our own hard-pressed team. My grave concerns about publicity met with surprise however: Andy, Jo and Helen all felt that Steve, who already knew about I.T. and Four Corners, was the right person to be Press Officer and I was overruled. Both Helen and Jo had worked in the office with Steve and although they admitted he was going through a rough patch they were convinced that once he was over it there was no better person for the job. As a result of this decision and the riders last-minute frenzied activities in the LDDC office making it impossible to concentrate there, it seemed a good idea to take myself off to work in the I.T. offices. Steve had expressed a lot more support for Four Corners and I hoped that by working in the same location communication would be improved and I would be able to give him the necessary help to enable him to effectively work on our press and publicity. I was fond of Steve and didn't doubt his ability, it was just that I had to ensure the job got done.

I used my contact at the advertising firm Young and Rubicam to gain more help and advice. David Emslie suggested we should form a 'Marketing Steering Committee'. This was set up and consisted of members from advertising, marketing, public relations and sponsorship companies. Young and Rubicam gave us several members of their staff, Burson–Marsteller gave us their Creative Director, Tim Forster, Michael Peters gave us Stephen Thomas and lastly there was Dirk Spiers, our in-house sponsorship man. Without money there was no more I could provide Steve with at this point.

Steve, Helen and myself and later Mark Sinclair met with these people every two or three weeks, working towards the press launch of the Americas Route Team in September. The meetings involved brainstorming, exchanging of contacts, press pack and presentation ideas and a good deal of action. There was also immense practical support from them with the mounting of the press launch, design and printing of press packs. The Docklands would host the launch and deal with the logistics such as venue and hospitality. In other words, the mechanics to do it were all in place.

The first press launch was planned for September 11th, two days before the departure of the Americas Route. Less than three weeks before this I was called into the Press Office at I.T. and Mark Sinclair announced 'I'm not going to allow this press launch to go ahead before everything is guaranteed'. I.T. weren't going to have their name associated with the venture until we had cash sponsorship. I thought we had done well to get over £100,000 donated in kind — and after all, part of the purpose of a press launch was to attract more sponsors.

I.T. were also concerned that some of the riders hadn't got all their travel and subsistence costs together; there were some bits and pieces of equipment that hadn't been donated; furthermore that we hadn't been able to secure flights. I pointed out that although the Americas Route were set to go, some of the rest of the teams had up to 5 months to get it together. I also gave voice to the opinion that the launch was the key for the riders to get the financial backing they needed.

'But Miranda, there isn't a story to tell,' Steve told me. He was deeply worried that there was nothing sorted out for the finale, no major sponsorship. Maybe we were naive, but we all felt we did have something to tell the world — even if it was just that four teams would be riding from the four corners of the world and meeting up a year later; that it was the first ever attempt of its kind, with a whole year of planning and organisation behind it.

I fought back: 'So let's tell the press what we have got; we've got the first of four teams of cyclists taking off to the highest capital in the world, La Paz in Bolivia, to begin their mammoth 13,500 km pedal back to London. It sounds a pretty good story to me.'

'The press will ask questions that we just won't be able to answer at this stage,' Steve protested.

'Not if we only work on what we have got' I re-iterated.

But our hands were tied: we couldn't go ahead without doing it for I.T. since I.T. was the reason for Four Corners existence, so we must compromise. I.T. asked that the Americas Route team should delay their departure until things had improved. After an initial delay they went off unannounced on September 25th.

The only noise created around their departure was down at Heathrow Airport with some celebration drinks, high spirits and the raising of voices from family, friends and supporters for the final four cheers for Four Corners. I would miss Jo and Meryl a lot and it would be a while before they would be replaced in the office.

We were now in a Catch 22 situation. Without publicity it made it difficult to convince potential sponsors of the coverage the event would attract, especially once the first team had left with none. As far as I.T. were concerned, without sponsorship they wouldn't have their name associated with the event. Very frustrating indeed — for both parties.

It was now the end of September '86. For the time being this problem was put aside to deal with another: one of the riders hadn't been able to secure his subsistence money. I suggested using some of our administration money on a £ for £ basis but this was rejected as undemocratic. Tempers were fraying by this time and I couldn't understand why some were looking to me to resolve the whole problem. It was indicative of the strain we were all under that some nasty things were said and that Willy of all people turned to me, summing up, I think the feelings of the people at the meeting when he said: 'You know that if Four Corners falls apart it will be all your fault'. Some days I felt as though my role was as a communal punch bag, an object to be used for everyone to take out their frustrations. At some points I'm sure I was at breaking point myself. A few days later Willy apologised and things were right again.

The send-off of the Asian Highway Team at the end of October '86 was quieter than the first, but then again it was a Sunday and one team had already gone. At one point however it nearly seemed that they wouldn't be going. The baggage was considerably heavier than the allowance. Everybody gathered round to cram as much as possible into 'hand luggage', but the day was saved by Sebastian who by coincidence had previously photographed the airline official — and the riders were let through and the threat of the £400 charge was waived. There was a good deal of sadness on both sides as they passed through the departure gate — everyone was hopeful that the differences that had occurred had now mended.

Publicity, or rather the lack of it, was a continuous saga. A suggestion that we should at least try to generate some local-press publicity to help the remaining riders with their fundraising, was dismissed on the basis that it would dilute the effects of the main launch. Everyone understood the logic of this, but it was less easy to understand why the launch couldn't go ahead in the first place.

There were only two or three main riders meetings before the third departure. They were very quiet affairs now. I'd now come to expect 'pre-departure letting off of steam and tension' but the African Trail departure was a happy one. They had developed a good team spirit and there appeared to be no problems at all. There was champagne to send them off and one bottle specially for Andy. He must have been feeling really good, if a little strange leaving all the chaos behind.

Now there was just myself and the Oriental Path team. It was coming up to Christmas '86. Things were getting extremely tense between Four Corners and I.T. Too much time was spent planning press launches that never materialised. The LDDC were also rapidly losing patience with us. I was desperately searching round trying to find volunteers to handle publicity, replace those who had gone and get some help on the management side. I.T. seemed to be withdrawing their support more and more. When I went once again to ask Steve how work on the press pack was progressing I caught him just as he was going to his quarterly fundraising meeting. I saw that he was taking along a 'Four Corners Update' which was months old and pointed out I should have been asked to prepare an up-to-date report. The meeting was a major one for us as we had been tabbed their biggest fund-raising venture of 1987. But when I asked about the outcome I was told 'Four Corners wasn't even brought up Miranda, we had lots of other things to discuss'. That evening I decided I couldn't work out of the I.T. office anymore and packed everything up and went home.

I was deeply sad. We had viewed the relationship with I.T. as a partnership. That's why so much time had been willingly spent in keeping them informed and attending meetings. It had been a major part of our already heavy workload and hadn't been begrudged, but now I felt our time could have been used much more profitably. At the same time, we were only a bunch of enthusiastic amateurs. Whilst it might have seemed we were giving a lot in terms of our time, energy and resources etc., were 16 very privileged people as against the millions of grossly under-privileged that I.T. tried to help. They did have a difficult equation to balance in terms of how much time they could dedicate to us. I would simply have to find some other means of support.

I desperately needed to get Burson–Marsteller, the P.R. company more involved in our publicity. I called a steering committee meeting for the 19th December '86. Mark and Steve arrived as did Dirk and Gavin of Young and Rubicam and Tim Foster from Burson–Marsteller. All agreed that not a lot could be achieved until we had money, full-time staff and a firm plan for the final event which amounted to more than just a grand finale ride. At the conclusion of this meeting Mark said he would try and get I.T. to release some of the money that had been donated to them as a result of Four Corners, so it could be fed back into the project (I.T. had already been funding myself and another to the tune of £50 per week for five months). This would allow funding for a Manager and leave me free to pursue sponsorship and generally promote the venture. Also, it was agreed that there should definitely be a press launch to tie in with the departure of the last team, the Oriental Path. Finally, there would be a brain-storming meeting on 30th December '86 to thrash out the form that the grand finale was to take. Mark and Steve left. Tim turned round and gave me a hug of relief that something positive was happening. He also assured me that he would try and get Burson–Marsteller more involved on the publicity.

I hoped that the coming year would see everyone replenished with new energy to continue.

1987 arrived and for the first few weeks things seemed to be going O.K. More volunteers were coming on board and there was backing from Burson–Marsteller. Above all Steve appeared to be getting the press pack together, providing outlines and lists of questions that we at the office had to answer. Dirk and I were whizzing round to meetings with sponsors and the last team were whizzing round getting everything done before they left.

Then I received a phone call from Sue Brown from the company LDDC had employed to work on our press launch. 'Look Miranda I just want to know what's going on because Steve has suggested the press launch is off again and I mean this is just ridiculous!' Ridiculous? It was outrageous and it was the first I'd heard of it and I was supposed to be running the project. I had hardly had time to draw breath when a guy from Burson–Marsteller rang. He was extremely aggressive. 'Look I know you lot are patting yourselves on the back down there in Docklands but you just don't have a story to tell.' What had he heard for him to be so unpleasant? Next the LDDC were on the phone. They were fed-up with being messed around and they threatened to pull out of the project; this would mean the loss of our office. I sank my head into my hands at this point.

Steve had gone to Burson–Marsteller with his worries. There was a Crisis Meeting. One of the Managing Directors and about five Account Executives were there along with Steve, Dirk Spiers and myself. I presented our case. All of Steve's objections for the launch not going ahead were answered and the only amendment was that they suggested we open a donations account, which I duly did. This hadn't been done before because we had assumed donations would go direct to I.T. as this had been the procedure for previous fundraising ventures.

A new day for the launch was set. The 17th February. This meant the Oriental Path would have to be delayed two weeks. There was immense opposition to this at first. Not surprisingly they simply didn't believe what they were being told anymore but once this was resolved (thanks to the persuasive power of Dirk Spiers), I got everybody involved in making absolutely sure the press launch went ahead. At last it did and this is the letter I wrote to the riders telling them about that day:

'FOUR CORNERS HAS BEEN LAUNCHED... and I am absolutely bombed out of my brain at this moment so I thought I would sit down and write and tell you all about it.

'It was a real slog getting there and we did it just by the skin of our teeth. You can imagine the sort of chaos the H.Q. has been in.

'It was alright on the morning — yesterday that is, at 10.30 (what were you lot up to at that time?). I will try and present a picture of things.

'We had a huge room in Docklands which was set up with a podium, table and five chairs with a microphone in each place. (Very smart!) This was backed by a huge 20 ft by 10 ft Four Corners banner which looked great. From left to right there was Steve Bonnist, myself, Aidan, Adria and Chief Executive of I.T. Dipak Nandy. Before us were a hundred seats, mostly occupied (by volunteers and I.T. staff!). There we were waiting to kick off but no riders! The Sun had nicked them to take photographs. Volunteers were going in all directions trying to find them. The press, started to fidget and I was having 'bloody nightmares' about them leaving for their next assignment with nothing on Four Corners. Finally they turned up and Steve did the introductions. First me as the

'Sandwich girl' that used to deliver door to door for small businesses and was now delivering to the door of the Third World the means to feed itself! Dipak inspired them with details of I.T.'s activities, I covered the stuff about the grass routes of the project and Adria told them what it was like to be a World Bike Rider. Everybody loved her and she was a real star. Aidan rounded off on a more serious note about the routes and publicity to be gained world wide. After all the questions were was lots of piccie taking (a Times photographer was there) and interviews for radio and T.V.

'This resulted in interviews with L.B.C., a Midlands radio station, World Service, B.B.C. Far Eastern Services and Radio One Newsbeat. The highlight was the slot on John Cravens Newsround which was truly brill and went on forever. Kate Nivison made sure there was stacks of stuff in the local press where all you lot come from and there were calls from the locals in the home counties too.

'Sadly, TUESDAY 17TH FEBRUARY WAS THE SAME DAY THAT THE N.U.J. WENT ON STRIKE and consequently there wasn't anything in the press today.

'... I'm in a bit of a crisis here at the moment. I'm waiting for the arrival of amendments for the press packs and then have to send 300 of the buggers out and Steve has decided to take off on holiday now! I hadn't counted on that on top of catching up with all my other stuff after preparing for the press launch!!! Anyway, I'll just try and do what I can, but that does mean added patience from your end PLEASE.

'Love for now Miranda.

'P.S. If you haven't heard from Steve please bear with him, he's having a miserable time at the moment with a divorce and obviously that means losing the kids — awful. I'm sure he'd love to hear from you.'

The slightly worrying thing about the day was the mention of £10,000,000! The press pack stated that this was the sum that I.T. needed over the next three years. Of course that's what everyone thought we were aiming to raise. Very embarrassing. One headline read, 'Miranda Out to Get £10,000,000'!

Other than that it didn't go too badly.

In a letter to Andy I wrote:

'... After the press launch, it was such a haul to get there, when it was over, it felt so odd ... You know when you force your arm muscles to tense for so long that they just float upwards — well that's just how it felt after the press launch.'

I didn't work that evening. I went out with some friends and afterwards it was late and there were very few buses so I walked most of the way home through the quiet city and toward Hackney. I was quietly crying to myself and I don't really know why, I think it was just sheer exhaustion and that floating feeling.

It was very late when I finally climbed into bed, first arranging for a wake call since it was the departure of the Oriental Path from Gatwick early in the morning. After only having had a few hours sleep, I was in a bit of a daze and I inadvertantly took the longest route possible to Gatwick and with lots of delays it took a lifetime to get there.

I couldn't bear it that I might not be able to say goodbye to the last team. By the time I got to Gatwick I was deeply anguished and only just in time to snatch farewells before they went through their departure gate. As I hugged Aidan, he just said, "You're on your own now Miranda". It felt very lonely seeing the last of the riders disappear behind the barrier. It was an inadequate farewell on my part and I quickly rushed to the information desk to ask that the Captain send them a message of good luck. It must have seemed very odd for them — it was so quiet after the frantic pace of the last few days and they didn't really get the send off they deserved.

PART TWO

The Routes

With the African famine so much in the news it was easy to forget that extreme poverty and famine had to be averted in all four corners of the earth. It was to be demonstrated that Intermediate Technology was doing just that through their work in over 60 countries around the world. Routes were therefore planned so that each team would go on fact-finding visits to I.T. projects, enabling them to return to Great Britain and spread the word about their work. It was imperative that we knew where the projects were before we finally pinpointed our routes. On the surface this might seem a very simple matter. But not so.

It wasn't possible to pick projects out of a hat at random for this purpose. For a start, since most of them were based in rural areas, this often presented a logistical problem of actually getting there, many being way off anything that even resembled a beaten track. More importantly, I.T. had to first consider their collaborators in the field and how they would feel about being on view to four cyclists on gleaming bicycles and the possibility of subsequent publicity. Some projects were politically sensitive and it was better for them to maintain a low profile in their own countries where governments might be unhappy about their country being portrayed at home and abroad as 'Third World'. Another factor which might categorise a project as sensitive was that it might be difficult to predict months in advance what stage the project would have reached by the time the riders arrived, and thus whether there would in fact be much to publicise or even look at (many projects only work in the dry season and lie dormant during the wet, and vice versa). Whilst many projects had proven to be highly successful, others were still in their development stages and therefore not ripe for visitors and publicity. Further to this, relationships with small communities throughout the third world had been carefully nurtured, sometimes over a number of years to a level of deep trust and we had to be careful not to undermine this. I.T. couldn't be expected to write to each one for permission to visit them and supposing an enthusiastic response came from a project we couldn't logistically visit?

I.T.'s reservations were understandable over this aspect so in the end we had to set the routes without their help — and when they did come up with a list of projects that could be visited it was too late. Few of them were along the planned routes, and major alterations were impossible at this late stage. Although we had hoped that the 4 routes would begin at points where I.T. operated, because of the above, route planning was done fairly autonomously within each team — the general concensus being that it would be better to begin at points which might have great fundraising or publicity potential. As long as they met the aims of the project and they could ensure as continuous a route as possible, all meeting up a year later in September 1987 that was fine. With this in mind each team set about amending and finalising the suggested routes according to such limitations as climate, diplomatic relations between neighbouring countries, wars and even the odd bit of guerilla activity.

The following extracts appeared in our very first sponsorship proposal and I couldn't resist giving you this 'travel brochure' version of the routes:

'The FOUR CORNERS WORLD BIKE RIDE' is an event of superlatives!'

'On their way to London the sixteen cyclists will be spanning every geographic divide, linking with virtually every race, culture and religion on the globe. They will cross four of the world's longest rivers and cycle over four major mountain ranges. Every climatic variation the planet has to offer will be encountered, as they pass over glaciers, steppes, jungle and desert.'

The Americas Route

'The world's highest capital, La Paz in Bolivia, provides an awesome beginning to the 'FOUR CORNERS WORLD BIKE RIDE'. From 3,500 metres, the group will cycle along the Andes before dropping precipitously down to the Pacific Coast and traversing freezing desert. They will go on to visit food processing projects where Intermediate Technology have been helping local farmers increase their incomes and providing employment opportunities.

'From Quito in Ecuador they will miss out Central America, the scene of so much recent anguish, to go to Mexico City, from where they will journey across the excellent roads of central Mexico. This will provide a restful interlude before crossing the desert of the Baja Peninsula on the way to California.

'The Golden Gate bridge offers a dramatic setting for the start of the coast to coast bike ride, which carries the cyclists over the Rocky mountains, across the vast emptiness of the great plains and into the greeness of Virginia; and finally onto New York. From here the four will cross the Atlantic by plane to Lisbon. With one last mountain range to endure, the Pyrenees, their tired legs will carry them down into France for the last stretch home ...'

The Asian Highway

'Beginning in Melbourne, Australia, this team will be starting off furthest from home. From Brisbane, they will go to Indonesia, island hopping through colourful Bali, Java and bustling Singapore. The journey continues on through the Asian mainland as they cycle through the humid jungles of Malaysia and Thailand.

'From Bangladesh, the group will ride steadily upwards along the banks of the Ganges. Here, the riders might stop to see how Intermediate Technology has been helping local communities with installation and design of more efficient and versatile textile looms.

'The route then leads through the Himalayan foothills to Nepal, where they will certainly stop and admire the awesome bulk of Everest (grateful, perhaps that they will not have to climb it!). Following the mountain range they will cycle into India through open rural areas and, by contrast, the busy cities of Lahore and Delhi: continuing into Pakistan, past the huge Mangla Dam they will cycle to the newly built capital of Islamambad.

'The Four will take to the air to miss out the war torn areas of the Gulf, entering Europe via the gateway of Turkey ...'

The African Trail

'This route strikes a fascinating balance between ancient history and untamed nature. Starting near the Victoria Falls and Kariba Dam, linking Zimbabwe and Zambia, the team will cycle through Malawi and Tanzania, heading for the great game reserves of Serengeti and Ngorongoro, culminating in a climb of Mount Kilimanjaro, at 5895 metres, the highest peak in Africa. For this drought ridden area of Africa, Intermediate Technology have designed windpumps, which have given thousands of people access to water.

'The Olduvai gorge, the cradle of mankind is a short ride from here, leading them on to the timeless Nile Valley of Thebes, Luxor, the Sphinx and the Pyramids. The ride then climbs up the 'boot' of Italy, passing through Rome and Tuscany, over the Alps and into modern Germany ...'

The Oriental Path

'From Hong Kong, a busy metropolis and business centre, the four cyclists will wind their way around the amazing limestone spires of Southern China, on to the eternal Peking and the Forbidden City. Just a day's ride away, a visit will be paid to the Great Wall of China, the only human artefact visible from space. Intermediate Technology is collaborating with the Chinese in developing, testing and manufacturing electronic control mechanisms for small hydro-electric systems.

'The team goes on to Tokyo by plane, where they will begin their six week tour of the rugged mountains of central Japan, which is timed to take in the cherry blossom season. From Kyoto they will cycle back via Mount Fuji to the skyscrapers of Tokyo.

'The Soviet Union is the next step, beginning with Moscow's Kremlin and on to Winter Palace in Leningrad. From here the team will be able to speed up as they pass through the flat pine forests of Scandinavia. From the fjords of Norway they will cross over to Copenhagen to take in the last stretch ...'

These grandiose descriptions of the routes are the penwork of Alex and Andy. Great aren't they? This went to print in April '86 and there are only a few amendments to add.

The first team to begin was the **Americas Route**. They left London on 25th September and started cycling on the day Christopher Colombus discovered America: 12 October. This route would be a test for the toughest cyclist's stamina, taking them over the Andes as they continued through Peru, Ecuador, Mexico and the USA. With little planned in Portugal, they remained in the States to exploit the fund-raising publicity potential and flew from New York to Madrid. They continued through Spain, France, Belgium and the Netherlands. If they reached London, over a year later, they would have pushed their pedals round 8,100,000 times over 10,551 miles.

The Asian Highway began their journey from Melbourne on 25th October. Australia had been selected as a start point by the team for the fund-raising and publicity potential. This, however, was not realised since they didn't have sufficient time to organise this in advance. Also, because of a late start, they only had time to pedal as far as Sydney and not Brisbane as planned. From here they went on to Indonesia, Singapore, Malaysia, Thailand, Bangladesh, Nepal and India. Despite ill health, this team kept to the busiest schedule of visits to I.T. projects of all the teams. In the end, continued serious illness meant Pakistan had to be given a miss and they went from Delhi, straight to Turkey and from here to Greece, Yugoslavia, Hungary, Austria, West Germany, Luxembourg, Belgium and the Netherlands. If they reached the end, each of them would have pushed their pedals round 5,200,000 times to get back to London having covered 7,400 miles.

The African Team arrived in Zimbabwe in time for Christmas and left the capital, Harare on 19th December. Just before their departure they were advised not to go through Zambia due to an outbreak of border skirmishes right along the planned route. They went on to travel through Malawi, Tanzania, Kenya and Egypt. Their's definitely was the friendliest of all the routes and in all countries they were met with incredible warmth and hospitality, passing down roads with hoards of school children singing to them. Sadly, they left Africa and bid farewell to the Pyramids as they entered Europe via Greece and continued on to Italy, Switzerland, West Germany and the Netherlands, where they were to finish the route. They each would have created 5,000,000 revolutions

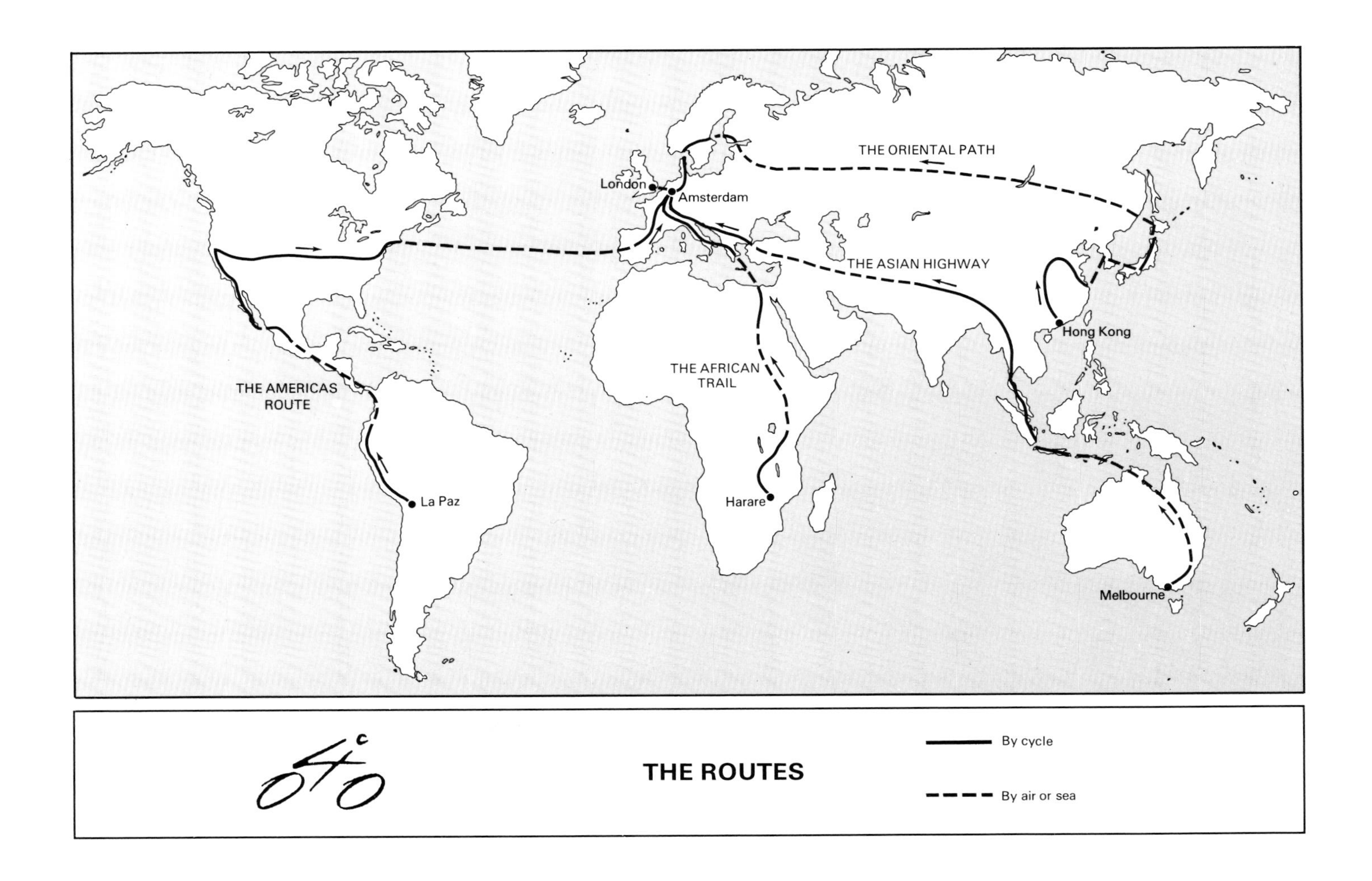
THE ORIENTAL PATH
London
Amsterdam
THE ASIAN HIGHWAY
Hong Kong
THE AFRICAN TRAIL
THE AMERICAS ROUTE
La Paz
Harare
Melbourne
THE ROUTES
By cycle
By air or sea

with their pedals to get them back home to London and covered 6,493 miles.

The main difference to the **Oriental Path** route was that Russia was excluded from the itinerary after lengthy attempts to gain them access to cycle from Moscow to Leningrad were unsuccessful. Leaving London on 18th February, their journey took them from Hong Kong and across to China. Sadly, their progress up to Peking and the Forbidden City and the Great Wall was thwarted by another 'unforeseen encounter'. Permission to cycle through closed areas of China, earlier seeming guaranteed, was not forthcoming in the end and with more time on their hands, South Korea was a last minute addition to their itinerary. In Japan there was a highly organised publicity schedule which meant they didn't see quite so much of the 'rugged mountains of central Japan' but instead, spearheaded a publicity campaign and gained fame.

They also had to contend with 4 of the world's most expensive cities for travellers: Tokyo, Helsinki, Stockholm and Oslo. If they were under constant pressure from publicity or expenditure, then for the oriental and Scandinavian part of their route there was a variety of massage and sauna on offer which they took full advantage of. Finland and Sweden provided a breathing space whilst in Norway they endured some of their toughest cycling as they made their way up (... and down, up and down!) to the Arctic Circle over snowy, stony passes. From here it was downhill to Denmark, West Germany and the Netherlands. Should they survive the Arctic Circle and make it home, they would have pushed their pedals 7,200,000 times and covered 9,000 miles back to London.

All teams had spent many months going through the same patterns of preparation, attending the same regular meetings and training sessions. By the time the Oriental Path team was on the road the teams were thousands of miles apart with thousands of miles to cycle before they would see each other again. Each route was to develop its own personality, shaped by the people, climate, terrain and events encountered along the way. And for each route, outside of Europe, this was to vary enormously.

For those who had worked 14 hours a day, 6 or 7 days a week for the months preceding their departures there had been little time to mentally prepare themselves for the route. The contrasts of the countries from which they were to begin their route must have been a strange shock for their weary bodies. Stranger still must have been when they pedalled off along that stretch of road at the beginning of their routes not knowing what was up ahead of them; so much that would be new and unfamiliar ...

Riders' Impressions

Each route would take in some of the world's most spectacular scenery so all the better that they were travelling by cycle since it provides an intimacy with the surroundings almost unattainable by any other means of transport.

The pace is not so fast that you miss things and of course it is extremely easy to stop and absorb the scenery and atmosphere or talk to people. Sounds and smells are also very much more a part of a cyclist's travel experience. With so much stimulation of the senses you get a more complete experience of the countries you are passing through and thus a heightened observation. Jane, of the Asian Highway, puts it more succinctly 'The good thing about bikes is you are forced to see everything so you get good impressions of where you are...'. Sometimes, as Jane would no doubt agree, this also meant contact too close for comfort with the worst, ugliest, smelliest and noisiest of places on this planet. However, often were they to find themselves cycling as fast as they could to get away from the latter only to turn a corner to suddenly be in heaven on earth. Concentrating on this, the routes will be unfolded with the World Bike Riders' impressions, capturing some of the joy, atmosphere, and incredible beauty of our world. If only we could re-produce the sounds too ...

The Americas Route

Jo, Meryl, Alex and Thomas wrapped up against the cold in all the clothing they'd brought with them, explored the crowded streets of La Paz to find quite a different picture than that painted by the media of a much more hostile South America.

Bolivia: 'I had not expected such a friendly relaxed city ... the people on the streets are smiling and laughing. We're staying in the Indian old quarter, the most colourful area of town.' (Meryl)

'It's everything you would imagine it to be. The Indian women with their hats and shawls sit by the sides of the streets from dawn till dusk selling anything from goat's heads and vegetables to coloured pills and sellotape not to mention gorgeous alpaca jumpers.' (Jo)

'... stalls with breads and cakes and shops full of brightly coloured paper toys and decorations. Most of the streets are cobbled, steep and full of battered cars and microbuses beeping their way through kids and dogs.' (Meryl)

'La Paz itself was special for its incredible expanse of Indian markets, working up the crater-side towards the 'altiplano', and the green, pink and turquoise houses of the *pueblos jovenes* further up.' (Thomas)

For a practise run Meryl and Jo took themselves off to a place called Viacha, some 30 km distant, where they had been told they would find a traditional fiesta: '... around the next corner was a bustling crowd and the sounds of brass bands ... The main square was full of dance troupes dressed in wonderful bright costumes, followed each by a small brass band and they in turn were followed by a large group holding cassette recorders on their shoulders. This phenomenon was explained to us as the Peruvians who had come from the villages to record the wonderful Bolivian music so that they could copy it!' (Meryl)

Back in La Paz, there was more similar activitity and I can almost hear Jo shouting her impression of this scene above the noise and commotion: 'There was a lovely procession through the streets from the church next door with statues of our lady being carried along and a brass band in blue surfer shirts coming along behind drowning out the prayers. The atmosphere was great, everyone greeting each other and being showered with confetti.' (Jo)

And finally, with La Paz left behind, they cycled on and up out of the city past 'The tiny little fields that had been tilled were at angles of 45 degrees or so and made the mountains look as if they had been patched up'. (Jo)

... and onto the Altiplano: 'I love the colours on the Altiplano ... green, red earth and yellow. Wonderful blue sky and clouds. It's a lovely feeling to be on a bicycle. As we get nearer to lake Titicaca it becomes greener. More water, lots of pigs, mules, sheep and bullocks.' (Jo)

Their introduction to **Peru** was via the border town of Juliaca, on Lake Titicaca. The lake is named Titicaca (three-coloured cat) because of its cat-like shape and the three colours of the blue water, the straw-coloured reeds and the green weeds: 'At this altitude, about 4,000 m, the sky is a deep blue which was reflected in the lake, the highest navigable one in the world'. (Jo)

'Lake Titicaca really was beautiful, very tranquil, fisherman drifting around the lake's edge swinging a 3-metre sickle through the deep blue water scooping up the lush green weeds onto their boats; quiet villages slid past.' (Thomas)

'This afternoon I lagged behind the others, quietly enjoying the ride. A few barking dogs and a goods train were all that disturbed the tranquility ... I spied a field of freshly shorn Alpacas. I had a little conversation with the guy on horseback looking after them and carried on up the hill. Next thing I heard a noise behind and looked round to see the whole lot about 3 feet behind me all staring at me ... they followed me all the way up the hill.' (Meryl)

Being in one of the world's most mountainous regions the team were to experience complete changes of scenery, sometimes from one valley to the next:

'As we dropped into the valley I couldn't believe the greeness. Fat, healthy cows grazing, water running everywhere and irrigation channels. And trees! It was like entering another world. I had to keep stopping to take in the lush surroundings. More villages and therefore more schoolkids calling out and chasing.' (Meryl)

'... hundreds of birds were chattering noisily above. They were green and looked remarkably like parrots. I really hadn't expected to see such scenery — giant cactus and eucalyptus trees.' (Meryl)

The Inca Trail and Machu Picchu inspired much excitement and imagination back in London at the American Route meetings and this was one part of the venture where the bicycles were to be locked away and the whole thing was to be taken very slowly, to be savoured for a lifetime. As Meryl said, they 'set off across the wobbly wooden bridge to begin the most famous of 'Trails' in South America. An historic moment ... The first day's walk took us along a river valley, over the little wobbly wooden bridge, up a steep valley with rushing water far below through the wierdest vegetation. Cactus flowers hanging onto sheer rock faces, trees of small hard leaves which have been almost completely taken over by predatory cactus plants and silvery lichen, (maiden hair fern one of many plants).' (Meryl)

'What I find about this scenery is that it's overpowering. Looking down through jungle spread over the steep valley sides and bottom, craggy mountains above, then the clouds in the distance clear and you see magnificent mountain ranges covered with snow, several miles away.' (Meryl)

Machu Picchu: 'The last stretch to Machu Picchu was along a gentle gradient about two hours away. I took it slowly, savouring the anticipation of seeing Machu Picchu, maybe around the next bend, also hearing the cracking of branches, birds singing . . . seeing the sun shining on the valley sides and the river rushing below.'

'The whole place is supposed to have been built, lived in and abandoned within the space of a hundred years. So much, in fact, nearly all of the information on the Incas is supposition.' (Jo)

'I turned a corner and climbed some steps to the Door of the Sun for the first view down. Everyone already silent. I'm not even going to try and describe Machu Picchu, everyone has seen pictures of it . . . It was magical looking down on the shadows, occasionally lit up by lightning.' (Meryl)

'Breakfasted in the growing light. The city below us looked really beautiful. The stonework may not be as impressive as some places but the setting is superlative. The river has cut a deep gorge round it and the city sits on the green saddle with Huaya Picchu (young peak) overlooking it.' (Jo)

'As soon as the sun had risen we rushed down to look at the ruins before all the tourists arrived . . . It was amazing up there, the view was magnificent, and we perched on warm flat rocks to sit and stare. The mountains around, which had seemed like big rounded animals last night were now jagged and sharp in the morning light . . . Machu Picchu was now swamped with tour groups, men blowing whistles, loud Italian tour guides. The spell was beginning to be broken so we left.' (Meryl)

Wondrous as Machu Picchu had been, it didn't succeed in reducing the riders appreciation of the beauty that they were surrounded by for a large part of this section of their journey:

'Sitting on the Altiplano — clear blue sky and a few wispy clouds in one corner of the sky. Jagged mountains far in the distance on all sides, some covered in snow. The heat was beginning to shimmer off the land. Grey-brown soil with loose stones dotted around a few clumps of spikey grass and soft to look at green moss. Silence so quiet you can hear it, only broken by the occasional gust of howling wind sweeping across. The road stretches on ahead, gently up and down, for miles. You can still see the dust of a bus which passed us 20 minutes ago, and a tiny speck of bright blue which is a lake.' (Meryl)

On the way to Nazca: 'We only saw people 2 or 3 times a day up there, perhaps a passing Indian striding purposefully across the hill, or a family living in virtual isolation around a tiny shop. We pass the town of Puqio fully expecting to fall off the edge of the world. In fact we had two more days of riding, past herds of graceful, skittering Alpacas, who were more scared of our slow silence than of the occasional truck or bus'. (Alex)

The Nazca lines had to be viewed from above and so the bikes were downed in favour of wings: 'While recuperating in the desert town we took time off to fly over the flat plains where the amazing Nazca lines lie . . . The astronomical figures and geometric patterns are little more than shallow scrapes in the gravel plain, yet are still clearly visible and impressive hundreds of years later.' (Alex)

Not that they hadn't done a good bit of getting up where the air is clear already: 'Just after Pativilca we turned inland starting the trek up to Huacaz — from sea level to 4080 m in 120 km. It was beautiful initially, cycling through huge fields of wind whispering cane.' (Jo)

After that, it was down hill to Peru's capital on the coast: 'We were shown many things in Lima, the fortified and guarded millionaires' suburbs with the shanty towns of the poor hanging like a death-threat from the hills above them.' (Alex)

Before they said goodbye to Peru, there was to be some real adventure cycling through the Canyan del Pato: 'The land became just stony and muddy mountains and we followed this fast flowing roaring river of mud . . . The gorge was absolutely stunning, 33 tunnels, a very narrow gorge, 10 cm wide at one point of the river and all you could hear was the thunder of water.' (Jo)

Ecuador: 'Green hills with lush forest, small fields . . . as we crossed into a new valley it became very barren, just stunted trees with hollow tree trunks and no leaves. Nothing else apart from red earth and the river at the bottom.' (Jo)

They were to see all sorts of activities as they pedalled on, miles from anywhere: 'We stopped for lunch at a place where there was cock-fighting and we watched them baiting the cocks. It seemed like all the men from miles around were there.' (Jo)

'Along the river were people panning for gold . . . we stopped in a small hamlet and everyone seemed to be selling meat — pigs hanging up and every part of them for sale.'

Here, particularly they were to see much evidence in the buildings of the rich Spanish colonial past: 'Many of the cities here are very beautiful with their colonial style architecture — a mixture of very strong Catholic and Spanish influences . . . Quito, the capital, was a picturesque old town with dozens of churches, open plazas, markets and narrow cobbled streets — fascinating to wander round, although a little unsafe — as carnival time approached children amused themselves by throwing water-filled balloons at people. Foreigners are a particularly enjoyable target.' (Jo)

Finally they were to leave South America behind them, with the sounds of out of tune brass bands still ringing in their ears. There was a stop for rest and recuperation between South America and Mexico, which Thomas thoughtfully sent word about: 'Greetings from sunny San Andres, where coconut trees, white beaches and beautiful turquoise pure water are the names of the game!'

Mexico: 'Raced the 400 km to Morelia in 4 days through fresh-smelling pine forest and Mil Cumbres (thousand-peak) mountains.' (All)

It became more and more apparent that they were getting very close to the USA and now the team would come upon such things as the local Mexican rodeo: 'They had a wooden ring set up with thousands of people watching, some sitting astride the fencing posts, others standing on the trucks outside the ring while others peered through the slots between the logs and crows stood on the railway line overlooking the ring. The majority were men wearing their stetsons, jeans and boots and half of them had moustaches and nearly all of them were drinking.' (Jo)

After cycling along sand-strewn roads amongst the cacti and rattle snakes of the Baja California, 'civilisation' was to be a bit of a come down: 'Ensenada was a dump — loads of clubs, pizza places, restaurants and knick knacks. A Mexican tourist place for US citizens ... The US influence is creeping down. There's loads of marriage and divorce bureaux ... it was the marriage and divorce places that shocked me most.' (Jo)

And the USA itself seemed like another planet after the low tech and remote Andes: 'It's all so big and spacy, wide avenues, loads of drive-ins ... such tremendous waste. All these fast-food places exist on throw-away plastic cutlery and polystyrene plates. Most buildings have automatic sliding doors and air-conditioning.' (Jo)

It didn't take them long to adjust though: 'Cycling up the coast it is so beautiful. You're right by the sea with stunning views over the hilly coastline. There are so many cyclists on the road all of them with helmets. We've never seen so many cyclists.' (Jo)

'We found somewhere off the road in the gathering dusk, wading through the long sea grasses with our bikes ... in the cove were a pair of sea otters playing and searching for food. We sat on the rocks watching them not more than

20 yards away and the sun went down in a magnificent rich red-orange hued sky. It was so quiet and peaceful save for the light slapping of the waves and the tapping of the otters. They float on their backs and crack shells on their stomachs with the use of a stone. I watched the moon come up and listened to the otter playing in the silver ripples. I felt really privileged to see these creatures ... it was one of the most idyllic nights of the trip.' (Jo)

'I fell in love with Montana — the big sky state. I have never seen skies like it. Vast, vast expanses, blue skies, small white dense clouds. How come the horizon stretches so far? I'm sure the sky is bigger than I have ever seen — it's more than just the far-reaching landscape of hills and fields of corn. Montana is a cowboy state. These small towns have just a granary, a gas station and maybe a corner store and a bar. It's a rough land but very beautiful; stretching wheat fields.' (Jo)

'All the small towns look and feel the same, sell the same things and give off the same sleepy vibes. However, now we are moving west it is changing, now we see cowboys in pick-ups crowding the streets and bars, and herds of cattle ranging on the grass.' (Alex)

The Asian Highway

The team's arrival in **Australia** was greeted by pouring rain, and home for the first week was a house in the Melbourne suburbs. It didn't feel quite like they were on the other side of the world. After a few days of preparation they set off down the coast for a four-week journey towards Sidney via the Princes Highway: '... this was our first long uninhabited stretch, it was quite hilly and almost all forested, there was a beautiful smell of eucalyptus from the trees ... this part of the route was beautiful, there were lots of deep gulleys full of long trees that looked beautiful in the evening sun, in other places the road was banked by high red rocks ...' (Jane)

Merimbula: 'Lots of villas and bathing costume boutiques.' (Jane)

'... we took a detour to a place called Bournda Beach ... huge and empty with crashing surf and white sand.' (Jane)

'... open country with fields and remote smallholdings ... at dusk we were at the most beautiful place called Tilba Tilba which was a small village set in huge wide, wooded hills.' (Jane)

'... A huge beach with white sand and great forested hills rising up all around, and down to the sand a wide area of short grass covered in kangaroos, there were blue and red, and green and red parrots swooping around.' (Jane)

Sydney: 'Cycled on along the main road into Sydney, stopping occasionally in stages to dodge torrential rain. The suburbs looked almost like London; just as busy but less dirty.' (Jane)

Indonesia was the team's first experience of the Third World and was quite a shock with its steaming heat, teeming people and mind boggling noise. Thus, their arrival in Denpasur was to make quite an impression: 'All the bicycles are big black things that people cronk along on with their knees sticking out! Everywhere there were palm trees and everything was very lush and green. Along our route to Kuta Beach there were houses all the way and they were mostly like huts with a few people standing around or sitting on the earth. Everywhere the children were pointing and screaming with laughter at us and yelling 'hello, hello' ... And everywhere there are smells: food cooking, people, bad drains, animals, all mixed up together and very strong. There are loads of dogs and cats everywhere too, the cats are lovely but noisy; they are mostly half wild but quite clean looking and fast, they are often flashing across the tops of walls and down from roofs. The dogs though are quite a different story, they are just horrible, most of them look as if they're rotting on their feet, covered in sores and mange with their bones sticking out everywhere ... The other thing here is geckos, little lizards that run all over the walls and ceilings and eat mosquitoes, I really like them, the way they dart about — and anything that gets rid of mosquitoes is fine by me!' (Jane)

In fact, to grab a moment of peace and quiet they had to get up at the crack of dawn before the whole lot started up again: 'I woke at about 5 to the sounds of women sloshing washing. It gets light at about 4.30 in Bali and by about 8 the sun is quite strong. Went to the beach by myself ... looking at the white beach and palm trees and trying to believe I really was where I was!' (Jane)

Further respite could be found by pedalling up into the mountains: '... up and up through palms and forest and with spectacular views ... downhill for about 15 km, wonderful views across hills with little field shapes over them, isolated villages, rocky outcrops and jungly palms ... As we reached the coast again on the north side of Bali, the air lost some of its humidity and the scenery all round became more brown and baked looking. The villages were dustier and less rural ... Found ourselves somewhere to stay on the coast. The beaches here are black sand, the water shallow and waveless and there are big palm trees leaning out at steep angles.' (Jane)

'... Borobadur — this is a very ancient beautiful temple, supposed to be one of the several extra wonders of the world. It *was* wonderful though — the whole thing was in a kind of pyramid construction with a long flight of steps right from top to bottom that you could leave at any point to walk round one of the many tiers. All the way up there was dense and elaborate stone work and many, many cross-legged Buddhas sitting enclosed in little frames ... The views from the top were spectacular ... out across the jungle and paddy fields towards the mountains and volcanoes in the distance.' (Jane)

Another change of country and scene as they arrived in **Singapore** for Christmas: 'Everything looked incredibly clean and rich ... a huge contrast to Java ... exotic plants and flowers jumping out everywhere.' (Jane)

In **Malaysia** they were to pass through miles and miles of palm oil plantations which they had been told were full of pythons and king cobras. Fortunately the only pythons they spotted were those that were 'dead and decapitated and in piles of tangled reptile' on the roads. However they were to spot other wild life of a gentler sort: 'Saw some beautiful birds — very bright turquoise with red beaks flitting among the palms.' (Jane)

For the most part the team cycled down the east coast of Malaysia. Not as scenic as you might imagine: 'This was our first bit of East Coast but most of the time we couldn't see the sea — just some scrubby grassland and endless scrappy palm trees. Also there was quite a bit of industry — at one point we ended up cycling into the middle of a huge Esso oil refinery.' (Jane)

A few days of this and things improved: '... for the first time the coast was beautiful — little *kampongs* (villages) by white, sandy palm-lined beaches ... sparkling beautifully in the morning sun.' (Jane)

One of the stranger sights for the team along the East Coast had been muslim women walking along the beaches completely covered up ... this was to fade in Bhuddist **Thailand**: 'Thailand — colourful, friendly and above all unveiled! The people were so beautiful too ...' (Jane)

'Came to a huge statue of a gold cross-legged Buddha rising up through the trees on the top of a hill — quite a sight, especially when you're not expecting to see anything grand. The 3 of us climbed to the top by the statue up the temple steps ... went to what we hoped was a cafe, but which turned out to be a Buddhist monastery! Lots of young boy novices with shaven hair sides and vibrant orange and lemon yellow robes.' (Jane)

Bangladesh was reminiscent of their experience of Indonesia, and before they'd even touched down they could see masses of people below them: 'The landscape looked brown and arid. Down below we saw a group of thin, ragged Bangledeshis scuttling across the runway to a waterhole.' (Kate)

Nepal was where they were to set eyes on the much anticipated Himalayas, there were a few other things to feast their eyes on as well: 'We arrived in Katmandu in early April. This is a beautiful city with wonderful medieval architecture; it is however, incredibly dirty. Rubbish and flies are everywhere.' (Kate)

'The scene is totally chaotic with rickshaws, autorickshaws and motorcycles announcing their arrival by blaring their horns. They are clever at manouvering around the docile cattle who sit in the middle of the road, oblivious of the obstruction they are causing. In the major roads we saw the same scene — cows lying nonchalently munching while steaming angry trucks race past missing them by inches.' (Kate)

'April is a bad month for visibility because the Himalayas are usually wrapped in impenetrable cloud. We felt very fortunate to be able to see the rugged outline of the Annapurna range glistening clearly in the early morning sun. We went rowing on the Polhara Lake and again the range could be seen mirrored in the tranquil water. It was very beautiful.' (Kate)

India was to provide them with an excessively busy schedule and little time to see much of the country itself, or record anything of it in their diaries however, busy schedules or not there was no way they could leave without seeing the Taj Mahal which Kate said 'exceeded all our expectations.'

The African Trail

Julia, Willy, Andy, Norman and Moira left London on a crisp December afternoon and arrived in Harare, Zimbabwe to find a very different Africa from the one envisaged: 'It's an open-spaced city with pastel-fronted colonial-style houses.' (Julia)

'This didn't feel at all like the Africa I'd expected. I don't suppose it was really, just a lump of displaced Europe.' (Norman)

The poorer quarters of Harare presented a rather different picture: 'This area had lots of people on the streets; Indian shops selling saries and samosas, cafés serving loud 'Sadza' music, garages etc.' (Andy)

'On sights like this Angels must have gazed in their flight' said Livingstone, not of Harare but of Victoria Falls and since the little Angels of Four Corners happened to be passing they stopped for a gaze themselves: 'Amazing sight as you round the corner to overlook Devil's

Cataract, a 100–metre dip from the wide waters of the Zambezi to the tumultuous boiling gorge below. The spray travels as high as the falls again and a rainbow crosses the view.' (Julia)

'No picture can do justice to them. You don't get a sense of their length or height, the amazing roar roar roar, the huge amounts of spray that fly up from the gorge, driven up by a gale like upside-down rain, and then curl over the edge to drench you in a fine mist or heavy shower.' (Andy)

Another watery sight they were to behold was Lake Kariba: 'This lake is beautiful, huge, the biggest man-made lake in the world, 200 km long and 32 km wide.' (Julia)

Africa turned out to be far greener than expected and in some places it was eerily like parts of England, with only the exotic wildlife to make the distinction: '. . . on the southern section of this route fertile grass and woodland ranches — surprisingly similar to English landscapes — gave way to sparsely wooded scrub. Chameleons and snakes in the verges and vervet monkeys, baboons and buck way off the road. Insects are frequent too, some of them the biggest I've ever seen. Beetles 2 inches long. Up to a dozen different species of ant. At lay-bys the trees are very often swarming with tiny ants. At the side of the road, termite hills up to 6 feet are not uncommon.' (Norman)

The first impression of **Malawi** was that it was even greener than Zimbabwe and there were more people: 'Lilongwe itself is very strange — a lot of roundabouts and signs saying 'Area 1, 2, or 3 but no houses. Big tar roads with lots of green in between them, and many poor people in rags or very cheap and bright synthetic clothes walking between them.' (Andy)

'Went exploring the amazing Lilongwe market; a vast expanse of stalls selling fruit, vegetables (huge selection of healthy-looking fruit). Although the overall impression was quite squalid and the smells were something else, it was exciting looking round and feeling that you could buy almost all the essential items of food or equipment you might need and there were enough craftsmen around to adapt and make it for you if not.' (Julia)

Out in the country there were lots of people and activity too: 'Came across the village flour mill with a queue of women waiting outside with their maize. Back onto the beach just in time to see a group of fishermen pulling their nets. The catch was fascinating — fishes of all sizes were flapping around catching their last breath before ending up on dinner plates. Villagers had flocked to grab the best of the catch whilst fishermen turned a blind eye as children picked up as many tiddlers as they could get away with . . . saw a fish eagle fly overhead and swoop down into the sea to try for a fish.' (Moira)

Livingstonia, on Lake Malawi was a mixture of another 'displaced bit of Europe' and Paradise: '. . . situated 2,000 feet above Lake Malawi — spectacular views across to Tanzania, like Cote d'Azur without the condos. Very odd though, it feels more like Scotland than anywhere else. Scottish missionaries founded it in 1894 and built houses out of grey stone, just like you find in Scotland.' (Julia)

Tanzania: '. . . a great country — huge open spaces and open easy-going people.' (Julia)

'The next 50 km took us from a cold, misty English highland down a breathtakingly beautiful river valley, green and lush with trees, and loud with the sound of rushing water and spinning tyres as we flew round hairpin bend after hairpin bend to a warmer, humid, flatter valley floor.' (Julia)

'The rest of the ride was a smart ride into Mbuyuni along the sunlit valley with beautiful grey scrubby mountains on all sides and clouds of bright yellow weaver birds feeding in the nettles by the side of the road while groups of kids skipped and sang as they went home from school.' (Julia)

'35 km ride down the Great Ruaha valley — probably the best part of any ride so far. The morning was fresh and warm and the huge river, brown with sediment, supported a thick fringe of tropical flora along its banks. Huge leaves dominated the baobab trees around and provided cover for more baboons than I've ever seen squatting lazily on the road in front of us picking at berries until we were nearly upon them when they scattered into the trees looking down at us as we passed.' (Julia)

Dar es Salaam: 'The road along the seafront is absolutely beautiful, curving by white sands with palm trees and the sea as turquoise as any travel brochure. Ocean Drive it was called and the end nearest the town was surrounded by a busy market with a fish auction, a good fruit market . . .' (Julia)

What awaited the team over the border in **Kenya** was something that would help them quickly forget their sadness at leaving Tanzania behind . . . it would also give them a break from pedalling, though not a break. A letter from Willy told the whole story: 'Climbing Kilimanjaro was the most amazing experience. We took six days to get up and down. The climb went through the stunning regions which varied from tropical rain forests to bare arid dust plains . . . The last night we slept at 15,500 ft and I didn't believe that I could ever get so cold — I slept in a sleeping bag in 3 extra jackets and 2 pairs of trousers. In fact nobody slept. We all lay there gasping for breath in the thin air. We were woken at 1.30 am for the final 3,000 ft to the top. We move unbelievably slowly and by the top were stopping to get our breath back every 10/20 steps. Willie (our guide) was an old bloke of about 60 who ran up and down, with a fag hanging out of his mouth, urging us on and singing hymns to us in Swahili. He was mad as a hatter but really lovable. Just before the top we met a Japanese climber who had a suspected oedema. He had literally turned blue and could not speak or stand. Willie (the guide again) massaged and pummelled him then two guides took an arm each and ran down the mountain dragging the poor sod behind them. Eventually we all made the crater rim and watched in gobsmacked awe as the sun rose behind Mount Mawenzi. We had the dawn on one side and the huge blue ice cliffs of Kibo on the other. It really was one of those magical moments I will never forget ... Andy got the nickname Doctor Death on the way up. Our guide had told us that the art of making the top (and only 30% do) was to do everything slowly. Andy had a fit of Germanic obsessiveness and took him too literally. Anything that would have taken a one legged geriatric one hour took Andy 3 hours. Willy, the mad guide, used to follow him singing "Pole Pole Kilimanjaro" — Swahili for slowly, slowly Kilimanjaro. The sight of both of them arriving at a hut four hours after everyone else had us in fits.'

And he ended that letter with: 'I must finish as I think the security guard has spotted that we are not residents at the Hilton and therefore shouldn't be lounging by their pool!'

More wonderful descriptions of Kilimanjaro followed: 'The clouds cleared, and we could see both Mawenzi and Kibo — they were both rising up lovely and high above, beautiful and white in the sun. The contrast between the two was especially beautiful — Kibo smooth and snow-capped, Mawenzi jagged, the snow contrasting with the black rock. It was very bright and sunny, with huge dramatic clouds racing up from the plains below and curling over the lip of the plateau thousands of feet below us ... the Saddle was absolutely beautiful — really weird and empty and absolutely still.' (Andy)

'The walk led through forest; trees dripping with water and festooned with lichen hanging like cobwebs from all the branches. Smells of coffee and lavender drifted over us although it was difficult to trace the source. After about an hour the rain stopped and shafts of sunlight pierced the gloom of the forest.' (Julia)

'The forest changed to moorland ... The vegetation changed too, the giant groundsels appeared towards Horombo and saw some beautiful flowers — otherwise it could have been any Scottish hillside.' (Julia)

'Below the hut were layers of cloud as though we were in a plane; above us the twin peaks of Kilimanjaro: craggy rugged Mawenzi and the smooth slopes of Kibo.' (Julia)

'When we reached the Saddle the alpine vegetation disappeared and became dry brown desert. Quite a spectacular scene with the snow-covered peak in the background.' (Julia)

'An amazing pair of dark blue birds flew off overhead revealing a crimson underside to their wings and furry monkeys screamed in the dense undergrowth.' (Julia)

Once back on their bikes and on the way to Nairobi, the landscape was a little less hilly(!): 'The road cut through vast landscape of rolling plains, we passed a lot of Masai — some working the fields and some herding cattle.' (Moira)

From the rolling plains to 'heavy culture shock' in **Nairobi:** 'It seems richer than London — hundreds of plush safari camp offices, bars, restaurants, bright lights, manic drivers, wide boys, prostitutes, Wuzungu tourists (whites), Norwich Union, Wimpy and Woolworths ...' (Andy)

As soon as they could they left the city behind and went back into the wilderness: '... viewed the game in the Ngorongoro crater and gazed in awe at the vast plains of the Serengeti.' (Willy)

(Andy and Norman went off separately to visit the Turkana desert: 'I wouldn't have missed it for the world. Turkana scenery is unreal. Vegetationless, barren in the extreme, remote and stunningly beautiful ... the surrounding hills of volcanic rock which glow in the afternoon sun, the sunsets and subsequent crystal clear night skies and the feeling that you are travelling through the edge of the Earth all made this the highlight for me of the trip so far.' (Norman)

Moira made a brief visit to Mombasa: 'Streets full of people, food spread over the pavement — piles of coconuts — I'd never seen so many in one place ... tomatoes in piles of 4 like pyramids. Women dressed in kangas added to the colour — men pulling carts — bicycles passing, weaving in and out of the crowds — bike workshops, mechanics busily straightening up wheels — inner tubes and bits of bike sprawled over the pavement.' (Moira)

Egypt was reported to be dirty, smelly, extremely noisy and anarchic — and the African Trail team loved it more than anywhere else on their route as their descriptions clearly indicate: 'The first few days were spent cycling up the Nile Valley — endlessly interesting and with a timeless quality that felt as though things hadn't changed much since the Pharoahs. Old men on donkeys, kids on camels on top of bundles of sugar cane, snarling dogs, dead dogs/or donkeys — (hard to distinguish the smells) green fields, water buffalos and, just to the side in either direction, bare desert.' (Julia)

'Little villages were built just into the desert, placed there to avoid taking up too much arable land. The houses were often made of mud, sometimes of wick. They were small and square and looked very poor. There was much more rubbish on the edge of the road than in Africa — and dead animals. Dead dogs in their scores, smeared across the road with their intestines red and sticky buzzing with flies. Dead dogs from a few days back, stinking like hell and half rotted. Dead dogs pressed flat as if run over by a steamroller. Disgusting and upsetting as they were, we preferred dead dogs to live ones.' (Andy)

'Vegetarianism seemed to become a valid option for me again as a few kilometres later we drove through a pool of blood in the road. Screeching to a halt we looked for the source imagining a traffic accident victim ... or a dead dog. Nothing so prosaic — a huge cow was being hauled up a scaffold by its back legs, its glassy eyes staring up at a crazy angle, the head half split off from the body by a huge gaping wound. The master butcher was already cutting off the udder, then running his knife inside the leg and peeling off the skin, revealing the pink sac underneath. A row of sheep in a similar state of undress hung upside down next to the cow, dripping blood from their severed heads. Sickened by this bloody sight, we struggled on, to be finally blown out by a huge bloated gaseous buffalo floating in the canal, whilst children drank and splashed around in it.' (Andy)

'... the desert was just that — flat rock and sand mixture spreading away in all 4 directions as far as you could see ... The grubbiness was a feature of much of Egypt, but especially this road. To our surprise we found a lot of buildings strung out along it, but they didn't add anything to the scene. They were always half-built, with bricks and rubble and barbed wire spread in a wide circle around them. The desert along the roadside was in fact just a dumping ground for all sorts of rubbish, and this took away a lot of its appeal.' (Andy)

'... the road became a bit more interesting, with craggy mountains on either side, and the occasional Bedouin encampment.' (Andy)

Part of the route in Egypt took the team across the Sinai, in the centre of which is St. Catherine's monastery. On the way to St. Catherines: '... huges hills and gorges between steep sandstone elphantine buttresses opening into vistas of desert floors and wind eroded isolated rocks of bizarre shapes.' (Julia)

And actually at St. Catherines: 'The mountain's the highest in Egypt, 2,600 metres and is where the angels are said to have laid the bones of St. Katerina, a fervant Christian in pagan years who was executed for her beliefs . . . We reached the chapel on the top and stayed eating lunch gazing across the rosy vistas of rugged jagged ranges stretching into the heat haze in every direction.' (Julia)

And finally at the pyramids: 'Visited the pyramids that evening, half an hour after arriving found ourselves half way up Cheops, the biggest! A watchman took us up despite 'forbidden' notices — fantastic sensation — dark grey blocks of ancient granite and wide angle views of Cairo . . . saw the son et lumiere from a sand dune and then crept by candle light round the tombs.' (Julia)

'The sense of history here is truly awesome . . . to sit in the Abu Simbel temple (one of hundreds) and look at paintings and hieroglyphics that tell stories of life and wars and loves of thousands and thousands of years ago is a really sobering experience. Everything is on such a huge scale. The Karnak temple goes on for miles and took 2,000 years to complete. The Cheops pyramid would dwarf modern buildings and pyramids made so majestic and full of feeling make European cathedrals look small and fussy.' (Willy)

The Oriental Path

The traffic, dirt, pollution and noise in **Hong Kong** were no worse than those Aidan, Rhoda, Adria and Sebastian had just left behind in London and of course with many signs written in English there was a familiarity about the place, but the humid air carrying unfamiliar smells and an awful lot else told them that they really had begun their part of the Four Corners: 'Hong Kong whirls and shuffles and shifts and crashes around you.' (Adria)

'No other cyclists on the roads, lots of buses, trams and cars all moving very quickly but fairly carefully. We are an immediate focal point for unselfconscious staring, gaping, smiling, laughing, giggling and often hear shouts of "bye-bye" as we whizz past . . . Distracted by the shops with lots on display . . . Sky rise apartment blocks rise up. Washing, flowers, bamboo scaffolding, wall paintings, street cleaner; a little lady with two wheeled barrow, with wicker baskets and a straw brush, totally regardless of the traffic.' (Sebastian)

China was to have been the most exciting part of the trip, but sadly permission to cycle through areas normally closed to tourists was not granted and so their trip was mainly restricted to the fairly well-beaten tourist tracks. However, they saw a good deal more of China than most tourists and even other travellers: 'Canton, 4.3.87 — I heard about the early morning market and got a glimpse of the leftovers this afternoon. They sell cats, dogs, monkeys, chickens, eels, fish, crabs, frogs, pigeons ... everything! Not just odd animals but very strange to see them eat seemingly every part of the animal's body; intestines, feet, eyes. On the market stalls they slice animals live to prove their freshness!' (Adria)

'First glimpse of rural China by bike. Off the road and up orange beaten track. Passing fields being worked by girls in blue and straw hats ...' (Sebastian)

'We saw some of 'real' China, the sort that most foreigners wouldn't even get a glimpse of except from a dirty train window. Everywhere we went we were welcomed enthusiastically by the locals.' (Sebastian)

The famous Limestone Peaks in the South of China had been much looked forward to and Adria describes the surrounding area as they come into view: 'Wuzhous to Yangshuo 8.3.87 ... To begin with in the early hours of the morning and as the sun rose we cycled along winding narrow roads over mountainous sub-tropical terrain. After a couple of hours the land flattened out and we cycled for many kilometres over the flat wide plains with views of the Limestone Peaks. Every little patch of land along the way was meticulously farmed and irrigated ... so much was growing. A lot of rice. Large areas split into tiny squares, perfectly sectioned off with little ridges to walk along. Many workers guided cattle harnessed to simple ploughs to turn the soil, soil is mostly very red. Cattle looked like oxen, long-haired, long curved horns and long rough looking noses.' (Adria)

'... we passed through the most beautiful mountains and lake scenery, a bit like the Italian Appennines in spring, but with every hillside blanketed in yellow rape, the local winter crop. The Chinese hillside terracing is unbelievable, creeping up the most impossibly steep slopes.' (Aidan)

'... wherever there was flat land there would be yellow ... interspersed with purple flowers — a yellow and purple quilt.' (Sebastian)

Other parts of China were to be reminiscent of Italy as well: 'Chongging ... dirty and well polluted but the old streets on the peninsula that leap up and down hill are enchanting. It's a little like being somewhere in

Italy. The main high streets are yukky but the tiny side streets are full of fascinating things ... Barrels and barrels of squirming eels, row upon row of dangling pork and pig fat, basket upon basket of ginger, potatoes, greens, mushrooms ...' (Adria)

Part of the journey was by boat along the famous Yangste river: 'The deck was wet, clouds whirled above over the tops of the rocks beside us that dropped precipitously to the thick heavy brown water of the Yankse around us. The sky was otherwise overcast. The formation of the rocks was fascinating. Thousands of years of pushing and shoving from the earth's crust had left them looking callously split, thousands of years of thrashing by the elements had eroded them in great stripey streaks that cut down to the water like streaks of lightning.' (Adria)

Their exit from China was via Shanghai: '... the facades of the buildings here I was told were a mix of neo-classical Chicago with a hint of Egyptian — sounds peculiar but the description was apt ... the streets were amazing. Little side streets lined with old terraced wooden houses. Every doorway was occupied with a different activity. Women sold eggs in egg-shaped wire baskets. Children toddled around in and out of the little grey doorways. Brightly coloured laundry, fun patched kids clothes dangled all over the place like flags.' (Adria)

Finally, Adria's main impression of China: 'There are always a lot of people around who only have the use of one eye ... come to think of it it's the eye complaints that seem the most prolific. Hygiene's pretty appalling. The loos are unforgettable; so are the filthy kitchens.'

South Korea being a last minute addition to the itinerary, there had been little time to visualise what to expect ... they weren't unhappy with what they found: 'We cycled the way around the beautiful peninsula, very mountainous, very green; lovely people, rich culture.' (Adria)

'Chejudo — one of the world's most mountainous regions, only 20% of the land is flat and arable. Solid granite and limestone base of the land is lifted and folded into mountains that on the east coast plunge precipitously to the sea and that on the southern and western slopes descend gradually to the coastal plains.' (Adria)

'The road glided through thousands of tangerine groves along the coast. The bright blue sea was rarely out of view.' (Adria)

Seoul, though highly westernised, still had traces of the past to be found: 'Behind the 14-lane highways that slash through the city and the huge masses of concrete, steel and glass are centuries-old Royal palaces, temples, pagodas and imposing stone gateways set in gardens where you wouldn't know the rest of the city existed.' (Adria)

Other large towns were also very westernised: 'Pusan ... the streets at night were full of life, with an almost European atmosphere. Stalls and markets in Korea certainly specialise, one shop selling just chains and padlocks, another full of a wonderful variety of nuts! Coffee bars and bakeries with sweet breads and cakes are very popular as are cinemas. 'Les Miserables', James Bond and 'The Mission' were all on when we were there along with a seemingly endless selection of gory violent Korean films.' (Aidan)

Rhoda and Sebastian went in pursuit of the old Korea and found it at the end of a rough track: 'Rhoda even persuaded me to go up a rough track to a temple and an old fortress wall. 2 km of agony beside a small reservoir, but cherry blossom, a last outpost, greeted us and a beautiful Kensai temple, quite deserted and with an evocative atmosphere — situated at the end of a valley, surrounded by steep rocky hill thick with foliage ... Pelicote trees and light breeze. Tranquil, calm.' (Sebastian)

They returned to Seoul to take the flight to **Japan**, where to begin with the team were hit with the hard and fast Tokyo: '... thick with traffic and striking sunset silhouetting roads, trains, sky scrapers, pipes, chimneys, pylons, water, rivers ...' (Sebastian)

Not surprisingly, industry was very much present in most of the Japanese cities they were to pass through: '... the city's just teeming with concrete blocks and factories ... it's odd to notice heavy industry, something that as southerners in England we had not been brought up with ... Cities packed with factories and chimneys belching thick smoke into the atmosphere. Yuk! In Japan these industrial plants smack themselves in and around every city.' (Adria)

Despite being highly industrialised, there were still many areas of extreme, untouched, beauty to be discovered: '... narrow roads surrounded by paddy fields filled with the noise of frogs croaking, or tea plantations smelling so potently of tea you think you're in a tea cup. And Buddhist shrines with strange little stone figures each with its own red bib ... I explored a small temple ... there are too many of them. The one I did look at had been badly maintained. The gravel was disappearing to mud, it had a wild feel like a forgotten grave yard, which indeed it might have been ... rows of little statues at knee level, images of Buddha, with character inscribed red bibs and bunches of withering flowers held, sometimes in a beer bottle or other logo'd receptacle that didn't fit in with the ancient worn stone.' (Sebastian)

'Nagoya to Kamamutju — the ride was just beautiful lifting us up over mountains along smooth narrow lanes through dense forests of pine and bamboo trees. I shall not forget how beautiful it was, even in the pouring rain.' (Adria)

'Flat flooded rice fields.' (Rhoda)

'Close to the coast. Undulating road . . . thousands of little islands, all greenery sitting on top of small lumps of sandy lands . . . Some had temples and were linked together by bright red narrow bridges . . . To look at the scene as a whole it resembled a map of the Greek Islands, but condensed into a smaller area.' (Sebastian)

'One of the most beautiful rides to date. Hakkoda San National Park over 1,040 metre mountain pass . . . The road followed a very fast-flowing mountain river that barged and splashed its way through newly-green woodland. The sun shone through the overhanging leaves. It was idyllic.' (Adria)

'From the lake we went down and down, a road that followed an idyllic mountain river . . . Gushing water over boulders, and forest, and bracken and ivy, waterfalls and small tributaries, and stepping stones and cool and very beautiful and extremely luscious — a sort of paradise.' (Sebastian)

Finland, the land of the midnight sun, caused some confusion: 'The absence of the night throws one's sense of time completely.' (Sebastian) The team were to spend some time in Helsinki before pedalling on through forested countryside: 'Much of the architecture is quite Russian with buildings a dirty yellow orange colour. Flights of steps lead up to many of the buildings, pillars and columns and Georgian windows and long straight facades.' (Sebastian)

'The trees change considerably. Sometimes pines which go up and up, rising from a fresh floor which is quite bare, to a forest where deciduous is richly mixed with conifer and the undergrowth is dense and thick and impassable.' (Sebastian)

'The houses are mostly wooden-built, planked outer walls, distinctive roofs, and sauna buildings in the garden or adjoining with tall chimney stacks.' (Sebastian)

The first stop in **Sweden** was the capital which was extremely enchanting: '. . . immediate impression of Stockholm is a fairy tale town — spires, crenellations and castellations and highly decorated domes, and impressive aristrocratic buildings, and trees and statues and yachts and ships and boats bobbing all over the harbour.' (Sebastian)

After this there was some dirt road riding through flat terrain surrounded by a sea of endless yellow rape or hay fields, contrasting with vast tracts of forest. At the end of the day 'various lakesides' would provide the campsite.

The team entered **Norway** just after the lakes had thawed, as summer had been late coming; in fact this meant lots of wild flowers they would have otherwise missed. There were many mountains to pedal up, but for this extra effort the team were rewarded with a breathtaking view - in fact the most beautiful sights of the oriental trip so far: 'Terrain suddenly got hillier. Very green. Lots of wheat and barley crops. Big tall pine trees ... excellent scenery, steep descending fjiords.' (Rhoda)

'You will cycle in the continual presence of mountains — some of them permanently snow-capped ... Some of the most impressive coastal scenery in Europe' (Rhoda quoting from Nick Crane's *Cycling Guide to Europe* and following one of his recommended routes).

'... climbed up through forest to emerge onto a plateau which was stunning. Trees bashed by winter, scrub grass. Road wound through. Patches of snow-capped mountains in the distance. Pancake lakes, sheep with cow bells, a stone church that had a turf roof, low slung and snug on the landscape.' (Sebastian)

Well that brings us to the edges of Europe with just a few of the enthusiasms and impressions of the teams — a gentle introduction to what cycling from the four corners was like. There were many beautiful and memorable moments and these provided an essential cushion against the stresses that the World Bike Riders found themselves having to cope with. Physical stress from the endless pedalling, harsh conditions, sleep deprivation, regular diet changes and constant illness, not to mention the mental stress of being so much in the public eye and, more importantly, from being in such close proximity with only 3 or 4 other people day and night. The wonders along the way, under these circumstances could be the best restorer of spirits when the need arose. As you read on you will probably come to the conclusion that this need must have arisen often.

Conditions

The conditions the riders were up against in many of the developing countries were harsh: they were exposed to extreme weather, the worst roads imaginable, gruelling mountains and deserts, and had to cope with limited food and water supplies, daily exhaustion and nasty tropical bugs. On top of all that it was often 'filthy hot 'n' sweaty!' But however tough it was, it was a reminder that many of these conditions were part and parcel of the daily struggle of the people from Intermediate Technology who had to work 'in the field'. That sobering thought was to carry the riders through the hard bits.

Before discussing conditions on the ride, it is worth mentioning the problems of flying out bikes for tours abroad. All the bikes were dismantled and packed in protective boxes for the flight. Alex wrote back with some sound advice when he arrived in La Paz: 'Tape stuff to the bikes and don't put too much in each box' — the Americas Route team found bits and pieces spilling out of the bottom of their bike boxes when they collected them from the airport. Then too, Nick's bike didn't survive the journey very well and after some rough handling, it arrived with a hole bashed in the frame and one of the mudguards almost tied in a knot. It took the Asian Trail team 5 hours to put their bikes back again — obviously not all attended those bike maintenance classes!

It is essential that tyres are let down before the bikes are packed for the flight: Adria's flight out was spoiled by a nagging doubt that she had forgotten to do this and of course if she hadn't, the tyres would have blown and she'd have had to have changed the inner tube on arrival.

At Dhaka airport, Kate was to make a grand entrance via the luggage conveyor belt — she'd just managed to rescue her bike in time before the porters tried to fold it through the luggage hatch!

Roads

In Bolivia, the **Americas Route** team began their journey by reluctantly pedalling their spanking new bicycles over the cobbled hilly streets of La Paz. The hardest part was the steep 5-kilometre, fully-laden climb out of La Paz, but doing this without stopping was a matter of honour since they had made a pre-expedition pact to do it with their route mentor Hallam Murray. (Hallam, they did it!)

It wasn't just the road surfaces or lack of them that were to cause problems either. Meryl found that the most disturbing aspect of cycling in Bolivia was that the drivers seemed to take perverse delight in driving as close to the team as they possibly could, only swerving to avoid an actual collison at the last minute. This happened several times a day, and often they would look up to see a band of laughing Indians jeering at them from the back of a truck or car.

At some points the roads were narrow and slippery with a sheer drop of 2,000 feet on the left-hand side. Then, the prospect of meeting a truck coming the other way was even more alarming. At one point, Meryl reported that 'truck upon truck started appearing in the bends of the road ahead, heading for a massive pile up. As all traffic stopped all the men took the opportunity to relieve themselves wherever they fancied before trying to remove the blockage in the road.'

For a while on the Peru side of Lake Titicaca, they were welcomed by fairly flat tarmac roads, but that didn't last too long. Jo found the road out of Copacobana to be one of the worst with dirt, sand, grit and stones — none of them packed down — making for difficult riding. Out of Puno they enjoyed a brief respite of relatively good, flat roads — until they hit the Pan American Highway. As Meryl said in no uncertain terms 'The Pan American is a complete joke and does not deserve such a lofty title', while Jo wrote:

> 'The Pan American out of Juliaca was terrible — stones, gravel and lots of skidding. But there were cyclists along the side of the road on a track and so we followed their lead. The track was about 6 inches wide running beside the railway track by the road and through fields where stones threw the tyres off. Thomas took the first tumble, then me. I was getting quite weak with no food and little the day before.'

They endured 17 kilometres of this, with sand and grit continually flying up into their faces. When the path began to slope down towards steep stagnant waters and both road and track proved too difficult, a third alternative had to be found and then they wheeled their bikes along the sleepers of the railway line. These were mostly single line though and so when they came to long bridges over gorges and rivers, they had to trust to luck that they wouldn't meet a train coming the other way — fortunately, as they were to discover later, trains only ran once a day.

It was with some relief therefore that they reached the tarmac road. The first few kilometres were great but then melted tar began to stick to their tyres and hamper progress. Meryl called the road to Cuzco 'foul' and she hated the 'smelly traffic' ... and worse was to come.

The stretch of road from Cuzco to Nazca was to be the toughest of the whole trip due to the large numbers of high passes they had to climb: 'The next week can be summed up by the chanted sarcastic refrain of "it's all downhill to Nazca" — it wasn't and it became a standing joke amongst us as we slowly ground up hill after hill and across bare and silent plains.' (Alex)

Meryl came off particularly badly: 'We met fords across the road; I fell into one and stepped in another. My legs were looking worse for wear: one sock on, bandages, bites, wet shoes.'

There is an assumption that riding downhill is much easier than riding up. In fact, it carries its own problems. Constant breaking puts an enormous strain on the hands and wrists. Greater control and concentration are required to avoid potholes and stones, and reaching the bottom leaves you far from exhilarated; often you feel more exhausted than when you reach the top.

'The road followed a river valley all day and was more down than up. The road surface was horrendous. For 4 hours we bumped along through the barren landscape ... I met an old lady who asked why we were undergoing this suffering!' (Meryl)

The team suffered 100 punctures between them over a period of 11 days. Jo and Thomas got completely stranded at one point, when having got through all their rubber puncture patches they had to resort to cutting up their other punctured inner tube to make more. When they ran out of glue supplies with just a few kilometres to go to reach their destination, they had to hitch a lift in the back of a truck.

From Nazca to Lima, the Pan American became a lot smoother with the added bonus that as it ran along the coast, the team were able to take occasional refreshing dips. However, once back on the road they did battle with '100mph behemoths slamming and buffeting us as they raced past'. (Alex)

Interestingly, when you're doing so much mountain cycling, you begin to lose your sense of the gradients. This can have a strange psychological effect whereby although you think you're pedalling on the level and in extreme cases possibly downhill, you find you are cycling as hard as you would if you were tackling a hill (which in fact you are but you don't realise it). You begin to question your strength. You can take the remedies — salt or iron — but still it's the same. This can be extremely deflating and certainly the Americas Route were to find this, though they cottoned on to it: 'It's difficult to gauge slopes and we rely more accurately on the effort required and the gear we're in to tell us.' (Jo)

They climbed to extraordinary heights as well: 'The top of the pass is about 4,300 metres, thin and cold air and almost up to the snowline', and at Christmas they climbed through the Cordillera Blanca reaching 4,080 metres.

Peru had provided an exhausting range of road conditions, over mountains through desert and latterly, over smooth tarmac roads of the Pan American Highway where 'instead of doing 40 km a day in the mountains on dirt roads we could do 70 km quite easily' (Jo). One day they did 90 km before lunchtime!

Ecuador saw a return to the tougher cycling: 'The first thing we noticed about Ecuador was that the roads, still with dirt surfaces, were even steeper than Peru.' (Meryl)

Need I add any more. From here it was on to **Mexico**, where they knew they could be sure of good roads virtually all the way. 'Down from Milcubre, steep cambers, winding, good tarmac road down through the pine forest and the mountains' (Jo). Though the team thought this the best bit of cycling they had done, those on four wheels were the worst they had met so far and buses in particular made playthings of cyclists. Obviously in the U.S.A., the roads couldn't have been bettered and there were few problems from other traffic.

The **Australian** part of the **Asian Highway** route was to be brief, taking the team from Melbourne to Sydney. However, since the team had not done much travelling it was a good acclimatizer. For the most part they travelled along or close to the coast along the Princess Highway which threw few problems in their path though traffic was often heavy and hazardous. The worst culprits were the log-carrying caterpillar juggernauts roaring by buffeting and sucking the riders into their path as they went. To get away from them and to break the monotony they left the road and cycled instead along rough tracks which ran close to the highway. This was to take them through rolling countryside where farm dogs, not wanting to miss the rare opportunity of biting four pairs of juicy ankles, would give chase. The back tyres were an added attraction. The latter stood up to their attentions; the ankles didn't fare so well.

The tracks were often a combination of baked earth, sand, stones and potholes. And the traffic wasn't any slower: 'I cycled on ahead of the other 2 and the track was just through dense bush. Occasionally cars passed and I was amazed that they didn't slow down; they just stormed by showering me with stones and choking me with dust.' (Jane)

However, passing vehicles were rare and that meant for the most part there was just the sound of birds and bicycles — worth the extra struggle over the stones: 'The surface was pretty awful in parts, just sharp stones that turned in very unpredictable directions, the weight of the panniers makes you feel very grounded and once the bike does go off balance it's hard to hold it.' (Jane)

At Denpasar in **Indonesia** it was more like the dodgems — the road was full of 'bikes and motorbikes and honking cars and all proceeding along in the most haphazard and hair-raising way' (Jane).

The roads had fairly good tarmac surfaces which they hadn't expected to find. That was a good thing since they did their first bit of serious hill cycling, climbing 2,000 to 3,000 metres high: '. . . a very long but steady mountain climb, the first part was up through villages and we were called to and followed all the way. Usually I wave and call back but on this occasion I was just grimly concentrating on plodding on up it. I was completely drenched in sweat and it was dripping all over my panniers and into my eyes!' (Jane)

Jane stopped to ask the way, and was told their destination was 3 kilometres away when in fact it was 30! This happened as dark was falling and in the middle of the Javanese jungle — and as Jane found out this can be pretty nightmarish: '. . . nervous impatience turned to pure fear as we pedalled totally unlit through the blackness, unable to see even the road beneath the front wheel and with nothing but jungle to either side. Occasionally lorries and trucks would hurtle past us and blind us with their lights. As we battled along I vowed to never get into such a pointlessly dangerous situation again.'

It was a great relief to find that in **Singapore** Jane's confidence was restored and she reported feeling 'safe as houses on the wide, well lit smooth roads'.

Again in **Malaysia** the roads were good and they almost glided along the coastal route towards Thailand. Mind you, they took extra caution not to topple over sideways — there were deep puddles at the edges of the roads which were full of water snakes! On the road there were rotting heaps of larger varieties of the species.

Whilst **Thailand** could also boast smooth roads with little traffic, occasionally things deteriorated: 'We did a full 40 kilometres without stopping — the first part of this was across endless roadworks. We were sliding about on loose earth and rubble, disappearing down potholes and sometimes crossing rivers on planky holey bridges.' (Jane)

The British Embassy in Dhaka strongly advised them not to risk cycling in **Bangladesh** because of the reckless driving. In fact, they found traffic less of a problem here than in Indonesia. The roads were tarred, and when they did encounter traffic they had to get off the road anyway because it was single lane.

In **Nepal** they covered their greatest distance in any one day when they pedalled 140 km from the plains of Nepal to Kathmandu on the flat dusty road of the Raj Pass. In the towns and cities, particularly Kathmandu, the streets were more like very narrow dirt roads. They were full of rickshaws, motorcycles, trucks and cattle which have to be carefully manoeuvred round. They experienced their toughest hill climbing in the foothills of the Himalayas up to Polhara where they would climb for up to 30 kilometres. Progress was occasionally hampered by piles of large rocks from rock falls. However, they also achieved their greatest speeds in Nepal — when cycling away from Nepalese dogs.

In **India**, once again their route was along flat and dusty roads all the way from Nepal to Delhi. Here, the most serious riding problem they encountered was when they arrived at a junction to find Kanpur, the place they wanted to reach, signposted in both directions!

At the end of this stage of the Asian Trail each team member had got through a set of tyres, and punctures had been so numerous they'd lost count.

In **Zimbabwe** the **African Trail** team were amazed at both the frequency and accuracy of the signposting and the quality of the roads: 'The road surfaces here are great, much better than in the UK, drivers are far more considerate too, often waiting behind for vehicles coming the other way, and giving loads of room when passing.' (Norman)

The exception to this was the stream of buses — up to 20 or 30 a day — of the 'Shoe Shine Bus Company'. Andy described the problem: 'These buses are crammed, crammed, crammed full of people all spilling out of the windows and doors. The roof is chronically overloaded with bedsteads, bikes, chairs, suitcases, mealie bags etc! When the bus pulls up at one of the stores all the unfortunate people spill out and rush off to the toilet and then into the store to buy "Chibuku" or "Lion Lager". The drivers drink the most, so you have to keep a good eye on the buses.'

To avoid the buses they took to the less dangerous but potholed cycle lanes, but it wasn't all flat and easy going as Norm pointed out: 'We were travelling East to West, against the grain of the mountains, which meant stiff climbs and lots of sweat. Luckily the surface was good and the traffic quite light.'

In **Malawi** the hill climbs involved dangerous hairpin bends too: 'Having completed the first couple of hairpins, I began to wonder whether or not we would make it to the bottom in one piece; concentration and constant pressure on the brakes and impeccable balance were needed. Throughout the descent my wrists were a constant source of agony — due to the amount of pressure put on the handlebars and brakes.' (Moira)

Tanzania proved to be a pleasant surprise for the reasons outlined by Julia: 'Cycled along excellent roads . . . the 93 km stretch turned out to be only 69 km. Found out the reason today, the Michelin map was revised in '79 and the road was built in the early 80s and greatly straightened.'

Even the worst roads provided some enjoyment as Andy recalls: 'The road was really rough again and the bikes took quite a bashing. The worst bits were the soft sand . . . sunk over the rims and we were immobile . . . Going very fast crashing from boulder to boulder, slithering and bouncing across the sand. Out of the saddle to save the rear wheel. The faster we went the more dangerous and exhilarating it became . . .

'There are six different types of surface on the road from Dar to the North. In ascending order of difficulty, they are:

1. Tar (apt to melt).
2. Tar with potholes.
3. Tar with bad potholes.
4. Washed away tar - very rocky, with occasional lumps of tar.
5. Washed away tar with corrugations. Very bad.
6. The worst - deep sand.

'For the latter it is recommended that you deflate your tyres and keep an eye out for the very deep bits - the aim is to stay on the bike for as long as possible, and hopefully you won't have to push.'

Tanzania had its own version of the Shoe Shine Bus Company and the team nicknamed them crab buses because they moved in a strange sideways gait across the road.

In **Kenya** again they were to find the two extremes: 'The Turkana was great . . . the road was THE WORST in the world — it was a lava field with occasional tyre marks in it. 18 punctures in one day GGGGGRRRR!'

They also enjoyed some of the best tarmac roads in Kenya, covering 270 km in two days easily.

Egypt saw some of the most difficult cycling of any of the teams: 'Up at 3 am, left at 4 am. Cycled across desert — moonlight — sunrise, sand, sand, sand and more sand ... Real effort and concentration. Pitch black no moon. Cars, buses, lorries approaching with full headlights.' (Moira crossing the Eastern Desert from the Nile to the Red Sea)

On the way to find the ferry port to cross the Suez Canal, they were completely mislead: 'This time it was a lesson in Egyptian navigation — the signs pointed clearly down one road then the next, the road got covered with sand — eventually trailed out into one big drive. Climbing to the top we could see lots of sand leading to lots of water but no El Shat and no ferry.'

In fact, that day got so bad, what with sand storms, not being able to find El Shat and the encroaching darkness, that all the team ended up having to hitch a lift.

Dogs along the road were another problem to be dealt with. They would wait for the riders to pass and then chase them in large packs, barking and growling wildly. Choosing to outrun them carried the risk of crashing if they hit a pothole at speed or even being knocked off the bike by a speedy dog. It took courage to stop and face them but it worked, sending the dogs off in a panic.

Despite having been through all this, the roads of Cairo were even more frightening. It wasn't only the mad drivers, (and when you learn that Egyptians only have to be able to drive between two posts to pass their test then you know we're talking mad here!). For Julia, the scariest part of the whole trip was the 14 km through the Cairo traffic 'up over flyovers the wrong way, down drain grids, across dual carriageways to the Siak Pyramids Hotel, and this is where I lose all sympathy. Ended the day with a huge buffet meal and sunk into bed watching television!' (courtesy of the hotel).

Far away in another city, Sebastian, of **The Oriental Path** team described cycling through **Hong Kong** as an 'incredible experience', since they were virtually the only cyclists on the streets winding their way round cars, trams and buses. Rhoda told us 'Our team hung out in Hong Kong for almost two weeks where we played that familiar city game "suicide or survive" amongst all that high tech transport on the highways'.

And in **China** the roads weren't too bad; tarmac and occasionally dirt roads. The latter at least gave them some challenging cycling as Adria described: 'The bikes went well on rough ground — I mean really rough ground where we were riding over huge loose stones, sometimes gravel, sometimes unpacked but laid stones, and sometimes just packed dirt.'

'Just as it was about time to stop to eat and rest under the blazing sun we were hit by the longest mountain climb we were to experience that day, only we didn't realise it until we were half way up! It was a hell of a long way but tremendous satisfaction was gained because all our effort was being put into it and of course the higher we got, the more fantastic were the views.' (Age)

South Korea '... turned out to be a blast. 800 miles in 14 days'. When they first arrived in Seoul, they were in for a shock after the quiet roads of China: 'A late afternoon flight left us fumbling around Seoul amongst city traffic of seven lanes each way. I'll never forget the sight of seven pairs of lights roaring towards me, and just making it to the middle of the road to see the same amount whizz the opposite way.' (Rhoda)

Most of their route took them along smooth tarmac coastal roads, albeit sometimes hilly and sometimes tricky: 'Dangerous windy roads not very wide and lined with sand that tumbled from the mountainside.' (Adria)

In **Japan**, roads were generally excellent, but traffic often very heavy and included many long and polluted tunnels.

For most of **Scandinavia** the roads were good except for in the towns and cities where they were cobbled and tramlined and these were found to be the most difficult roads of the trip.

By **Norway** all the team were into their second set of tyres. Here they took the E6 — a surfaced road but narrow and broken in many areas: 'I'm amazed at its poor state, but it doesn't carry that much traffic' (Bas). There were more very long tunnels which were often unlit and treacherous as Tony Redpath, Adria's boyfriend, discovered when he ended up crashing into the side of one of them; the longest was 7.7 km just South of Bodo.

There were of course lots of climbs as they made their way up to the Arctic circle. Trollstigen was a succession of climbs, U-turns and zig zags. Roads became stony and snow covered and altogether very difficult to cycle over.

Struggling against the Elements

Having crossed the equator to La Paz, Jo, Alex, Meryl and Thomas hadn't expected to be greeted by snow. After all, this was summer time in **Bolivia**! And it wasn't only snow but 'a gale force wind, rain, sleet and hail'. Fortunately they had taken thermals which they quickly changed into. They also came in very useful for the Andes, when scorching sun during the day could change to freezing conditions at night.

This was especially the case in **Peru**, where Jo wrote in her diary: 'It was COLD last night, lots of ice on the fly sheet ... We washed in the river; bloody freezing, enough to make your limbs blue within seconds.' The other problem at that height was the ultra violet light and it was important the team protected themselves against sunburn and peeling — Alex's thermometer read 105 in the sun and 100 in the shade — but at least the mountain stream and waterfalls provided an abundance of water to work off dehydration and offer welcome baths and showers.

Before departure they had been positively warned by 'experts' not to risk travelling through Peru during the wet season because of the landslides. In fact the only time when they seriously felt threatened by this was in the Canyon del Pato, where Jo records: '... stones were continually falling from above in the high wind. There were obvious signs of land and rockslides on the road and later in the afternoon I found myself pushing the bike through heavy mud and the mudguards got completely blocked up so I couldn't push it any further.'

However, in **Ecuador** they didn't escape the wet and experienced such heavy afternoon rains and hailstones that they were often confined to only cycling in the morning. Winds of 30–35 mph were a problem throughout the Andes.

In **Mexico** 30 mph gusts of side winds challenged their attempts to beat a fast trail through the Baja California desert under blistering sun. In the USA the winds were only slightly reduced on the West Coast ... Meryl was to write home of other difficulties: 'I stopped breathing on the way to Omaha in over 100 degrees fahrenheight heat and lots of humidity. The papers were warning people not to over exert themselves in the humidity and we were doing 100 miles a day. Contrary to popular belief, the mid west states are *not* flat. I was picked up off the side of the road by a passing policeman and allowed to recover in his air-conditioned car.'

Meanwhile, in **Australia** at least Nick, Jane, Katharine and Pete had good roads, but once again, in the Australian summer, the heat was intense. The journey was broken up by their having to keep stopping to take shade under whatever scraggy shrubs were available on the dry red earth and rock banks lining the road. But they too were to suffer from strong winds — especially on the coastal roads when the wind was against them all the way, causing additional tiredness.

In **Indonesia** there were other problems to contend with. Inside Danpasar airport Jane hadn't realised it was air-conditioned since it was so hot 'But when I went outside for a cigarette ... the air was so humid I couldn't even light the match!' At least there was the odd East Asian thunderstorm to relieve the pressure. One of these erupted on the day the team had to pedal 150 kilometres. over 13 hours with a lot of the route including hilly roads: 'All afternoon it was cloudy and cool and half raining which was great after the usual burning hot sun . . . A big thunderstorm came at about the same time as we reached the main road along which we had to travel the last 20 kilometres to Yogya — the rain was just tipping down and the traffic dense and sloshing — I once got a great wave of water whooshed right over me by a truck — it was such a battle to fight along through the rain that it almost became quite good fun.'

Weatherwise, **Singapore** was much like Indonesia. In **Malaysia** the team were told stories of the floods that they missed by two weeks and which had seen several of the places they were to pass through submerged: '. . . floods so bad that the river had risen up . . . when the waters fell again they left two big crocodiles stranded on the bridge! Again we realised how very lucky we've been to miss the flooding as the area we'd come through on the West Coast is now flooded; Jahore, Baru and Batu Pahet making headlines with villages having to be evacuated etc.' (Jane)

Here and in **Thailand** they were to be battered most of the way down the coast by strong head winds, though there was at least one day let-up from this: 'I think for the very first time in the whole of this damned ride, the wind was square behind us . . . it took for once less than the usual amount of effort to propel ourselves along.'

After the extreme heat of **Bangladesh** the cool air of the **Nepalese** foot hills was very welcome. Whilst here they experienced the lowest temperatures high up in Darjeeling where, for a change, they shivered whilst wearing every item of clothing they possessed.

In **India** they were told 'You have chosen exceedingly the wrong season to come to India'. This was amply confirmed by record temperatures in Calcutta in Uttar Pradesh of 45 degrees centigrade. By this time they were well hardened!

When they had arrived at Harare airport in **Zimbabwe** Julia, Willy, Andy, Norman and Moira were surprised not to be smacked with sweltering African temperatures. Sunny, it was but with light breezes — perfect — but not for long: 'We had to set off into the sun — mad dogs again! Until then we had always cycled at midday — like those other mad dogs the Cranes we discovered that the wind kept you cool as long as you kept moving. In addition we all wear hats and scarves round our necks, and spray water from the bottles over ourselves.' (Andy)

At one point Moira's thermometer went off the top at 120°F and her pump melted in the sun and the team burnt on every exposed area of their bodies: 'It's so easy to burn in literally minutes. Backs, ears, feet and noses seem to suffer most. We're all sporting all sorts of stripes and colour schemes.' (Norm) They were blasted by heat from the sun above and by the heat being reflected back up at them from the road surface. Whilst the Africa team were experiencing this slow roast effect, back home, Britain was experiencing the bleakest winter on record!

Overcast weather was to be the norm throughout **Malawi, Tanzania** and **Kenya**, with occasional days of 100% humidity followed by some wonderful dramatic storms. From Lake Malawi Andy wrote: 'Storm blasted, thunder, pelting rain and lightning and high winds ... held down the outer tent which by now was flapping like a torn sail in the wind.' Three hours later when it all subsided, Andy went outside to see the shore of Mozambique, 30 km away, lit by lightning so powerful it looked like daylight. Often the weather would change in an instant: 'It was great watching the lightning strike the peaks all around, feeling the wind, then 5 minutes of *torrential* rain, then sunlight more wind, and the heavens would open again.'

In **Egypt** there were microwave conditions accompanied by the dreaded sandstorms. 'At 6.30 am the sun would already be creating a furnace inside the tents making them unbearably hot, the only way to keep cool = sea' (Moira). Andy added: 'It was so hot (44°C) that the tar melted and stuck to our tyres. Worse, the stone chips on the road started sticking to the tar, so we were cycling with a ½ inch thick strip of tarmac attached to our tyres. This didn't do much for our rolling resistance, and we kept on having to stop to scrape it off.

'Egypt: at 12 noon, the hottest part of the day, the road led out into the desert. The air there made the 42°C in the shade seem cool, deliciously cool. Unless you've been in the desert you can't realise what no shade means — it's scary. There is nothing to protect you from the sun — it just beats down on you. It gets reflected off the sand and the rocks and temperatures rise to a staggering intensity — it was at least 50°C out there. In addition there was a huge wind blowing, a real hot desert headwind which raised the temperatures even more. Lots of people have cycled down the Nile (Nick Sanders, Neil Clough, Bettina Selby). The difference is that they cycled in December/January, and more important, from north to south. No-one we knew of had cycled the other way — with good reason ... it was a hellish wind and we were fighting it all the way. I was wearing climbing goggles. Willie had skiing glasses on. Even so, sand got in our eyes as the wind whipped up dust devils and we could see on-coming cars only by their headlamps peering through the gloom. It was the nearest to hell I've ever seen. We'd been hot in Africa, but not hot and sandblasted at the same time and then into a hellish head wind with no shade! ... Over the hill and down again, the wind hammering you full in the face at the crest of the hill so you had to push harder going down than up.'

'... 12 hours into the ride and I decided to hitch. Willy nobly agreed to join me. The others continued into the dust storm, heads down and looking good.' (Julia)

In order to reduce resistance to the wind the team cycled bumper to bumper taking it in turns to be the one at the front taking the full brunt of the wind — but as Moira said, being in the middle wasn't much fun either: 'slipstreaming is as boring as hell — you can't talk, watch the scenery or relax at all at snail pace speed using 15–18 gear speeds.'

In comparison to the first three teams, Aiden, Rhoda, Adria and Sebastian had very favourable weather indeed, though the humidity and heat in **Hong Kong** was a bit uncomfortable. **China, South Korea** and **Japan** all proved to be 'a bit hotter than an English summer' with occasional 'woolly jumper days' or wet and windy days no worse than the worst of those back home. **Scandinavia** provided some 'gloriously sunny' days of cycling and even up near the Arctic Circle there were blue skies.

Food and Drink Supplies

With all this dehydration and energy-burning pedalling going on, drink and food become a pre-occupation. Generally, liquid refreshment was not too much of a problem. Certainly they avoided the local water unless it was puritabbed which Jo told us was 'disgusting and warm to drink day in day out'. There were local alternatives; usually the local variety of coke or fizzy drinks or some form of tea.

Some of the cyclists, despite all the exertion, actually put weight on. Willy wrote home that 'The whole logistics of the trip revolved around Andys' next meal ... I had no idea he had such an insatiable appetite.' However, to avoid getting ill, they were wary of eating any foods that appeared the least bit unhygienic. A balance between this and enjoying the variety on offer along the way was struck.

All the teams had small gas stoves to cook on, some using them more than others. The Americas Route team could probably write a cook book since they were well endowed with culinary skills and would regularly stock up on herbs and spices. A typical camp breakfast in South America would consist of cinnamon porridge, figs and nuts. Lunch was often just nuts, raisins and biscuits while an average supper would be rice, a couple of vegetables and a mug of soup plus a packet of chocolate biscuits. Paw Paws, oranges, bananas and avocados grew in profusion along the way so fresh fruit was always available. If they felt like a change from their own cooking then there were lots of inexpensive bars and restaurants, even in the villages. Here they could get deep fried potatoes, potato balls with peas and carrot in them, potato pancakes fried, cheese and waffles etc. On the coast there would be lots of fresh fish available too.

Just before they left Peru they were treated to an amazing national dish called Pachamanca which Jo describes as being cooked in a '... fire in a pit in the ground with stones in it. Burns for several hours until the stones are hot, sacks of potatoes poured in, about 40 lb of lamb and pork, corn with a maize flour and sugar mix inside, beans, cabbage and finally alfalfa. This is covered with sacks after having interspersed the food with hot stones, and then the earth is shovelled on top.'

This was a real favourite of Jo's - something to do with the fact that during the hours it took to cook, everyone danced and drank and got very merry! 'After the pisco sour, we had papaya and pisco, pineapple and pisco and finally hot coconut and pisco.'

In **Ecuador** guinea pig was sampled but it didn't prove too inspiring, Jo reporting that it tasted like chicken although it had more bones than meat.

In **Mexico** hot cakes and syrup provided excellent cyclists' food and they ate 'fried beans and tortillas ad nausea ...' However, when they were racing up the Baja California it was 50 km between roadside inns, and then they would simply eat as much as they could to replenish the energy just used and store some for the next stage. This was during their toughest cycling stage of the journey, when they were battling on the bikes from dawn to dusk.

Once in the **USA** they were suddenly faced with a vast range of foods and there was huge overdosing of peanut butter and cream cheese sandwiches. In one state which is famous for its potatoes they even ate potato ice cream, which apparently was very good.

In **Australia** there was no problem with food. Kate and Nick, keen muesli consumers, stocked up on the stuff though a little birdy told me that Pete and Jane fed it to the pigeons! Even in Australia though there was a need to keep a watchful eye on water levels — as the team discovered when they were cycling through great sunbaked valleys miles from habitation: 'I began to realise for the first time the need for water in heat, I started to get obsessed with not running out and timing myself between gulps. Like an idiot I'd started off pouring water in my hair and all over myself ... now there was only one bottle left.' (Jane)

In **Indonesia** warm artificial fizzy drinks were downed by the gallon to stave off thirst, so in Bali it was a real treat when villagers scrambled up trees to bring them coconuts to drink. Less appealing was 'Durian' which was to be 'avoided at all costs — foul smelling South East Asian fruit — once described as "like eating an ice cream whilst sitting on the toilet"' (Kate). A very old goat curry and an unidentified Satay in banana leaves were other Indonesian delicacies which didn't find favour with the team.

Christmas was spent in **Singapore** where feelings of homesickness were heightened by the traditional (ish) lunch with roast turkey and curry and ... a Marks & Spencer christmas pudding!

The **Malaysian** Satay went down a treat though with skewers of chicken, fish balls, tofu and squid to dip into a boiling peanut sauce. Breakfast was good too: noodles and fish balls. And for fuel, there was '100 plus' the equivalent of 'Lucozade'.

The staple in **Thailand** was Roti Chanai Taloth, a bready pancake with egg fried on top of a black metal plate, in actual fact, an Indian dish.

A food shortage in **Bangladesh** meant emergency rations provided by the British Embassy of baked beans, Mars Bars, twiglets and corned beef. Other than that they survived on bananas and biscuits, the latter could be spread with '100% artificial' jam!

Appetites took a nosedive in **Nepal** where the team saw 'piles of flesh and entrails covered in flies and grit being sorted through like a stall at a jumble sale'. (Kate)

On the hottest day in **India** each team member consumed 15 cans of the local chemical fizzy drink! They also sampled one of the most awful fluids: a drink which tasted 'like a combination of raw mushrooms and Turkish delight' (Nick). This was about as welcome as the local brew: very sweet stewed tea dust. Breakfast didn't come highly recommended either: '2 chloroquinine and 2 salt tablets washed down with heavily chlorinated water and followed by a bony fish curry with chilli sauce and all before 7 am' (Kate). The best foods of the journey were the abundance of pineapples, rambutans, coconuts, watermelons and fresh figs which would often be given to them by people at the roadside.

I somehow don't think one of the local relishes of **Zimbabwe** would have appealed to the Asian Highway team: '... nearly ran over some big fat, blue-patterned caterpillars on the road which the kids were collecting in squirming cartons to make into relish!' (Julia). In fact, food was not a problem and could be bought at the bottle stores along the route; though sometimes these were thin on the ground and the team would stock up with fresh produce at markets. A lot of cheese and tomato rolls were consumed and the odd plate full of steak and chips was devoured.

In **Malawi** bananas were a mainstay and the team polished off 50 bananas in a day! If they got tired of bananas though, they could always sink their teeth into fried flying ants. There were many other insects which crept into the Malawi range of cuisine: 'On the horizon of the lake we could see what looked like clouds of smoke; apparently they were swarms of insects which — when they fly over land — the locals catch in nets and make into relish'. (Moira)

In **Tanzania**, the food was reported to be excellent, with masses of fresh produce available — cheaply: 'every small village has a hotel (not with accommodation) which serves chai and chapatis or *brown bread* or half cakes. The chai here takes some getting used to although I really like it now. It's brewed with condensed milk and sugar — no option on these — and often has added cinnamon. Really gives you a quick glucose rush for only 5/ (5p)'. (Julia)

'We had heard innumerable scare stories about theft in Tanzania, so we normally took our bikes into the chai shop with us. The shops are great — really bizarre. The owner stands behind a glass-fronted counter in the corner. Through the glass you can see samosas, imitation doughnuts, and "half-cakes" rock hard little cakes with a groove in the middle so you can break them in half — hence half-cakes. The tables and chairs are simple wood or plastic the floor is swept concrete . . . The walls are plastered with beautiful smiling white faces selling ice cream, soap powder, riding motorbikes. We sit there sweating and drinking hot super sweet chai, whilst hundreds of kids crowd the doorway, running away occasionally when the owner bellows at them.' (Andy)

Most important was liquid though which they just couldn't get enough of: 'Almost fainted with thirst — for the first time on the trip my lips cracked then bled . . . No water so Coke after Coke after Coke . . . what this does to your metabolism I shudder to think. Extreme dehydration followed by injecting lots of concentrated sugar water . . . The psychological reactions when cycling in extreme heat and humidity whilst drinking Coke are very odd.' (Andy)

In Dar es Salaam they encountered a very strange sight indeed, though not totally unwelcome under the circumstances: 'I spent the afternoon chilling out in the Sno-Cream ice cream parlour. It's the most surreal thing on the trip so far . . . Dar is a poor city; bang in the middle is this tiny place with millions of Donald Ducks, Mickey Mouses, "have a nice day" placards, home made tarts, maple leaf syrup, Daffy Duck. A real Hollywoodland with Snow White and the 7 Dwarves, plastic statues of Bambi and ice cream peach melba splits, coffee — you name it, they have it, they have 17. Outside the cripples and beggars sit moaning in the dirt and we sit inside listening to muzak and paying a week's wages in 10 minutes. Roll on World Bike Ride ...' (Andy)

In **Kenya**, Nairobi, the team were treated to a meat feast of giraffe, zebra and other unidentified species ceremoniously served up on spear heads. As guests they ate on and as semi-vegetarians suffered the consequences the following day.

By now the team had got food acquisition tactics down to a fine art: 'We had breakfast full of Oliver Twists. An Oliver Twist is asking for more and by now we were past experts at squeezing the most coffee/tea/fruit out of whatever unfortunate establishment we happened to be in.' (Andy)

In **Egypt** in the Sinai desert, the need for water reached urgent proportions: 'We pulled into the little village feeling very hot indeed — and discovered our salvation. Big earthenware urns full of lovely cool water. We could splash it all over ourselves and also drink it (after purification). What bliss. We poured it over our heads, down our shirts into our shorts into our shoes (a great trick your socks stay wet for hours).' (Andy)

There were stores and cafés along the way so they could either stock up with food such as yogurt, bread, mango juice, beans, biscuits, cheese, or sit down to a meal, a typical lunch being lentils, rice, chicken salad and 2 litres of water.

As for the **Oriental** 'gannet' **Path** team, by all accounts they ate their way from Hong Kong. As for Adria, if she wasn't eating, she was writing about it: '... hot tasty soups piled high with delicious filling noodles and topped with squid or spare ribs or beef or chicken. To watch the Chinese cook food is fun too — in huge woks over enormous flames in tiny filthy kitchens while business goes on as usual in the market places all around them.' (Adria)

China was full of temptations the descriptions of which could be endless so it's over to Rhoda for a characteristically brief run down: 'Food in China was excellent, good, bad and unknown. Rice always being with everything. Common to be served a dish of guts. The unknown would send questions through your mind — am I eating cat or dog or both? Where are those kittens we just saw in the cage?!'

South Korea was an unknown quantity in many senses, certainly on the food front there were to be some wonderful surprises. When they arrived they were taken out for a slap up meal by one of their sponsors: 'A lunch of local specialities, 'except insects and snakes', dumplings, fish in rich spicy sauce, thick flabby noodles that wallowed in a fish soup, and rice balls, and little wooden arrows onto which were skewered good-tasting bits and pieces ... and beer.' (Adria)

Or another meal:

'Unlimited dishes of rice, soup with beancurd and chilli, mushrooms, dried spiced fish strips, vegetable curd, cold greens, fried eggs, mussels in half shells, whole chillies, celariac (hot) and the usual spoonfuls of chillied somethings, beer, Korean whisky and cold coffee-tea (neither coffee or tea). Rhoda and Bas also had noodle soups ... every time we finished off a dish at the table it was replaced by another full one.' (Adria)

There then followed round two as their host, a famous Korean comedian, stocked them up with more food to keep them going — KEEP THEM GOING WHERE is the question! They went away with 8 bars of chocolate, 5 packets of lemon biscuits and 4 packets of nut biscuits.

Days later this eating ecstasy was to soar to even greater heights: 'Undoubtedly the best Korean cuisine. We enjoyed delicious specialities. White cabbage salad with thousand island dressing, whole garlic cloves and green chillies to dip into a nutty chilli sauce and crunchy, chillied salad with onions, fresh lettuce leaves and pickled (Japanese) lettuce, boiled peanuts (plain) and the centre attraction, barbecued succulent beef carved in long slivers and cooked before your eyes in the middle of the table. This you grabbed with your chopsticks, dipped into sweet sesame seed oil and rolled in a lettuce leaf. Just delicious. Though we filled ourselves quite enough with all this, it was important (?) to try one other Korean speciality — cold buckwheat noodles in cold vegetable soup and garnished with pickled cabbage and spring onions ... freshly peeled and cored pears followed. Pears a curious cross between apple and watermelon.' (Adria)

With that kind of hospitality, I should think that that little lot will cause a rush on tickets to South Korea!

Japan wasn't always so inspiring: 'The usual choice on the menu — spaghetti, curry, salads, pilaf, pizza, fried this and fried that, ice creams and cakes. The one good thing I will say about these Japanese restaurants offering Western food is that the salads are always very fresh and as crisp as if they'd been picked from the garden that morning.' (Adria)

Actually, Japanese food was very expensive. Fortunately they had been sponsored and were supplied with food vouchers, otherwise there would have been four very hungry and unhappy World Bike Riders.

Scandinavia was another exhorbitantly expensive part of the world to be travelling in and they mostly existed on bread and cheese here. A sad come-down after what they had got used to. However, in Sweden they were treated to: 'Avocado and Caviar, Reindeer, new potatoes and salad, and coffee and yet more sherry and wine in the drawing room.' (Sebastian)

So, life on the Four Corners wasn't all bad Eh?

Off Colour

It would be tedious to go on about how many tummy bugs and effects of sun stroke they all got — they were endless and accompanied a lot of the riders for the greater part of their journey. Absolutely no-one escaped these unpleasant side effects. Often, unwell or not, there was nothing for it but to continue pedalling on to keep up with deadlines and meetings. If anyone was really unwell, then they flagged down a passing truck, threw their bikes on the back and accepted a lift. Occasionally the whole team would stop whilst the fellow team member recovered from the latest bout of something or other.

The worst hit however was Kate on the **Asian Highway**. In Indonesia she suffered severe sunstroke and later in Nepal, there was an outbreak of dysentry which all the team went down with. However, Kate developed amoebic dysentry and in India was admitted to hospital in Lucknow and again in Delhi where she wrote home from the hospital bed: 'I hope to be able to join Nick and Jane. I'm in hospital (2nd admission to an Indian hospital for a week). I have severe diarrhoea and anaemia and dehydration. No dainties have passed my parched lips but I have the bruises of many attempts to replace my intravenous drip to show. In such a state I'm not fit to join totally in the procedures but I hope to be let-out tomorrow to greet Jane and Nick at the border.' (Kate)

The British High Commission contacted London with a doctor's recommendation that she have at least two weeks' rest. The team flew to Turkey and went on to the Antalya coast in Southern Turkey for 10 days where she was able to convalesce.

Something else that no team escaped was altitude sickness. Obviously the Americas Team had to endure this most, but the most extreme case of it was experienced by the African Trail team when climbing Kilimanjaro. Andy already had suspected malaria and with temperatures dropping to freezing, Julia had developed a very bad cold. This topped with the feeling of nausea and piercing headaches must have been intolerable. Then Moira went down: '... everything seemed to hit me at once. I came over hot and cold — felt nauseous and developed a headache. All I wanted to do was collapse on the spot. William (the guide) picked me up off the ground — telling me to bend over and take deep breaths whilst he rubbed my back. I felt much better . . . to help me further he walked behind me pushing me up the scree . . . Jules was feeling pretty rough and also needed a push.' (Moira)

Sleep generally came easily at the end of the day but sometimes mosquitoes, cockroaches or some unexpected noise would keep them awake: 'It is a bit of a problem though, trying to cycle all day on top of very little sleep — if it's not the family or other guests you can bet that at 4 in the morning the local mosque is going to blast you half way out of bed!' (Jane — Indonesia)

Adria had the knack of falling asleep just about anywhere but the worst case of exhaustion was Jo. This was less from cycling than from over-work in the fund-raising office in the USA: 'Because of my tiredness and the stress that I was under, I definitely had a catch in my voice — you become so vulnerable and sensitive to emotions when you're so weary.'

A great worry was knee problems. Again with so much pressure in this area most of the teams had varying degrees of strain and damage to the ligaments. The two that were the worst affected were Andy and Aidan. Andy received treatment for his at Kamuzu General Hospital, where the physio told him he was to do no cycling for 3 weeks. A couple of weeks later he was back in the saddle. Aidan's was worse still. It was in Japan when the first signs of trouble showed, but finally, in Norway, there were weeks when he had to resort to buses and trains, though this allowed him to work on team publicity.

In Africa Andy discovered the consequences of falling off his bike were a lot more serious than if similar happened back home: 'I had fallen off in the sand, and had big suppurating sores on my back and elbows. At the hospital, everyone else seemed to have suppurating sores.' (Andy)

(Some of these, children, had half their toes missing and Andy was told this was because they had been eaten by rats.) Over the next few days the wind made the bandages work loose and then, when the pace of cycling was slow, flies would alight on the wound, delighted at finding such a feast.

Talking of flies, there's a particular variety in Africa, the tsetse fly which gave the team a lot of trouble with their 'red hot needle penetrating the flesh'.

Mosquitoes eventually sent Julia down with malaria. The symptoms; a blinding headache along with shivering, aching limbs and a high temperature. A visit to the hospital and a shot of chloroquin put this to rights and after a few days rest, though thinner and weaker, she was back with the team cycling — though she had to take prophylactics for the rest of the ride.

Fortunately no-one went down with any incurable tropical disease and of course before departure all the recommended innoculations were done. However, once out there, everyone was glad they had had a rabies jab when faced with wild packs of hounds in various corners of the world, and the few who hadn't wished they had — luckily no-one got bitten badly.

Accommodation

All the teams took two two-person tents with them and the team to make most use of these were the Americas Route team, mainly in **Bolivia, Peru** and **Ecuador**. Sometimes they were to hanker after a good bed and a solid roof over their heads: 'We were surrounded by barking dogs who, as soon as we'd gone to bed, came nosing around the camp site to eat our leftovers. Rustling through plastic bags, growling at odd noises, their barking kept me awake.' (Meryl)

Having been told many tales of robbery, the teams always tried to camp away from roads and would ask people if they could camp on their land. They got some wonderfully idyllic camp spots as a result and it was much more secure: 'I can't think of a more perfect campsite. The views into one valley below were spectacular ... Jo had strategically placed our tent so that we could just open the flap in the morning and watch the sunrise over the mountains.' (Meryl)

'We camped the night in a wood with cows grazing and what looks like broom growing ... the smell is delicious.' (Meryl)

'... camped in the garden of a lovely house with water running through and geraniums growing everywhere. Soft grass, wind in the trees and the sound of running water made a very pleasant change.' (Meryl)

In **Mexico** in the Baja California desert they didn't even have canvas over their heads: 'I really enjoyed sleeping in the desert amongst cacti under the stars, but I was terrified of scorpions creeping into my sleeping bag seeking warmth.' (Jo)

But Mexico also saw some of the worst places they stayed at: '... a terrible hotel — I think it was the worst one we've stayed in on the trip — dirty sheets, pokey room, no water, filthy loos and showers and in a street with all the strip joints, the tarts, the vomiting incoherent drunks.'

In the **States** the team stayed in schools, church halls and community centres for most of the way.

For the **Asian Highway** team, the first part of their journey took them along the Australian coast where the tents were used but often they opted for cheap caravan accommodation in one of the many caravan parks along the way.

In **Indonesia** they stayed in *losmen* (cheap hotels). These were usually run by families who seemed to have little regard for their 'guests': '... terribly noisy back at the *losman* — there were 2 colour tellies on full blast outside our room and the whole family and half the neighbourhood gathered around about six inches from the screens yelling their heads off at each other. Guests really seem to be a bit of a sideline in some of these hotels and *losmen* we've stayed in!'

And a few days later: 'Finally got to bed and honestly it was like a bad joke — someone was doing repairs to their lorry at *midnight* right outside our window — clunk, clank, crash, hammer, scream, yell, rev! As if that wasn't bad enough a dog set up howling and barking and a group of kids came and started singing and playing guitars ... At one point Pete got up and dug out his whistle and did one great almighty blast on it — there was a moment of stunned silence and then the hubbub and racket surged back again ... Indonesia could definitely drive you right off your head!' (Jane)

The saving grace of these losmen was the *mandi*; tanks full of cool water which the riders would 'splosh' all over themselves.

In **Singapore** the team were guests of Ilsa from the Nature Society and some V.S.O. workers, so didn't get to sample the local guest houses.

In **Malaysia** after sampling a variety of accommodation, including the expensive government rest houses, the team conclusion was: '... the Chinese hotels are definitely the best value for money — even if they are cockroachy. The linen is usually clean, you get boiled water or chinese tea and always a fan. In this particular place we had it going full belt and our washing strung up and blown flat against the walls ...' (Jane)

In **Thailand** they found themselves staying in Buddhist monasteries. Accommodation could be pretty frugal and at one place they slept on planks in the woodland — though, for the most part, like **Nepal, Bangladesh** and **India**, once again it was cheap and cockroachy hotels.

In **Zimbabwe** Julia, Willy, Andy, Norman and Moira were warned of robbery and so would always try and find a camp site away from the road, often seeking help from the local police in locating the safest sites.

This was to be the case in all of Africa, interspersed with staying in the cheapest guest houses along the way as well.

In **Malawi** the team would be woken many a time, either by a ravenous rat munching its way through their panniers and into the food supply, or by encroaching cockroaches. 'Ugh — the feel of their dry scaly bodies and dirty feet scuttling noisily across your naked body is not much fun' said Andy. The other night-time menace was the 'Dive bombing mossies'. It has to be said that this wasn't the norm throughout Africa. In fact, after they had read hellish accounts by other 'hairy chested' cyclists who had written about conditions in this area, they were amazed at how their experience of Africa completely contradicted this. In Livingstonia, on Lake Malawi they saw 'Holiday Cottages' signposted and found themselves transported to somewhere on the edge of a Scottish loch around the turn of the century; to grey stone cottages with paraffin lamp lighting. And in **Tanzania** they booked into a £1.50 a night Norwegian log cabin where they enjoyed such luxuries as mosquito nets, duvets (!), freshly-baked brown bread and homemade marmalade!

In Dar es Salaam they were absolutely elated when offered an 'AIRCONDITIONED (!) flat, with FRESH WATER (!) a FRIDGE (!!), a CRATE OF BEER (!!!!), CHEESE (!!!!!!!).' (Andy)

In **Egypt**, accommodation could be found for a mere 50p a night and ran to such luxuries as a mattress on the floor with broken springs in it, plaster falling from the ceiling, disgusting loos, constant noise outside, muddy brown trickling water from the 'showers' and the inevitable mossies. I should think this gave them an added appreciation for the 5-star luxury they had in Cairo where they ended the day with a huge buffet meal and sank into luxurious beds watching television: 'from the hotel you can see the pyramids and you can cycle there in 10 mins — so we did after a very lazy day by the pool and in our airconditioned room.'

In **Hong Kong** Aidan, Rhoda, Adria and Sebastian were given free beds in exchange for 'mowing the lawn with a pair of blunt hedge clippers'.

Accommodation in **China** was a lot more entertaining and didn't cost them much more: 'The cheapest hotel we managed to find costed(sic) no more than 18p each. It consisted of wooden beds padded with a layer of straw. A bowl of water for the four of us to have a bird bath out of. Torn plastic bags holding the window frames together. The loos were a classic — just head for the nearest pigsty. But there was a choice. You could relieve yourself with two fully grown snorters, or go in the pen next door with four grunting weaners . . . and . . . once you've done ya business you get to witness a mad scramble of pigs fighting over your loo paper! Of course, the whole ordeal is more of a challenge when it's pitch dark and you get the feeling that upon crouching down, some curious pig is going to creep up and tickle you with its whiskers. Next thing you're leap-frogging up into the cobwebs above and to finish it all off you put your hand on an upside down broom while trying to feel the way out of the bog . . . Still on the subject of pigs . . . an almighty death-defying scream came from outside our room window. That's funny, Adria's still here I thought! Sebastian stuck his eyes out the window and confirmed a huge fat pig (not Adria, she was in the room) had just been slaughtered.' (Rhoda)

South Korea provided a few more comforts of life with a combination of camping and cheap, very clean hotels. In **Japan** hotel accommodation was very good and at half price for a special cause. The Japanese take hygiene to squeaky clean extremes. Sebastian sent home laments as to how they will cope with camping in Scandinavia: 'We are all rather unsure as to how we are going to cope under canvas. No buffet breakfasts. No unit bathrooms with 'Disinfected for your protection' strips of paper around the loo seat. No telephones. No mega big and just as soft sofa beds. No air conditioning which doubles as a tumble dryer if you can master the knack of twisting plastic coat hangers and stuffing them into the grill. No televisions with coin-op naughty videos . . .'

Every day linen would be changed regardless of whether the team was staying for more than a night. Adria refused to let them change hers so unnecessarily.

In fact camping in **Scandinavia** on the edges of fjiords in clear mountain air had its compensations . . . that is, except for the mosquitoes and midges which were the bane of their lives for the duration of their stay.

So, life out in the Four Corners required immense stamina, more for some routes than others. I'm sure the Oriental Path team would agree that theirs was not the most difficult to endure in terms of these conditions and the time that they had to remain in the field. However, the other three were fairly evenly spread and would do well to make it home in one piece!

Adventures and Mishaps

The Americas Route

One of the exciting things about travelling from the four corners would be the unexpected; the funny, the unusual and the downright terrifying and sometimes all of those and more. Each team was to have adventures, and some individuals were to have more than others. Thomas was one of the latter. His began by learning how to get himself out of a sticky situation. This took place just outside Lima in **Peru**: '... slum, rubbish tips, noise, dirt and pollution — we came to an enormous petrol station, flame burning high, licking the wet air from a tall chimney, huge storage tanks, refinery and queuing up petrol trucks. It all looked very interesting to me so I got out the old contax ... and snapped merrily away. Got back on the ol' steed and cycled onwards towards an army control post. Just as I was passing an officer steps into the road and motions me to stop. Just another control stop. Like countless others I thought.

'He asked me to come inside. I was alone "at the back" and was a bit worried. I wheeled my bike in. "Do you have a camera?" he asked. "Oh shit" I thought, Steve Bonnist's warnings about taking pictures of official looking places were ringing in my ears. "Yes" I answered, he asked me to give it to him and of course I did. We walked into an office like any other post in Peru, a desk, a man behind it a couple of chairs (no swinging bright, shadeless lamp though!). "Did you take photos of the refinery?" he asked, "it is forbidden!" ...'

After lots more questioning, handing over of the camera and film, Thomas handed over his passport and, as an afterthought, he showed them the London Peru Embassy letter, guaranteeing the team's safe passage through Peru: 'He looked at it for a long time, meanwhile I had decided bribery was out of the question (!). He still looked determined ... suddenly ... he said with a smile "would you take *our* photograph?" I almost burst into hysterical laughter . . . Of course I said yes and soon I was outside the office, passport back in my money belt, focussing the contax on 8 soldiers all in uniform.' (Thomas)

A close shave for the youngest of the World Bike Riders.

The first we heard about the next Americas Route encounter was when Meryl's local Bournemouth newspaper printed a story with a headline 'MERYL FLEES KNIFE GANG'. They were referring to an incident in North Peru, when the team had been racing towards the border before their visas expired. They were doing some hard cycling, were tired and stopped at a town to rest: 'There was a strange and scary interlude in the market at Sullana just short of the Ecuadorian border. It was a small crowded market much like any other, except that kind-hearted people kept approaching us, miming or whispering "the area is full of thieves, knives are used, you must get out!". Glancing round at the inevitable crowd of curious children and onlookers it seemed hard to believe but we soon became nervous and jumpy as the warning was repeated more and more urgently. We fairly leapt onto a truck for Las Lomas our last stop before the Peruvian border.' (Alex)

The reason for this was later explained as involving drugs and tribal discordance. Apparently even the local police felt it necessary, for their safety, to be off the streets by dusk!

Shortly after this when the team was travelling in pairs, Meryl and Jo were cycling alone and dark was falling fast as they climbed up through cloud over stony tracks. They were desperate to find a suitable camp spot and finally when they did, miles from anywhere, their part in the Four Corners World Bike Ride nearly came to an unpleasant and abrupt end: 'Cycled on through another drunk village. I stopped to fill our bottles at a lovely stream where it would have been really nice to camp as it was about 6 pm but Meryl wanted to go on to a house so we went on in the mist with me in a bad mood, my knee hurting and the bike squeaking. No houses, no nothing. We heard a bell and some voices at one point which was eerie but couldn't find a track off the road.

'Eventually at about 7 pm we followed a track off the road and camped in what looked like a field. By then it was cold so we quickly put up the tent and put on some warm clothing. We were having soup so I set about lighting the stove which I put on the grass fairly near Meryl's bike and the tent which had both our sleeping bags in and all my clothes. The gas bottle has two tops, one with a thin pouring spout which I screwed on in order to fill the stove. The bottle takes a litre and I filled it that morning. After filling the stove I primed it by pouring a bit of petrol on and lighting it. Then once it goes out you generally have enough pressure and you can light the jet. However, that didn't happen this time.

'The gas bottle with the pouring top fell over towards the stove and the little fuel that poured out caught light. I picked up the bottle and swept it away from the stove but it was going to catch light. I wasn't sure if it was about to imminently explode or not. We both jumped up and Meryl started running, calling to me. We ran about 50 metres or more away and sat behind a rock expecting an explosion. I was a coward, I watched the reflections of the flames in my glasses instead of looking at them directly. They must have been 2–3 feet high and it went on and on. I expected us to lose tent, sleeping bags, and almost everything except for bicycle frames but when it came down to it Meryl and I were far more important and I wasn't going to risk either of us getting badly burnt in the middle of nowhere at night in a thick mist with very little traffic passing and the nearest hospital 70 km away, so we stayed put...

'We must have watched it for about 20 minutes with all sorts of thoughts going through our heads. It started burning lower and it was getting darker and we, colder. I went forward a bit for want of something to do and started feeling for and picking up grasses with the idea of smothering it or using them to save the tent etc. Then I thought of the earth bank next to the tent and with a bunch of grasses under one arm and cupped hands filled with earth, I walked quickly back and dropped the earth over the neck of the bottle where the flames were and to my total amazement everything went dark. It was out!

'We were incredibly lucky and afterwards we both talked of what we had imagined the outcome to be — taking a truck that night with a bicycle frame in our hands and not much else.' (Jo)

The following morning the pressure and anguish of the previous day lifted as they woke and found themselves in a beautiful spot. They breakfasted in sunlight, accompanied by the sounds of Indians going to work in the fields. 'One boy was whistling a traditional tune and it sounded beautifully clear in the morning air.' A neat way of rounding off the episode with a timely reminder of life and its magic.

For a different sort of challenge in **Ecuador** the chance to play Tarzan and Jane came up: 'We left our bicycles in Ambata for a week while we went to Banos, a holiday resort with natural hot baths, and then down into the Orient for a few days' adventure on the fringes of the Amazon Basin. We were led by a Shuar Indian guide and his father, who have a history of head-hunting behind them, and who also walk incredibly swiftly through the thick vegetation avoiding all the muddy patches. We were not so adept! We ate the fruits and leaves of the forest and saw the odd snake and animals tracks. We played Tarzan and Jane on enormous llianas and built our own palm-leaf shelter which proved very waterproof considering the amount of rain we had. What proved most fun was crossing rivers. We built a raft of logs lashed together with creepers one day, baled out a sinking canoe with wellington boots another day; other days we swam, crossed slippery tree trunks and waded through the undergrowth. Needless to say we were quite a sight when we finally emerged from the forest.' (Meryl)

Back into the fast lane once again and a 'hit and run' in Mexico where a drunken driver's game of 'dare devils' went badly wrong: 'The next thing we knew was that Thomas had been hit by a large green car which was swerving drunkenly about the road. Of course the car didn't stop. Luckily a doctor was visiting a nurse in a nearby house; he rushed out and with Alex's help they got Thomas into his car and to hospital. Thomas was given good treatment, although Meryl had to run off with a shopping list, to buy the drip and sutures at the local pharmacy, while Thomas lay waiting on the operation table!' (Jo)

Thomas wrote explaining his side of it: '... I was lying down. Meryl was now there as well. Both she and Alex were giving words of encouragement, touching and reassuring me, telling me what was going on. I would have been terrified if they hadn't been there.

'Someone gave me a drip, I felt groggy but not ill or suffering, pretty aware of what was going on around me now. They were cleaning my arm and my head had been badly cut and I was going to need stitches. The next 1½ hours were spent head on one side, with someone above me struggling to thread a needle through my thick scalp skin giving me injections, 24 stitches in my head in all. A great haircut to boot.'

This was rounded off by the nurse and doctors dropping their masks and giving each other a kiss over Thomas's prostrate body! Things took an upward turn from here: 'I guess I really can't complain, in Mexico city as I was resting, I had 2 maids, TV, video and a chauffeur at my service!!!' This luxury aided a quick recovery and a couple of weeks later he was back pushing pedals up the Californian coast.

As Thomas was nearing the end of the coast-to-coast crossing of the States, he used up another of his nine lives. He was racing with another cyclist and crashed into the back of another going over the top of him in a double somersault, ending with a severely torn ligament. He virtually hobbled into New York where doctors told him he would not be able to continue ... and so close to the end too. He stubbornly insisted on going on, but was persuaded otherwise when he was told that to do so might result in lifelong ligament problems. He returned to London for surgery vowing to join up with the team again in Paris. After having got so far, we certainly hoped he would be joining the other World Bike Riders for that last leg.

The Asian Highway

For the Asian Highway team, Australia provided some light encounters, the first of these being with the biggest hairy spider they'd ever seen. This was when fellow keen cyclist John, invited them to stay in his garden shed. Since it saved them the trouble of putting up tents etc, they gladly accepted. When they arrived John introduced them to a funnel web spider which he tipped out of a jar to show them. It was very impressive, with its brown, big fat body, fangs and long strong legs. At a glance it looked like something from a joke shop.

'That could kill you if it bit you' he told them reassuringly. Luckily this particular specimen was dead, but there was a lot of other life in the old carpet. Red-back spiders for instance: 'Oh yeah, they're poisonous as well, but they won't kill you' he said leaving them to settle down for the night. At least Nick and Kate had some sort of bed to sleep on, but Pete and Jane were down amongst the carpet life on the floor: 'Pete was convinced that even if he put a holy circle of jungle formula insect repellant round his bed the spiders were going to leap down on him from the ceiling! We did up the drawstrings of our sleeping bags very tightly round our heads so that only our noses showed and slept very lightly.' (Jane) In fact, they survived that night to go on and meet a real live funnel web spider. Kate found it in her sleeping bag and enlisted the support of the others to get rid of it, whereupon it immediately became a dead funnel web spider!

They much preferred the two legged creatures of Australia, though sometimes they became just a bit too friendly: 'this "thing" came hurtling after me out of the darkness and chased me right back to my tent ... Pete emerged with his head torch and hissed dire threats at it ... a possum!' (Jane). After its third attempt at joining them in the tent for the night Pete had to use brute force to persuade it otherwise, throwing his torch at it to frighten it away. The possum took revenge, while they were asleep it must have returned to the campsite, because in the morning Pete found his freshly washed Four Corners t-shirts had muddy possum-shaped foot prints all over them!

The kangaroos were a little more endearing: 'They were into everything, thumping and hopping everywhere and stuffing their heads into tents and panniers; one even succeeded in grabbing a bite of chocolate cake ... I love the kangaroos, they're very funny and bouncy but fairly gentle and dignified at the same time, when you push them away, however hard, they just push you back with their front legs while averting their heads in a completely unconcerned way! The babies are great, all sixes and sevens, just shoved into the mothers pouch leaving bits of themselves hanging out, sometimes just a tail or back leg. They do get very pushy though and then the only way to get them hopping is to make a colossal fuss. Pete was charging at them flapping his karrimat and Nick at one point was bashing one marauder round the head with a paperback book — a typical scene of Four Corners at one with nature!' (Jane)

Surviving the wildlife of Australia, they went on to Indonesia where a mini expedition to the top of Mount Bromo to view the crater nearly had them minus one team member: 'As we reached the crater rim, a great load of sulphur smoke came straight up at us out of the volcano — it smelled terrible and after the steep climb sent me halfway to an asthma attack ... the sight of the middle of the volcano was a bit horrible — it was very wide and deep and at the bottom was bubbly thick mud. Out of the cracks and holes, thick yellowish sulphur smoke was drifting upwards ... It was strange being up there right on the edge of all that space with the bubbling and boiling going on to one side and nothing to the other — quite dizzying after the climb and no sleep. The path was very crumbly and often terribly steep both up and down ... I had a really bad moment when I thought I was going to slide right off the path ... afterwards I was shaking for about an hour — it struck me that if anyone had told me a year ago that I would be clinging by my toes to the edge of a volcano at dawn, I'd have been sceptical to say the least!' (Jane)

Finally, the most alarming moment happened in Bangladesh. Shortly after arriving the team decided to let someone else do the pedalling, and took a rickshaw out into the streets of Dhaka. There were crowds of people demonstrating and the air was tense. Suddenly a mob turned on them: 'We made the mistake of riding in a rickshaw because we had not been informed of the strike. After only a short way down the road we were bombarded with stones. Not a very encouraging welcome.' (Kate)

Unbeknown to them, the demonstration was for better pay and conditions for taxi drivers and there was a ban on any form of public transport and anyone who didn't obey this was a source of hostility. Thus, this little excursion was brought to an end and they gladly took to their own bikes again.

The rest of their trip didn't exactly proceed without incident but these were only a few of the trickiest.

The African Trail

The hero of the African Trail team was Nick Sanders, a world cyclist who had ridden part of their trail on his Journey to the Source of the Nile. The team had read his book religiously, hoping to pick up all sorts of useful tips about what to expect along the way. For camp fireside entertainment, they would recount their day's events through the eyes of this cyclist, which made good nightmarish sleeping-bag time tales, but didn't quite match the reality of their own experience.

Anyway, here's what happened when a drunken police woman was in charge (?) of Moira's bike — (a very precious possession when you're relying on it to get you from one of the four corners): 'Arrived Mvuma about 3 pm when we rode round the corner to the market place, full of people but with a strange lifelessness about it. We stopped at the bar, hanging short of riding through the market, testing the atmosphere before going further. Here people seemed less interested in talking to us although crowds gathered to stare. I tried to shrug it off but felt mildly uncomfortable. Willy and Andy went off and secured a promise of safe land to camp at the police station so off we all went. When we got there everybody was well drunk from the party the night before. A police woman called Angelina commandeered Moira's bike and weaved her way back into town with me in tow. She fell off as she dismounted in front of the bar to the onlookers amusement. After some lewd proposals from one of the drinkers, we cycled back to the station. By this time quite a little crowd had gathered to watch us put our tents up, I went for a wash and Angelina took the chance and weaved off on my bike, this time with Moira in hot pursuit. It took Willy and Andy to search the village before she was escorted back. We made a pact never to let anyone ride the bikes!' (Julia)

Malawi proved fairly quiet whilst Tanzania offered plenty to write home about. What was generally dreamt about at the end of an oven temperature day of cycling was cool cool beer. At Margots Andy went in search of this rare liquid and found himself in a disreputable sailor's bar, full of 'ladies of the night': '... A beautiful 6 ft 2 inch Masai prostitute in a silver lame top and red leather trousers. She grabbed my arm, leered at me, and asked for a drink. "Heh heh poor cyclist, no money heh heh" ... She tightened her grip and leaned forward to fondle my neck and head. "Very nice, very nice" I stammered, twisting my arm violently this way and that. Luckily I was sweating enough to loosen her grip and eventually slithered out of her drunken clutches and ran away

'I looked around. One of my companions was being pinched on the buttocks, the woman in our group was fighting off a marriage proposal and tables and chairs were flying around in the corner. "Great" I thought as a little 14 year old draped herself over my arm and looked up at me and said "please dance?".'

Tanzania seemed to offer a good selection of alternative life and one aspect Andy enjoyed the most was changing money on the black market, also known as 'sheep selling': 'I would have a wonderful time winking at strange men in public toilets, tapping my nose ...' he reported. Andy made many 'friends' in Arusha where he and the others were constantly greeted with 'Hello my friend, how are you my friend? Change? Change?'

Whilst being chased by three different groups of these 'friends' their 'best friend' rescued them in a taxi. The get-a-way took them to 'Big Maws' house in a slum area of Arusha for a 'sheep deal'. As a couple of wealthy Westerners they stood out like sore thumbs and people gathered round the cab, staring at them in a none too friendly manner. 'No problem my friend' they were told as they sat sweating with fear and not knowing where on earth they were.

Also in Tanzania a semi-arrest occurred which fortunately whilst frustrating, was more funny than fearsome: 'Our first arrest — I was keeping up with our great leader for life, heroine, friend of the people, Julia. We were shooting downhill through a dozy joint called Matingu when a tall skinny cop rushed onto the road waving his arms about and jumping up and down. Julia shot past, but I stopped and was led off to the station. For the first time African officials were not friendly — I was sat in a room with 3 guys all looking suspiciously at me and asking dumb questions. Their English was bad, so they couldn't make sense of the official letters from the International school of Tanganika and the Tanzanian High Commission. They're very sensitive about S. African spies and so the questions went on; "Why are you travelling by bike?", "Where are you going?", "Where have you been?" etc etc. After half an hour Willy turned up and got the same annoying treatment. To cut a long story short, we managed to talk our way out of it, just as Julia arrived.

'... So, sorry to disappoint you all again, but we can't repeat racest crap that all African cops are gun-toting drunks who beat the men and rape the women. On the whole they're much friendlier than British ones — not good copy I know but there you go ...

'I got arrested again. The main problem is that they are badly trained, suspicious and can't read English. It therefore takes hours to sort out.' (Andy)

After being 'terrorised' by the local Bobbies Andy's next fright came from the elephants and buffalo in Mikumi Game Park: 'I asked the locals about the road ahead. "Don't go — very dangerous". The next 50 km ran through Mikumi Game Park and our destination lay right in the middle. Undaunted, I set off. We'd cycled in Hwange Game Park and around Vic Falls, so I had no fear, not even as I passed the elephant and lion warning signs. Like magic, from 1 km to the next, game appeared. Mikumi is a real garden of Eden — beautiful flat plains and lots of impalas, buffalo . . . buffalo?! Shit, there they were, only 20 yards to my left grazing peacefully. Buffalo can weigh in at 1½ tons and charge at 60 kmph. They are also liable to charge any threatening smell without warning. Cars they are used to — but bikes? I just didn't know. Elephants can also be unpredictable, and there were plenty of those around. I grew more nervous. A petrol tanker passed, and I waved it down.

'The friendly people in the cab strapped my bike to the top and imitated lions eating cycling *wusungu* (white person) whilst laughing uproariously. Very funny. Crunch — the gears and brakes groaned and we shuddered to a halt "the camp's left up the hill mate" the grinning driver was indicating. "Waaw, rrrrrr" went the passengers and almost fell out of the cab laughing. "Heh Heh" I chortled and bravely climbed out. I looked at the road. A steep uphill with high grass on either side. There could have been an army of buffalo hiding in there and I wouldn't see it. My mouth felt dry as he handed me the bike down from the top. I strapped the panniers on whilst they held the bike up for me. Last favour for a condemned man. I've never felt quite so lonely as when the tanker pulled off, leaving me totally alone in dangerous bush country.

'I looked at the road again. Apart from being up hill and framed with buffalo hides, it was rough and stony. No chance of pulling away from a buffalo, even if I did see it. Oh well, here goes. It was dusty, it was up hill and I was covered in tsetse flies, inflicting their painful bites and crawling into my eyes, ears and mouth. Worst of all I was scared. The scene had that weird dreamlike quality of adrenalin highs. I kept on saying that if I ever got out of this I would never be so bloody stupid again. Every bush, every rock was a lone and angry male buffalo. I was standing on the pedals all the way both to move faster and to see better, heart pounding.' (Andy)

Andy went through all this to reach his destination, a hotel campsite, only to be turned back at the gate and sent to the next site down the road he'd just come from: 'Elephant 10 yards off the road, didn't pay a blind bit of attention. The buffalo did! Short-sighted and bad tempered, it lifted its massive head and sniffed. My legs whirred like helicopter blades, and I was gone before it could decide whether to charge or not.'

Andy reached the next camp site where he was promptly told of a Japanese tourist who had been killed, speared by the tusk of a rogue elephant in the grounds of that very same hotel that had sent him on his way!

There were a few other hiccups between here and Egypt, but they were generally caused by the gin and tonic consumption! (I hear it comes with ice in the African desert!) However, it was Willy who was the next to write home of his ordeal and I have to say the office was in hysterics — only Willy could go on a world bike ride and end up having a fat horse fall on top of him! It was in the Eastern Desert in Egypt, and happened when he was offered a ride on a beautiful white Arab stallion called Snowy. As he rode away up and over the dunes and round the pyramids, he impressed the owner, a sheik, so much with his handling of the beast that he was invited to ride the following morning:

'When I arrived the next morning, Snowy was not there, so I mounted another stallion called Whiskey — an appropriate name as it looked completely alcoholic. I was warned that Whiskey was prone to attacking other horses, but wasn't worried as I would be mainly riding alone. I had been riding for 20 minutes, trying to kick Whiskey into some semblance of life when over a dune at a full gallop comes Snowy. Joy of joys the Sheik had arrived late and was coming out to meet me and swap horses. Unfortunately nobody had warned him of Whiskey's erratic temperament. As he came alongside me, Whiskey at last burst into life. He reared onto his hind legs so that he could kick Snowy with his front legs. At this point I made a stupid mistake. Instead of sliding ignominously to the ground, I held onto the reins. This had the effect of bringing Whiskey's head higher and higher until he toppled over backwards. So there I was lying on the ground with this big, fat, alcoholic horse lying upside down on top of me kicking its legs in the air. To cut a long story short, I was helped to a Bedouin camp, passing out and being sick on the way. I was resuscitated with hot sweet tea and a fag as there was no G & T available. Anyway I have no permanent injuries and should be back on the bike in three or four days. Sorry to go on so long about my little accident. It may be a laugh for you lot, but I think I may have been traumatised. The others have been really sweet and are looking after me well; I even get my G & T brought to me in bed!' (Willy)

Bashed and bruised, Willy returned to his loyal steed — his bike — and bravely battled on towards Europe, with the team, as a mark of respect, following slowly at the rear ...

Oriental Path

Considering the Oriental Path was only pedalling for seven months, they had more than their fair share of misadventures. They decided to make an early start on this front, by getting lost up a mountain in the dark in Hong Kong: 'Desperate for some fresh air we spent a weekend out on a nearby island where we had our first adventure. It involved the 4 of us carrying our bikes up a mountain, losing our way in the dark, daring each other to knock on the door of a haunted monastery containing huge golden buddhas, threatened by a pack of growling dogs (why didn't I get that rabies injection?!), until we finally took shelter in a half-constructed Chinese hut. We were woken by the monks early next morning, who were travelling to the mountain to attend their sunrise worship ceremony.' (Rhoda)

In China whilst on a boat from Canton to Wuzhou, Sebastian woke in the early hours and was very sick. Not an unusual occurrence amongst all team members, but he seemed to have a bone caught in his throat. Gesticulating madly, Adria was able to communicate to the boat ticket girl and then some cooks on the streets that they needed a doctor.

They were directed to a hospital near by where they were passed from doctor to doctor trying to communicate their problem with the use of a phrase book. Sebastian takes up the story of his ordeal: 'Seated on a wooden chair, he clasped my tongue between some lint with his fingers, and wearing a round concave mirror holed in the middle for his eye, directed a beam onto another mirror which he briefly sterilised by holding it over a flame from a meths burner, testing it afterwards against the palm of his hand. The mirror inside my mouth went farther and farther back. I wretched; he directed me to a tiny bucket at his feet. There was an eerie light of dawn, yellow, flooding into the room . . . This examination was repeated a couple of times. No joy. He could not see down far enough . . . A small child had come in with a tooth problem. Another doctor was looking for a piece of string.

'X-ray was the next option. My case was gathering a collection of medical students. An interpreter appeared. And also someone either from the bus company or Public Security who badgered the doctors, asking why we hadn't bought bus tickets to Yangshou . . .

'Pale green hospital walls. No Spitting signs . . .

'One of the doctors grasped my head; shoved it this way and that, into the right position. They were very undecided and seemed to take innumerable shots. Lots of discussion between them all.

'We went back to the main x-ray room where there were light boxes in rows against one wall and waited. My mouth was foul with barium. The

Public Security girl had left us, but in marched a young chap with a gun which he propped up behind the door, sat on a bench beside ours and waited. One of the doctors, glasses, large jovial face, removed the gun when the boy had left the room for a while, and hid it behind a screen . . .

'The rest of the ordeal was by far the worst — taken up to yet another room . . . My fears were realised when I was first given injections at the top of my bum, which I was told would make me thirsty, and then told to hold in my mouth a yukky grey syrupy liquid, for five minutes; and then to swallow it in three stages. An interminable age went by — the whole of my mouth went numb.

'Another injection, then led into an adjoining room, laid down in foetal position on a couch, plastic bit inserted into my mouth by a masked nurse . . . I have visions of this black tube being pulled in and out. The white markings moving back and forth. Lots of conversation and debate. It suddenly became too much. I heaved and grasped the pipe with my hands — I felt I was suffocating and sicked up barium.

'They wanted to insert it a second time . . . it was easier. I tried to relax and breathed deeply and closed my eyes to the horror of the experience.

'Throughout there was a hand on my leg . . . I made a point of holding my hands firmly behind me. It was a personal fight to keep them there, tense, rigid, braced. I thought the hand was that of a Chinese nurse — but no it was Adria — bravely comforting, God knows I would have run a mile!

'. . . Afterwards, in the two-bed ward, Age said the doctors and nurses were squealing with laughter whenever I appeared to be in agony. Certainly when I was given the injections up until the end of my stay they didn't suppress any smiles behind white masks.

'. . . The next 12 hours; sleeping, drowsing, chatting tiredly to the others, when they popped in from their excursions around the town. English lessons. One chap who learnt English entirely from the radio and television, brought his girlfriend along — very elegantly dressed in pale cream suit and light turquoise shirt. Large legs though and those pumper (?) stockings which finished below the knee. She had a deep voice and was very shy. They were off ballroom dancing.

'On the first day I was given two litres of glucose by drip. Painful injections — thick needles with metal clips pushed into the back of the palm. After ¼ of litre one side of my hand puffed up and the needle was transferred to the other side. Two litres in all.'

After photos were taken £30 was paid. Sebastian felt this was cheap for such an experience!

After that a little gentle treatment was needed (if not for the cyclists, for the reader!). So, a tale of the pleasurable. Near Yangshuo in Southern China, the team tried out the local version of massage, known as Jiou: '... an alternative to acupuncture and none medical. Described in guides as massage but no. They call it 'fire bottles' — fat cups made of bamboo and poked with a ball of fire then plopped onto the skin on an area of tension. The guy either takes these off immediately and plops them back on or leaves them there for a few minutes if the muscle seems particularly taut. They say that if dark red blood rises to the surface when one of these hot cups is sucked to the skin, then the body is tired or unwell. The backs of our necks came up dark red. The man did massage a while and also took two burning pencils of herbs that smelled like incense and held them close to tight skin while he pushed and stroked it with his fingers — lovely.' (Adria)

Well, that would keep their cycling muscles happy for a while. Their next source of tension however wasn't physical; the problem arose through their confusion over where they could cycle in China and where they were prohibited to go: 'At 10.30 we reached the outskirts of Zunyi, a place marked on the map as Zunyi County — Zunyi Municipal was the main city (through which the Great March passed in 1934). In the middle of the high street stood a policeman who waved us off the road and into the Public Security Bureau. We stayed there until 5.00 pm that day when it had been established that we had inadvertantly disobeyed the Chinese law and in punishment were to have our bicycles sent to Shanghai until we exited from China ...' (Adria)

Sebastian takes up the story: 'We had to fill out flimsy forms for Foreigners — then they took us up to our rooms to escape the crowd. The officer in charge only had two forms, so disappeared to get two more, and an ex-English teacher to interpret. It was late — we were tired, but tried to be as ingratiating and co-operative as possible. And they seemed genuinely apologetic they were putting us to the trouble. They kept on shaking our hands and whilst saying firmly that we would have to leave Tongdao, repeatedly welcomed us to China ...

That was just a taste of what was to come. Ten days later they were arrested in Zunyi and taken in for questioning again.

'It took some time to decipher what our options were and the officer had to disappear to either telephone or visit his senior officers for their opinion.

'We were treated very civilly. Next morning the interpreter arrived again, this time Mao-jacketed, not suited, and took us to breakfast in the hotel dining room, some distance from the hotel itself. The waitresses and kitchen staff were changing out of their gum boots and back into high heels.'

Shortly after this their bikes were loaded onto a bus by a 'bevy of Red Army troops'. A small crowd had gathered to see them off and so ended their cycling in China. They were reunited with their bikes at Shanghai after travelling down the Yangtse river.

Aidan, relieved to be in Seoul, South Korea, commented 'As we left the polluted city behind, we cycled with a strange freedom, knowing that we wouldn't be stopped.' But South Korea wasn't to be without its tangled mishap. Adria, whose sign language had worked so well for her in China, didn't fare so well on this occasion and ended up on a mammoth wild goose chase: 'I'm sure that at about 10 I saw Rhoda over my shoulder close on my heels as we reached the top of a hill. From there I didn't look back and at 11.10 I was in the centre of Sunch'on alone. I stopped to buy an apple and wait for the others . . . Five minutes later a taxi driver pulled up beside me in his car and explained as best he could in babbled Korean with the occasional peculiarly pronounced English word that Rhoda had had an accident further back.

'I sped back – all power to my pedals. The taxi man suggested she was 2 km back. Maybe he meant 20?! I backtracked 12 miles and saw nothing of Rhoda or Sebastian. Where could they be?'

Adria stopped at a garage where a girl said she'd seen them on their way to Sunch'on. Adria threw her bike in the back of a lorry that had pulled in and had a lift back to Sunch'on where she leapt back on her bike in search of a hospital. A dozen conflicting sets of directions finally took her to a Catholic hospital where the English-speaking nun drew her a map with all the place names on it in Korean. 'The map was sadly wildly innaccurate and seemed designed to send me off on a wild goose chase.' Eventually, many crossed wires and an ambulance ride later, Adria arrived at the third and final hospital of the area: 'My energies were draining fast. It was past 3 o'clock and I'd had very little to eat all day. They took me back to their hospital and we all sat and looked confused. They made a couple of phone calls. I took their photograph and asked to leave. I was free again and decided to hitch to see if I could catch up with Rhoda and Bas, assuming that by that time Rhoda's accident couldn't have been that bad and that they were on their way to Wando.' (Adria)

Adria didn't have much trouble getting a lift. The first lift flagged down the second lift who flagged down a policeman who flagged down the third lift. All charmed by Adria's smile, youth and her press clippings book. Eventually with this relay of rides in various trucks she found herself a place to eat. Now well and truly split from the others, and worn out from all the frantic activity, she had to find somewhere to sleep. She had the tent but Aidan had the poles, so bed that night was beneath a cherry tree in full bloom. But it turned out not to be such an ideal spot and she viewed many bare bottoms that night as people leapt out of cars to relieve themselves by the side of the road!

The next day in Wando she caught up with the team. Rhoda wrote back home of the event: 'There was one time when we accidentally lost each other for two days. All 'cos of me who decided it was time to bowl over a pedestrian and leave some skin on the tarmac. A passing taxi driver saw the spill and informed Adria who was 5 miles ahead at the time, being told "your friend back there's had an accident" ... After being painted in iodine I cycled on, somehow missing Adria who'd come back looking for me. I continued thinking she was still in front... As the day progressed Sebastian and I put the non-appearance of Adria down to the fact that she'd received a sweaty T-shirt from a package, courtesy of 4C man, Tony Redpath [Adria's boyfriend], the excitement of it all was so much that she set off dreaming for the day and forgot to stop cycling. 100 miles further on, "Powerhouse" rolls up safe and well. We find Aidan just coming out of a Korean hot bath. This Oriental Yoga freak turned his ankle over while taking his jogging shoes for a run, and had to test out the Korean buses for two days.' So, whilst Adria had been chasing all over the place looking for Rhoda, Aidan had been doing far more damage to himself.

Their next adventure took place in Japan, on Mt. Fuji: 'And so we started to climb. Up and up and up. Mt. Fuji is 12,388 ft and it took us from 8.15 to 12.00 to climb from Shin-Go-gome on the south side to the top, mainly following a rope linking metal stakes ... It was very steep and the volcanic scree and rubble under your feet made the climb harder. One step up, two steps down as you slid back. 20% of the mountain was still snow covered. Mt. Fuji is divided into 10 points — 10 at the top, 1 at the bottom. [The team started at point 5.]

'We all got headaches because of the high altitude. Rhoda suffered a headache such as she had never before suffered and was very sick right on top of the mountain. Sebastian can be quoted as saying "I hate this. I really hate this" as he scrambled up in the second hour over ever tumbling volcanic scree.

'... It was on this day that I had the most frightening experience of my life. I was nearing the top where the air was thin and the temperature low. There were quite a few snowy slopes at this point, a couple of hundred feet from the top. There was a choice — snow slopes

Above: **The complete team of 4 Corners World Bike Riders at Millwall Park, 20 September 1987, on their return from the 4 expeditions. (Photo: Eric Paulton)**

Right: **Dick Crane and Miranda Spitteler – all smiles with the cheque from Flora, received 17 September 1987, just in time to save the Finale.**

Right: **Miranda Spitteler working in the 4 Corners office at London Docklands.**

The Americas Route team: Jo Doran, Meryl Channing, Alex Sfakianos and Thomas Harding at the British Embassy, Madrid, after Thomas's accident. (Photo: Amanda Harding)

Thomas at the top of th
pass in the Peruvian Al
after the team rode fron
sea level to 4080 metres
in 120km and 3 days.
(Photo: Jo Doran)

Pig meat on sale at the market in Huaraz, Peru (Photo: Thomas Harding)

Thomas cycling past Lake Titicaca, Peru. (Photo: Jo Doran)

Jo Doran pushing her bike through the mud on the way down the Canyon del Pato, Peru. (Photo: Thomas Harding)

Alex, Meryl and Jo riding up the coast of Peru along the infamous Pan American Highway. (Photo: Thomas Harding)

Above: The African Trail team – Norman Carr, Andy Hansen, Julia Leeward and Willy Taylor. (Photo: Moira Poulton)
Below left and middle: Easy days and hard days – on the left, Norman cruises past the Indian Ocean in Dar Es Salaam (Photo: Moira Poulton); middle – having climbed 2,000 metres in near 100% humidity, Moira finally succumbs to heat exhaustion in Malawi. (Photo: Norman Carr)
Below right: In Lilangue market, Malawi, a polio victim makes sandals from worn lorry tyres, his home-made wheelchair standing close by. (Photo: Norman Carr)

Taking a break on the exposed road to Suez in the Sinai Desert, after suffering heat and headwinds. (Photo Norman Carr)

The team celebrate 4000km covered on the Red Sea coast. (Photo: Norman Carr)

The full team and their guide William rest having climbed 5685 metres to Gilman's Point on Mount Kilimanjaro, the photo taken by a self timer.

The Oriental Path team: Aidan Prior, Rhoda Morrison, Sebastian Be[illegible] and Adria Stubbs at Shanghai. (Photo: Sebastian Best)

The team enjoying some of China's fine foods at Guangzhou. (Photo: Sebastian Best)

Cycling through the rap[illegible] at Zunyi, China, (Photo[illegible] Sebastian Best)

The team pause at Hiroshima, Japan near the epicentre of the bomb. (Photo: Sebastian Best)

Rhoda and Sebastian at the Arctic Circle. (Photo: Sebastian Best)

Difficult cycling conditions near Finse, Norway. (Photo: Sebastian Best)

Above: The road to Kathmandu 'like a twisting snake', in Nepal. (Photo: Nick Walker)

Left: The Asian Highway team – Nick Walker, Katharine Walker and Jane Evans outside a Raleigh bicycle shop in south-west Malaysia. (Photo: Nick Walker)

or scree slopes with a little rock climbing. I, like Sebastian, went for the latter. Our breath was short and we were terrifyingly high. Somehow I found myself under an unassailable cliff having stumbled around over crumbling rocks concentrating on just moving forward, not looking ahead as any experienced mountain climber would — or anyone for that matter with an ounce of common sense would. I decided to "hang a right", as Rhoda would put it, across a small strip of snow to a climbable area of the peak. After just a couple of uneasy steps I slipped, for the snow that looked so pure and gentle was a killer in disguise. Hard and icy. In my Goretex I slipped easily and it was *no* joke. I fell suddenly for about 15 ft and miraculously was able to get a grip — in pure desperation. It's amazing what you can do when you think your life is about to end! At the moment when I fell all I remember is a flash of lightning across my eyes and a scream louder than I have ever heard before. It was my own voice ... I sat gibbering like a baby ... I was absolutely and literally scared stiff. I had screamed but nobody came to my rescue ... Nobody *could* hear me and so I was alone. Left alone to save my own life. "That's just great" I thought. So I had no choice but to pull myself together and grip that ice like there was no tomorrow. I was on my bum and I had to concentrate on keeping my heels in the holes that I'd thumped out (with my heels) and willing the warmth into my hands so that my fingers would press test-tube-shaped holes in the snow and ice willing warmth into my bum so it would mould a little shelf to support me. I looked down, swear words were my only comfort — and saw that slippery slope descend smoothly for about ½ km. I could see myself flying over the snowy horizon like greased lightning. The view of the land at sea level was like a view from an aeroplane. I asked myself "shit, what am I doing here?". Eventually I made it to the guide rope having had a couple of breakdowns along the way. I weakly hauled myself up the rope, still shaking like a leaf.' (Adria)

Kogi, 'our man in Japan' appeared. Adria could not make him understand what had just happened to her and he just kept repeating 'yes, yes' to whatever she said. When she reached the top Aidan gave Adria a great big hug — Rhoda was too preoccupied with being violently sick by this time, and Sebastian had already taken off at high speed down the slope.

'The crater on top of mount Fuji was magnificent' we back at our safe base in London were told. Obviously it was worth the trouble! After this everything else would be down hill to Europe ... Or would it?

People

Travel by bike certainly leads to intimate contact with people. As Andy was to comment after passing through a few countries on the African continent 'The nice thing about bikes is that people are almost as interested in you as you are in them, and that breaks the ice very very quickly'. All the teams reported unprecedented friendliness where ever they went. This has a lot to do with the fact that people of the countries of the Third World aren't trapped inside offices, factories and their homes; there was so much activity on the streets of the towns and villages, in the fields and along the roadside. Often it was their curiosity and amusement at 'Gringos' travelling on bikes that made them interested enough to make the first approach. The great advantage in this for Four Corners, was that it gave the riders far more opportunities to talk with people and thus find out more about their cultures and circumstances. The curiosity that 'Gringos' on bikes inevitably attracted wasn't always welcome though.

The Americas Route

It was inspiring to receive reports of the fantastic response of many of the people in the Andes. They were the kind of people that I.T.'s work was all about, and who we were all working for: the descriptions of the fiestas, of how people lived were a great tonic.

As they pedalled on across the Altiplano they would often spot a poncho-cloaked *campesino* Indian with his herd of llama or alpaca. They would pass women outside their homes spinning wool, or slowly making their way down a track carrying bundles on their backs, or mothers with their children waiting for their man to return from the fields. A lot of these were Aymaran in the Lake Titicaca area and spoke very little, if any Spanish. However, one encounter was particularly special for the extreme generosity shown by someone of very humble means.

The team had asked an Aymaran if they might set up camp in his field and had invited him to join them for supper which they indicated by offering him a spoon. Conversation was restricted and carried out with a combination of gesticulations and pigeon Spanish, but he managed to convey that he would like to return the compliment. The following morning Thomas and Meryl got up before sunrise and went across the fields to his small home, a mud house with a courtyard enclosed with a roughly built stone wall. A striped blanket was laid on the trodden mud floor and life just carried on around them as they were served a breakfast of grain and vegetable stew. Mangey dogs, two bulls, sweet grubby ponchoed children wandered about and a sprightly old grandma was tripping round the courtyard collecting together the dried dung for fuel. They ate like kings — baked black potatoes and fire potato pancakes followed the stew. It was difficult to vocalise their gratitude and for the man to express his pleasure and there were beaming smiles all round. All too soon they had to get on their bikes and be on their way.

In **Ecuador** one of the most memorable nights for Meryl and Jo was when they stayed with a family in the wooded hills near a place called Catacocha: 'We pitched our tent amongst the chickens, the parrots, the dog, the cat, the goat, the mule and a horse (it wasn't the quietest of nights). The mother was overwhelmed by our tent and stove and brought out the best chairs for us to sit on. When the father came back from the fields later that night we sat on their balcony with them helping to shell peanuts by gaslight for the next day's planting, and chatting about our respective countries. I don't think I've ever met such a warm hospitable family.' (Jo)

This incredible sharing by so many who had so little was to happen many times in many parts of the world for all of the world bike riders.

On occasions encounters weren't quite so relaxed. The team will not forget Juli, and I should think Juli will not forget the team on their gleaming bikes. They entered a small town near Lake Titicaca at the same time as school was breaking up and found themselves being chased by excited screaming kids. They dived into a café, bikes and all. The owner found the whole episode very amusing, her café surrounded by about 200 pairs of peering curious eyes all wanting to get a close-up view of these blonde gringos on bikes!

There was another lively occasion around Christmas when Jo inadvertantly became the centre of attraction at a fiesta: 'We spotted a whole crowd of people in a square of a village just off the road and went to investigate. It was present giving time for the children. Meryl and I wanted to be inconspicuous and just watch and not detract from the event by diverting people's attention to us. Well, we wandered up and there was a traditional music group playing Andean music. We were in the Acash region where they are obviously very proud of their culture. The women wear straw hats like boaters with flowers in them and lovely green shawls with brooches. They were just playing music when we arrived but one of the older men wanted me to dance with him while Meryl took photos. I don't think it is that easy to dance to the mountain music and I was hesitant of making a fool of myself in front of the whole village in my T-shirt, cycling shorts and clomping shoes but I duly obliged. We danced on the raised platform, me mimicking his actions. The village was in uproar, people splitting their sides, never having seen anything so funny in years. For entertainment value, on a scale of 1 to 10 I must have scored 20! When we finished they gave me a big round of applause and bravos. Then it was Meryl's turn to make them laugh as she took the stage for a turn or two. We very much added to their enjoyment of the whole event I think and I loved it. What wonderful friendly people, and dancing and singing was a great way of communicating and sharing.' (Jo)

If I've painted an idyllic picture so far, things didn't always go so well. We've already been told tales of mean reckless driving and there was another incident too that wasn't so pleasant. Up on the altiplano the Americas team was riding along when a man stepped out holding a rock in each hand. They stopped. He threw the rocks away and held out his hat for money. They paid. But this kind of thing was rare and as for the media image of the gun-carrying drug-dealing South American, they saw very little evidence of this kind of activity. That's not to say that it doesn't exist, but that it isn't so rife as the media would have us believe.

Something which is particularly Andean is the wonderful array of hats that people wore. They were usually a variation on the bowler hat though occasionally flat caps would be spotted in an area. Hats vary from valley to valley, so that when people gathered at busy markets in the local towns you could tell where they came from by their style of hat. They also wore beautifully patterned alpaca jumpers, ponchoes and embroidered shawls; these things were all too tempting for the team and they soon learned the art of bartering with the vendors, usually finding that the first price given was actually twice as much as the seller expected.

In Southern Ecuador the clothes of one group of Indians was noticeably different from all those that had gone before: '... the most interesting Indians I have seen so far. They all wear black, the men wear ponchos and shorts with wellies. They have long black hair, plaited under a white brimmed hat. They are stunning, very handsome. I could quite go for a few of them. They seem a proud, noble race, the way they conduct themselves. The women too wear black shawls and huge circular brooch pins many of which are silver. They have big heavy earrings and necklaces of coloured beads.'

Just before they left Ecuador the team spent a few days in the jungle. Their guide, Sebastian, was of the Shuar tribe and told the team something of the history. Thomas relaid this back to us in a letter: 'Let me tell you a bit about the Shuar tribe — a pretty old Amazonian tribe spread across Peru, Ecuador and Brazil without religion or faith, superstitious, quite a warring tribe. They have a reputation for being head hunters [Sebastian's grandfather, a famous one, shrunk over 50 heads, still doing so 15 or 20 years ago when missionaries put a stop to it in Ecuador — but in Peru . . .], a tradition which consists of cutting off the head of most famous head hunters (doing so at odds of 3:1, 4:1, etc) by which means, both the victor and the victim gain honour and fame. They then shrink them. They never do it to outsiders and are not cannibals (there aren't any traditional cannibals in any of the thirty or so Amazonian tribes); they put their stick vertically through their lip for beauty's sake (I didn't see this), use blow pipes and are extremely knowledgeable about the flora, fauna and animals in the jungle.

'Now for the sad part. There are only 250,000 left in the Amazonias; none live the traditional life nearer than 400 km from where we were. Sebastian's father's village used to have over 150 houses, but as the road and the outside society moved further and further into the jungle this number has decreased, some people leaving and joining society, others retreating further into the jungle (now a reserve), to preserve their way of life. Everyone wears jeans, carries a gun and a machete and wears wellingtons.

'Sebastian himself, like all Shuars, had to go to school and then into the army. However he then went to college and studied the jungle in Panama, Brazil and Ecuador; now completely Ecuadorianised, but still retaining (only part) knowledge of the jungle, how it works and how to survive in it, Shuar style. One day he says when the economy collapses, he will tear off his clothes and once more blow-shoot monkeys, eat heart of palm and live with 8 women, shrinking his heroes' heads!'

A quick dash through Mexico didn't give the team much opportunity to learn a great deal about the Mexicans, though it was clear that they took great pride in their culture and once again were most generous to the team. However, as they got closer to the border, the hard influence of the USA became apparent and the friendliness faded somewhat. In the States the speed of everything, the false sincerity of 'Have a Nice Day' and the extremeness of their consumerism made the previous six months seem almost like a dream ...

'It was very difficult going into the States having led a simple lifestyle on the bikes amongst poor people. To go into this affluent consumerist society where so much waste of energy, food and resources was apparent, I for one wanted to turn round and go South again.' (Jo)

All was saved when they met up with the kindred spirits of 'Bike Aid', an organisation working towards the same aims as Four Corners. Then their enthusiasm welled up again as an energy that could only be found in the USA began to capture them too.

The Asian Highway

The Asian Highway didn't encounter quite such a contrast of culture at the beginning of their ride along the South East Coast of Australia. When they'd arrived at Sydney airport they had been met with the sight of Australians drinking Fosters lager for breakfast and an Australian spotted on a bike came complete with surf board, bare feet and surfing shorts! The team also found that Australians were generally friendlier and that there was a greater readiness to help than one would find in England; bike shops would check all their bikes over for free for example.

After the uninhabited open spaces of Australia, **Indonesia** with its throngs of people came as a real shock: 'As we left the airport in Bali, children rushed out to wave and shout all the English they knew — "Hello Mister", "I love you", "Where are you going?" This was a familiar pattern throughout Indonesia' (Kate), whilst Jane told us 'Sometimes you feel like some kind of comedy act the way everyone just collapses laughing as soon as they set eyes on you.'

Kate, observing Balinese people said they: 'don't just have a culture but actually live it ... Balinese life centres around religion from birth to death. Their temples are open cheerful places and wherever you go there seem to be thousands of them. Each village must have at least three. In the morning offerings have to be made to Bali's prolific spirits — on high shelves for the good ones, casually placed on the ground for the baddies.'

'In Ubud, the cultural centre of Bali, we witnessed a funeral procession. Even this was a fun-filled occasion with crowds of people and brilliantly decorated towers. A cremation is a release of the soul so that it can go to its afterlife, and therefore is a cause for celebration. To confuse the soul, the funeral tower containing the body is bounced, shaken, spun, twirled, splashed and run all the way from the deceased's home to the cremation field. The guests and onlookers sprint along behind. If the soul isn't sufficiently confused it might find its way back home which would be very annoying!' (Kate)

The people of Indonesia made a real impact on the team. In Java, however, things weren't so idyllic as they had been in Bali. The team found themselves a great source of fascination, especially in areas where few other tourists ventured. When they thought they were safely within the sanctuary of their bedrooms hoards of faces would appear at the windows: '. . . the people were all over everything, almost crawling through the window vents to look at us.' (Jane)

They were now in a Muslim country and loud 'reverberating' prayers were being broadcast five times a day from the mosques. These would begin in the early hours of the day. Also, the girls would occasionally be asked to cover up their arms.

Indonesia is just packed with people, many of them extremely poor with lots of beggars. Jane was approached by one for the first time: '. . . she was an old woman with a terrible deformity all the way up her leg which she pulled her sarong up to show me, I found it very upsetting. I thought of the fact that she looked the same age as my grandmother and of the kind of comfort she lives in. Actually, as my grandmother is about 87 she couldn't have been the same age as I've been told that people don't live much over 50 here . . .'

Some of the wealthier members of the community seemed to be of Chinese origin running their own businesses and restaurants etc. The population is 166 million which is startling when you look at it on a world map and compare its size to that of Great Britain with its 55 million population. It's not that much bigger. So, it was hard to get away from people, and when they were cycling up the mountains they would be followed by crowds of children grabbing their bikes and calling out after them. Noise, constant noise was the result of so many in so small a space and this was compounded by the addition of music blaring out on loud speakers, even in small villages.

In Malang, the team were shown amazing hospitality by an English couple called Alison and Clive. They would be leaving the island soon and had to arrange for their dog to be left with a neighbour's servant. 'Indonesians aren't altogether tender-hearted towards dog and cat type animals, so the neighbour's servant was asked carefully if he liked dogs, to which he replied "neither dog nor pork"!' (Jane)

A brief stop on Singapore didn't leave much time for the team to explore, especially since most of their time here was spent with the

Nature Society which comprised a fairly multi-cultural bunch of people.

Soon they were in another Muslim country, **Malaysia**, which meant that the girls were occasionally requested to 'cover up'. As they were cycling down the coast the temptation in the heat to don a bikini and race down to the sea had to be resisted: '... near a huge wide sandy beach. Nick, Katharine and I rushed straight down for a swim only to find that all the women were going into the sea with clothes on — something that hadn't occurred to us before ... Felt a bit odd going into the water with trousers and shirts.' (Jane)

Malaysia offered luxury of luxuries: Kentucky Fried Chicken. The manageress, a Malaysian called Marcia took them under her wing and helped them find the best of the cheapest hotels in town. Before they continued their journey she insisted they come in for a last chocolate milk shake on the house: '... we sat and talked to Marcia for a while — told us that her brother is married to the Sultan of Brunei's daughter and that one day they'd all shown up at KFC! She said she was quite surprised but that it wasn't actually that odd as royalty in Malaysia move around and dress quite normally, and that it's much safer to do so.' (Jane)

In Kuala Lumpur a taxi driver nearly moved Jane to tears whilst another nearly frightened the life out of her. Both were being friendly, they just had different ways of showing it as Jane told us: 'On the way to the High Commission we had the most amazing journey — the taxi driver was whistling something and Katharine joined in, recognising it as the 'Just one Cornetto' song(!), at which point the driver started to sing the real Italian version in the most wonderful voice — he sang on and on as we drove — it was so beautiful and so unexpected I was close to crying. On the way back it was a different story. I was sitting in the front with the driver and he got himself worked up into a terrible frenzy about when he was in London how a taxi driver cheated him at Heathrow and that he 'showed him this' — waving clenched fist under my nose! I thought he was about to get nasty with us but it turned out he *liked* English people.'

Thailand provided a quiet interim, though people were friendly enough: drivers overtaking them would blow their horns and give them the thumbs up and there was much smiling and waving from people in the fields as they cycled by.

The **Bangledeshi** people were really enjoyed. Initially in Dhaka they experienced some pretty harrowing scenes of poverty: 'We had become very used to people watching us intently but this was the first time we had been touched and squeezed. From all directions hands and stumps reached out eagerly for money. Beggars pressed themselves closely against us. We escaped in a mini-bus but still the crowd grew. Many people pushed their faces against the glass and others thrust their heads through the open window.' (Nick)

It was different out of the city though: 'The Bangladeshis were really friendly, more than any other people we met. There would always be cyclists accompanying us along the roads, not cycling behind or in front but along side of us, conversing with whatever English they had. Also, we would have lots of invitations to drink tea in people's homes and once, there was this completely impromptu invitation to meet a school. We were garlanded, introduced to all the staff and taken round the school to meet the children. They were so unused to visitors in their country and kept thanking us for being there — I liked them a lot.' (Jane)

The **Nepalese** were used to travellers: 'We didn't have so much contact with the Nepalese. This was partly to do with the fact that we were so ill here, and had to maintain a strong cycling pace, but also, they are used to tourists and so weren't as interested. As always, out in the country this changed and we did meet with some kindnesses there. The other thing is, Nepal isn't nearly so populated as Bangladesh and we could go for miles and miles without even seeing anyone.' (Jane)

In **India**, once again they were to come into contact with people in a big way: 'Calcutta was our next stop. It has over ¼ million pavement dwellers who are desperately poor.' (Nick) As one Indian gentleman asked them passionately 'Why do you come here to this tormented, confused, corrupt, futile and exasperating place?' (I should think that there are enough reasons there to visit any country!) 'When we arrive at a roadside tea-shop (or rather a tea-shed comprised of odd boards and sheets of galvanised iron) we sit at the table placed on a mudstamped floor the crowd doesn't take long to swell into an unruly mob of young children and men — where are the women we ask ourselves?

'Everything nearby appears to come to a standstill, not that there was much industry going on anyway. All conversation stops then begins again in an animated fashion. We pick up occasional snippets in English such as "It's a disco bike" or "Raleigh cycle" or "3-speed". Everyone loves to squeeze the grab-ons or turn the pedals — woe-betide them if they touch the gear levers — though usually it makes the audience laugh if we attempt to chastise them.' (Kate)

They found overwhelming kindness at the Gandhi Ashrams and amongst the people who had turned out to support them. Also, in Faizabad they were invited to a Sikh wedding: '. . . a flamboyant and expensive occasion. Nick had to wear a head-scarf which looked ridiculous. In the evening there was a party and we were asked to demonstrate "Western dancing" A Boney-M tape was selected and we started to move ... later we insisted that they should show us how to dance in an Indian way. Fortunately they were no better.' (Kate)

Finally Jane was to write home of Turkey 'It was easily one of the most friendly places on our route.' A particularly glamorous Turkish woman informed Jane 'You are wasting the best of your body in this undertaking!'

The African Trail

The African Trail team seemed to have a special rapport with many people in most countries. Was it Andy's talent for languages or Moira's endless supply of 'fags' that she carried as her 'friendship tokens'?!

As with everywhere in Africa that the team went, they found the people to be extremely friendly and warm. One of Andy's exuberant letters told me of their early exchange with Zimbabwians: '... We look really freakish, wearing Bodyfit skin shorts and tops, Thomas Cook hat with scarves sewn on, shades or goggles.' (Remember this was in heat between 35 and 40 degrees centigrade, and though their get up must have looked really strange, it was necessary to protect them from the fierceness of the sun.) 'The locals love it' Andy continued, 'they cluster around us when we reach the little bottle stores, asking loads of questions "Are those spare tyres?" "Where are you going?". When we say, "all the way back to London", they roll their eyes, whistle, slap their thighs and laugh.'

In **Malawi**, puritanical laws required the girls to cover their legs and they went along to a Tie-Dye Centre to buy some fabric for this purpose. The centre was staffed by handicapped people including the blind. Despite their handicap, the people were cheerful and interested and the team's visit filled the place with chatter: 'We got talking to a number of employees about Four Corners. They were fascinated by Willy's bike when he wheeled it in. Quite a crowd gathered and the blind were very keen to touch it whilst Willy explained what the various parts were for.' (Moira)

Generally, the Malawians seemed on the reserved side: 'People don't have the same natural exuberance that the Zimbabwians do — tend to stare and only react when we shout hello at them.' (Andy)

If the Malawians were reserved about some things then religion seemed to be the exception to the rule: 'We rounded a corner to cross the river and came across a group of maybe 15 people singing and chanting on the road. They turned out to be led by an African healer and were singing to the spirits of the valley for healing, both physical and mental. The singing was beautiful and the people were obviously very involved in it.' (Julia)

They were to meet with these bands of singing people a number of times in Malawi. However, one rare meeting took place in a quiet corner in Livingstonia. This provided the possibility of some juicy controversial political exchanges, even more so had they been aware of who they were talking to, though I don't think the others would have been too keen on the idea: 'At breakfast with two South African women. Immediately got into an argument with them when they said that the Malawian had less freedom than the South African! They then got very upset and hysterical when we argued with them. They just wished that people who hadn't visited RSA didn't have an opinion on it and then argued that anything is better than communism and they, of course, knew everything about communism, even though, as we pointed out, they had never been to Russia. It ended in tight lipped silence and they promptly left the rest house contrary to their former plans! Later that day Ben and Biddie, two more likable South Africans we had met at Nuarta bay, turned up and told us that the two women were in fact Pic Botha's daughter and friend!!' (Julia)

Julia, as a school teacher, had a personal interest in the education in the different countries and wrote of this and one of her visits to a school in Malawi: '... We were then shown an incredibly involved totally boring talk on the constitution in Malawi ... Despite disruption from the children, on he droned and afterwards asked questions of the kids, who in their eager to please way actually answered them but in a way that made me suspicious of weeks of drilling. If those kids could be given the same opportunities as English children they would all be high achievers given the level of commitment and enthusiasm they have for such a desperately numbing education. Only 6,000 out of over 78,000 each year go to secondary school and very few to university ... All schools are expected to aim for the dizzy heights of Banda's own Kamuzu Academy where classics are the favoured lessons and all the teachers are white! All are educated in English — I can just imagine the level of success if all English kids were educated in French! It made it easier of course for us to be understood in Malawi, but hardly progressive.' (Julia)

Soon after arriving in **Tanzania**, one encounter with people didn't provoke the usual cheery banter of the African trail and really got their backs up: '... we ran into a car crash — a lorry crash to be more exact. A tanker truck had overturned three times after a burst tyre. Amazingly no-one was badly hurt. We used up all our precious first aid supplies patching people up. Loads of cars were stopping and offering the injured lifts! Some baptists from the mission of Iringa stopped. They didn't get out of their car. When Willy asked if they could take an injured man to hospital they said they didn't know where it was and roared off as soon as he turned his back. We couldn't believe it. Of all the people who passed they were the only ones who didn't help.' (Andy)

Tanzanians they found greatly refreshing after the reserved manner of many people in Malawi. They wrote home of the Tanzanians: 'Very interesting both politically and culturally. I found the people to be much more interesting than either the Malawians or the Zimbabwians. Proud, and they treated us like equals rather than as superiors, as most of the Malawians and Zimbabwians had done.' (Andy)

'People were great — continually amused and incredulous as we pulled up at chai stops on our space age machines. But always restrained in their interest and there was usually a self appointed 'Askari' (guard) if children looked as though they might get too interested.' (Julia)

On arrival in Tanzania, there were lots of cries of 'change' and people shouting at them in Swahili '*Wazungu, Wazungu*' (white person) and falling about laughing. Altogether a much more assertive people, and sometimes even a bit aggressive: 'Many of the shouts seem less friendly, and I'm often glad that I can't understand them. We found though that if you react with humour and laugh and toot your horn and act very ostentatious and slightly mad, people will laugh even more and leave you alone. There's no point in trying to fade into the background, *Wazungus* on bicycles are space creatures in places like Tukuyu.' (Andy)

Their encounters with suspicious Tanzanian Bobbies had totted up but few of these were quite so pleasant as that with Godfrey: 'We were rather unsure of what to make of him at first — he invited himself into Willy and Jules room and sat on the bed chatting away, determined to be our escort for the evening. It turned out that he was a Masai, having left the tribe when he was 18. Apparently — all Masai in whatever area speak the same language. They don't recognise the border of Tanzania and Kenya, casually crossing in the bush, herding their cattle.' (Moira)

Godfrey showed them the best 'dives' in town, including the most up-market restaurant. He entertained them with tales of Africa all evening: 'He described his childhood when he lived as a nomadic Masai and drank only milk and blood and ate only meat until the age of 18.' (Julia)

At the end Godfrey made sure he got his worth and turned the other way when the bill for the meal came!

Soon after this, the riders were once again to be on the receiving end of incredible hospitality from Isaac Nkwabi. His nephew had greeted Andy as he rode into town, and told Andy to follow him to a school. This nice surprise was a result of a letter Julia had sent out to contacts from London. They were fed absolute feasts by people who themselves lived very sparsely. The women spent the whole time cooking while they were there but they didn't join the riders to eat. The men did of course. One very much appreciated treat was some cool beer. This is a very rare commodity in Tanzania and consequently expensive, so it was a treat they enjoyed.

In **Kenya**, as they cycled to Nairobi, in the few bottle stores that existed along the road, they would come across young Masai *mordu* (warriors) who came to inspect these strange white creatures on wheels: 'They were carrying long spears their hair plaited and coloured with beaded head bands, neckbands and earrings hanging off long distended ear lobes. Traditionally their role is to protect the tribe and as this role becomes eroded they seem to stand around with all the pride of their position but not much of the action. They showed most interest in the mirrors and the bikes. The sight of these young warriors queuing up to check their hair had to be seen to be believed!' (Julia)

Shortly after this in the 'lunar landscape' of the Turkana Desert Andy and Norman were amazed to discover that there were people living in these extreme arid conditions: 'I couldn't believe it — there were people living here — little huts made of grass (where did they find it?!) and 6 guys fishing; what a crazy place to live — it's so dry here. We later found out that these Turkana people live off fish, fish and fish. Once maybe twice a month a truck with some vegetables arrives. Cheers. The (very) occasional goat supplements this varied and healthy diet. Amazingly they don't look too malnourished.' (Andy)

We can't really say goodbye to the people of Africa without mentioning William the guide. When our own Willy had written home about an old man called Willy, rushing up and down Kilimanjaro, puffing on a fag and singing Pole Pole Kilimanjaro (slowly slowly Kilimanjaro), I thought he was referring to his own youthful efforts of being able to climb Kilimanjaro, smoke a 'fag' and sing all at once (I don't think!). In fact William really did exist and at 53 he did do all those things at once: '. . . a beautiful song in Swahili about Kilimanjaro, and he runs up and down the straggly line of tourists rubbing backs and gently encouraging you along.' (Julia)

The climb was very special to the team and they were so grateful to

William that apart from a whacking great tip, they left him bundles of clothes (he had 11 kids at home). He presented them with their certificates and all the porters burst into a round of applause.

I'm beginning to think this consistently overwhelming friendliness that the African Trail team met along their route had a great deal to do with the African Trail team and the way they interacted with people. Perhaps, whatever the knack is, they became more practised at it as they went along.

They reached **Egypt** during Ramadan; the period of fasting which lasts a month. It is something that is taken extremely seriously. The time they could eat began at 6.30 pm and ended again at 3.00 am. At 6.28 restaurants would be packed full of people, plates of food in front of them, poised to eat, and as soon as the mosque let out a cry of 'Allah-uh-Akbar', they ate furiously to make up for more than 15 hours without food.

Despite the stressful effects this food deprivation had on the population, the team found the Egyptians even more friendly than the Africans (... is this possible I ask myself?). Wasn't this friendliness of the Egyptians sometimes tinged with an ulterior motive? — maybe just occasionally anyway, but what the hell: '... The Egyptians also live up to their reputation for being friendly hustlers — there is always some smiling guy in a *galabeah* shaking your hand and calling you friend "Hello my friend, you want trip on Felucca?", "You want change?", "You want good room, cheap price, special for you?", "I make special price, O.K., come look, looking costs nothing". My favourite was the guy who shook my hand for half an hour running through the whole list of goodies — felucca, donkey, trips, hashish, genuine hieroglyphics, water pipes etc. When I said no to all of these he asked me in an exasperated tone "Look, is there anything I can do to get some money out of you?". The nice thing about these hustlers is that they aren't heavy — as long as you enter into the spirit of the thing and reply with a smile you won't have any problems — in fact they are quite likely to forget about selling you anything and start chatting about things, inviting you in for tea, or if it's after 6.30, some food. I learnt about 50 words of Arabic and such is the nature of the people that they were ecstatically happy whenever I spoke it — they would grin hugely, ask if I spoke Arabic, tell me how well I spoke it(!) and tell everyone else about it.' (Andy)

'The people here in Egypt are something else — hospitable, surprisingly gentle, kind, easy to talk to and completely anarchistic — we never know what's going to happen next. You eat a meal (never ask the price first), then they quote an outrageous price, we give them what we think it's worth, they shout and curse and call us sons of donkeys and call upon Allah then burst out laughing and welcome us to Egypt. One jolly innkeeper always shouted the same thing (his only English) "Happy Christmas, happy aida, welcome to Alaska" (sic). Cycling in the Sinai we were often 100/160 km between shade and water. It was comforting to know that Nomads on the way would *always* offer tea/shade/ sympathy and not want money.' (Willy)

This anarchic character was more than apparent in their style of driving: 'The roads here are unbelievable, everyone drives as though they're in a dodgem car and surprisingly they do dodgem, even the Egyptian cyclists who break every rule in the book — 3 or 4 to a bike (including under 5s), no lights, invariably cycling the wrong way, even on flyovers, often no hands — IT'S TRUE! On the main road up the Nile the story was the same and only in the Sinai did we get any peace and quiet (and then we could have done with the odd hornblowing, gobbing-out-of-the-window driver to break the monotony.' (Julia)

'Islam is the world's most dynamic religious/contemporary force, and we saw the remarkable spectacle of millions of people thirsting and starving for one month during Ramadan — in 45 degrees centigrade! "My God gives me strength" said Ahmed as he poured us tea he was not allowed to drink. The Islamic culture lives in a way it is hard for us Godless Westerners to understand — it's motivating force is I think unique in history.' (Andy)

This boundless enthusiasm for the Egyptian people would only wear rather thin when it came to asking the Egyptians the way to some place. The team were desperately thirsty from many hours cycling in the desert against the wind and asked a man standing by the road, how far it was to the next chai stop. He told them 3 to 4 km. 'So on we forged despite being desperate to stop but surely he couldn't have made it up? Eventually, 13 km later it appeared and we sunk into a zombie-like trance till we were fired up by a couple of Mazbuts. At this point in comes the same man — "you told us 3–4 km" we threw at him. "Well you would not have liked it if I had said more" he replied. A lesson in Egyptian psychology I guess.' (Julia)

The same exasperation occurred with Egyptian bureaucracy. It took them four days to buy their ticket to Crete and they all felt like they needed valium to recover! They were nevertheless very sad to leave: '... Add to that the ever-present beautiful Nile, the desert, snorkelling to rival any in the world — and above all very friendly, open and *fun* people. I wish the Western media would stop writing s..t about Arabs and Muslims — in England you get a terribly tainted view.' (Andy)

The Oriental Path

What shocked the Oriental Path team in Hong Kong was the juxtaposition of extreme wealth and poverty. Below the glistening glass towers of power were beggars, and in the harbour were the floating homes of the Vietnamese refugees. Around the harbour were International hotels with Rolls-Royces and Bentleys in the forecourts. In the more depressed areas of town there were high grubby towers, housing labryrinthian sweat shops in operation at all hours. When the riders rolled up outside a jeweller's shop a friend of the shop assistant, dressed in rags suddenly disappeared like a flash of lightning for fear of putting off trade. They felt like aliens from another planet and were the source of much staring. The Hong Kong Chinese had a word for foreigners, *guilos* (spoilt foreign devils). Under these circumstances it was difficult to get a real feel for the people of Hong Kong. On the other hand the British they met who had gone out to get rich and had succeeded, were extremely hospitable.

The riders didn't exactly fade into the background in China. Here the expressionless staring became almost oppressive. The attention was also very cheering: '... Slowly climbing, and only slowly being overtaken by a bus. I hadn't looked back to see who was behind me; then it was parallel — saw faces out of the windows, pressed to the windows, leaning out, and all shouting encouragement, smiling broadly.' (Sebastian)

'One village we came across was amazing — packed as if it was market day with thousands of men, women and children milling around exchanging sugar cane sticks, hundreds of different sorts of beans and nuts, meat and vegetables. All the people were dressed similarly in mao caps, plain cotton jackets and trousers — mostly of navy blue. The women had bright coloured materials. Some people had flat stiff shawls that looked as though they were made of ox mane and were embroidered and worked together at the shoulder.' (Adria)

At the top of another steep climb, the riders came upon what they thought was a tiny mountain village, but where were all these people coming from?: '... almost immediately some 100 if not 200 people crowded round in a tight circle to watch us. This happened from the moment we arrived, while we bought something to drink and drank thirstily, while we ate and as we left. It was really funny. Everybody looked pretty dishevelled, ragged and grubby. They were mainly children who stood there — of all ages — and only one or two adult men and women. Communication was as good as ever; hand to mouth as if eating, hand to mouth holding imaginary bottles as if drinking, numbers on paper for bill and "shi shi" repeated constantly meaning "thank you". On our way out most of the children ran along up the road following after us for a little way and then dropped away, giggling uncontrollably. It was almost sad to leave so soon the town where we'd seen so many smiling faces.' (Adria)

In Areas that were definitely closed to foreigners the team would take a train or a bus. On one occasion between Tongdao and Luizhou: '... this day we spent eight hours on the train to Luizhou, having the good fortune to travel with some Dong women who are from one of China's 60 or so minority groups, this one living around Tong Dao. Their dress was mainly black with white cotton headscarves. I could only see women, their long hair beautifully tied at the backs of their heads. One women had a baby back sack that was made of a bright pink and red flowery material. They all had lovely smooth brown skin. I wondered where they were going. They originally came from Taiwan.' (Adria)

'In China teachers, researchers and translators can often be quoted as saying "In China everybody has job but nobody given much money". True enough. It's good to see that everybody has a job but then people have more time to themselves during the course of a month — though they work 6 day weeks and what can they do with their time if they have no money at all to spare? Furthermore, the jobs for the most part look unnecessarily strenuous (breaking up the road surface with a small mallet or sweeping the sides of the country lanes), monotonous and unrewarding.

'In this little village, therefore, as with all the others, there were many many people and from what I could see few with any incentive or motivation ... Though people are poor they seem happy.' (Adria)

Friends were made along the way. They met an English teacher, his English name was Johnny: 'They really enjoy trying to please us. We went afterwards to the school, followed by the crowd, where Johnny took us up to his cell-like room where his girl friend — the schools' physical teacher — laid out simple stools, and there was the one narrow bed for us to sit on. Small radio. One electric light. Rough wooden desk. Rough concrete floor, weird western poster ... other teachers came in to join us and there was "Dick — the Philospher", with long side burns, bulging eyes, and a stilted way of talking — where it sounded as though he had prepared exactly what he was going to say, before it came out, rigid in his mind ... guitar. American tunes, and the physical teacher sings Jingle Bells in English accompanied; sounded like Nico, with Lou Reed strumming in the background. We attempted a party piece but we need practice. Aiden very bravely sang Bohemian Rhapsody with his ghastly cold and it sounded awful, but we all applauded — I couldn't have forced myself — thought about offering Donna Donna but was unsure of the words.' (Sebastian)

On the boat down the Yangtse River Sebastian's chance to sing came but maybe helped a little by the rice wine: 'I was approached by a Chinese fellow, and we tried communicating. I was invited into a dorm, offered a cigarette and rice wine, and with a Chinese who was better at written English, talked through the pen and played with questions about work and companies and ownership and co-operatives. I had to sing a song and the only words that sprung to mind were "She'll be coming round the mountain when she comes" — English campfire lyrics!' (Sebastian)

(Let's hope he didn't have to translate the words!)

On that same boat trip, the team was horrified to see poor people, going round eating the leftovers on tourists plates, scraping up every last bit. They found themselves incredibly well looked after, though sometimes the priority treatment they received was almost embarrassing especially when they were shown to the front of the food queues, or when seats would be given up by people who were in the middle of eating.

On their arrival in Seoul airport most of the people milling around in the lobby weren't other travellers but military and security. In the streets they were also to find this strong military presence. However, the people of South Korea were extremely open and friendly. Once when Sebastian stopped an old lady to ask her the way he found himself being enthusiastically embraced and his hand being kissed! They also seemed to have more zest for life; early mornings would see the parks full of hundreds of people exercising. They were more colourful too, both in terms of character and appearance.

Talking of appearance, on the way from the airport, there were masses of 'boys in blue'. Not the subtle darkest navy blue of our own bobbies, but bright blue and they were everywhere: 'I decided I couldn't take the police force seriously that dressed itself in the bright blue which appears to be the country's national colour' (Seb). In fact, they were very helpful and on one occasion, when the police waved them down to warn them not to ride on the motorway, they flagged down a vehicle to take them to a road they could ride on.

As they cycled along roads people would beep their horns and the riders would turn round to find broad grinning faces, people frantically waving and giving them the thumbs up signs. As they became almost well known the greetings became more frequent and grew into cheers, shouting and applause, something that would be repeated later in Japan. This was such a welcome change. Not that people hadn't been warm and hospitable in China, but there had not been the same display of openess.

An absolute favourite of all the team was a Mrs. Kim, from the Hong Kong and Shanghai bank. She was a terribly well turned out South Korean lady with a lovely coy laugh. Sebastian fell ever so slightly in love with her and described her as 'interested, keen and delightful' . . . and a few days later when it came to their departure; 'Mrs. Kim was gorgeous and our parting was rather emotional with invitations to England. She envied us greatly and we wanted to take her with us . . . she handed us a plastic bag bulging with tins of coke and orange juice and chocolate for the trip to Yessou.'

One of the most extraordinary things they saw of the Korean people was when they were on the island of Chejdu. This was a honeymooner's haven where couples would walk about this natural wild beauty spot in droves, decked out in the brightly coloured national costume, carrying tripod and camera for self portraits against a backdrop of lava rocks and sea. Did these rocks pass on some kind of power relating to fertility?

When they took a ferry from the island of Chejue back to the mainland, the team individually entertained themselves, reading books, writing letters. On deck however, there was a great deal of commotion: '. . . the old men and women — many not so old, in their 50s — were leaping up and down swinging their hips, rocking their heads, whirling their arms and shuffling their socked or stockinged feet. They sang at the tops of their voices with gay abandon. Folk songs I think. The music was their own. They bumped into each other and pushed each other around. It was so wild and so liberated I couldn't help wondering if they hadn't been on the bottle . . . You couldn't help but grin as you watched. The happiness was infectious. I was invited to join in but declined. My fun was in watching. Thinking back I should have joined in.' (Adria)

Just occasionally they would chance upon the South Korea of old. People in traditional dress, not for a special occasion but part of their way of life. Usually it would be an old person: 'An old man dressed in traditional costume — pastel coloured silk jacket, white shirt, cumerbund, lace socks and flared silk trousers tied with a ribbon around the ankle; upturned toes on the shoes' (Adria). He was rather annoyed at Adria in her cycling shorts exposing so much of her body in his country — but cycling would be a bit difficult in any other gear.

Another scene of the Old South Korea, fast disappearing with the rapid economic progress there, was that of rural life, which Sebastian found a quiet moment to observe: 'It was so peaceful to just stand and watch the farmer direct his cow with its simple wood-plough, there was such empathy between the two of them. The cow anticipated his every instruction — there were no harsh words — no strong lash of the whip. He frequently spoke to the cow — encouraging it along, and stopped for a rest at intervals caressing it, giving it a break from the harness, and he went and sat at the edge . . . They both seemed so content and at peace with their pace. No sense of urgency, no desperate drive to get the job done — very calm, another task in the slowly unfolding year. The ploughman's wife was at the other end of the field seed-sowing. She didn't look so comfortable bent over the earth, wrapped in headscarves.'

South Korea came to an end all too quickly. The last utterance that Adria heard from a South Korean security guy at the airport was 'Yu tunz mi onz'. Her grasp of the language didn't extend to this vocabularly, perhaps he was reminding her to let her tyres down before she put her bike on the plane, or maybe he was simply wishing her a safe journey. Apparently, he was a 'very handsome young, super-healthy-looking military man'. My own interpretation is that the speaker had been overdosing on gin-seng!

South Korea was a last minute amendment to the itinerary. Important in its own right, it also provided a good bridge for the riders going on to Japan. Had they gone straight from China it may have been hard to adjust to the stark differences, for in China 80 per cent of the population lived in rural areas and were very poor, whilst in Japan 80 per cent of the population were urban and extremely wealthy.

There was an incredible pristineness about the place which seemed to be all pervading. As they went on through Japan, the team noticed more and more how much this applied to people's dress, and need to create the 'right' image. This began with their everyday dress which was almost a uniform in the way in which it conformed to trends; it also embraced sports, and even artists painting by the side of the road were all dressed similarly and neatly. It was all taken very seriously. All the cyclists who joined them along the way were 'better' dressed than the riders themselves, with outfits colour co-ordinated with their bicycle frames. A member of the staff at the British Council said the Japanese only do things if they can do them in style.

In Japan, they developed much closer working relationships with people of that country through Japan Aid. Japan Aid had at first been a little reticent, and no doubt the language difficulties helped create this situation. In fact, the ice soon melted and they all became one big merry band. There was Massayuki, Kazumi, Kogi and Noryaki, Mr. Motozu and Toshi Hattori. Very little was seen of the latter two who remained in the office in Tokyo, whilst the rest of the team joined them out in the support vehicles. Kogi and Kazumi were more involved in the day-to-day running of things, but Kogi became really encouraging when the going got tough, especially with Adria. When she wasn't feeling well one day and was faced with a lot of high gradients, they switched seats, Adria in the support vehicle and Kogi in the saddle for the rest of the day — and in his jeans which must have been extremely uncomfortable. On another occasion Adria happened to be belting along at a record breaking speed — way ahead of the others. Kogi was timing her and stopping to give encouragement 'Today you go very fatht, very fatht'! Masayuki was a great morale booster as well, keeping the riders all linked together, letting the slow ones know how far the team were apart and 'There's only 3 more kms to go' etc. Lovely. Noyaki was fun too.

Generally, the team found the Japanese quite difficult to get to know. Other foreigners living there told them that you always feel an outsider, never know what they are thinking. When they did get to know individuals, they were, in Adria's words, 'gentle to the extreme'.

So there we have the riders' impressions of the people in the Four Corners. The ones that are remembered are those who, despite their often dire poverty, possess something magical which we in the West with our immense wealth, and 'education' are tragically lacking; a wonderful *joie de vivre*, humbling generosity and a precious thing called time.

Meanwhile Back at Base . . .

After the excitement of the press launch in February things went very quiet in the office. There were no riders, very few volunteers around and there was much follow-up work to do if all our labours of the last few weeks were to be exploited. This and the back log of work which had built up as I had given priority to ensuring the press launch happened, all had to be dealt with.

Kate Nivison was a great help with this and she and our Photograph Librarian, Simon Grosser were the only volunteers around, each for a couple of days a week. Sadly, Harriet, the other day-time volunteer had to attend a 5-week course, thus leaving a gap. I was trying to deal with all manner of things: sponsorship, publicity, riders, initiating UK rides. Japan Aid needed regular attention with promises of sponsorship, volunteer recruitment, access for the Oriental Path team to cycle through Russia, secondement of a General Manager. An answer to all of this lay in the possibility of £1,000,000 from Sony for a Grande Finale concert in the Docklands. I.T. were just as keen as I was to secure this sum, which Hiroshi Kato who'd raised $1,000,000 for Live Aid was organising.

Just holding the whole thing together was extremely daunting and with my energies dispersed over such a wide area things were happening slowly. It was just a case of nudging everything ahead until there were more hands on deck. Each morning I was propelled out of bed, by telling myself that I.T. needed this £1,000,000! It was a very effective stimulant and there were lots of dawn starts. When I got home there were letters to be written to the riders and diaries to be read, work often running on after midnight. Weekends were spent working out staff requirements, organising office systems and general planning and catching up. At the time I wrote to the teams 'All considered, things aren't running too badly, though it's more of a squeaky machine rather than the well oiled one I'd like it to be. If only there were 48 hours in the day!'

So, up at six and to bed after midnight, six to seven days a week was often to be the norm for the first few months of 1987. As time went on with more people getting involved, the mornings began at a more civilised hour and occasionally there would be a sanity-preserving weekend free for the odd lie-in which was bliss.

Something that did restore my sanity was meeting all the parents. I felt strongly that the riders' parents should be involved if they wanted to and we had family open days. One of the riders had mentioned that his parents simply weren't interested in what he was doing and I particularly encouraged them to try and come. To have disinterested parents must have been rather sad, but in fact, virtually all the parents were to become incredibly enthused. The first open day was at the end of February. They arrived from all over the country and visited the office one Sunday. We gave a slide show of all their kids spread out across the globe. They were all very excited about the first wave of publicity that had been gained in the previous week. They went off clutching press packs with masses of information about Four Corners and Intermediate Technology and were to be some of our best ambassadors. I wrote to the riders on the Sunday evening after the mums and dads had all gone home: 'It's so odd, only yesterday I hit an all time low. So tired I could hardly think and yet I had to be at the end of the telephone. I just dragged myself home and to bed last night dreading getting up and preparing for an 8.30 am meeting. That's the last I can remember of feeling gloomy and exhausted. Today has been wonderful . . .

'Your mums and dads all came to Docklands and were truly delightful. So much enthusiasm all in one room I would have thought too much. They were so eager and keen to know more about things, and, BOY, were they proud of their sons and daughters. How can a bunch of people just doing what they always wanted to do make so many people so happy? And their being happy has made me happy again — (isn't that nice!).

'What you realise is that Four Corners is for anyone who wants to take part and it seems there's a good few who do. And if the energy of those gathered today doesn't get others thinking the same then nothing will.'

I continued 'I can't tell you how nice it was to meet most of your families and how inspiring their enthusiasm was. They seem well and truly locked into the Four Corners grip, and really tuned into the spirit of things. It was just so nice to be climbing into bed with a smile on my face and it was only then that I remembered the contrast of yesterday — write and thank them for me.'

So the mums and dads, aunts and uncles, sisters and brothers and close friends of the riders were beginning to get drawn in as well. The riders wrote back, all thrilled at this development, some of them saying it was the first time in years that parents had got involved in something they were doing. Others were overjoyed to receive letters from their proud Dads, another first in years if not a first ever!

Crisis on the Routes

Out on the route there was lots of activity and not a few crises: on the Americas Route Thomas had had a pretty serious accident; on the Asian Highway, the team were in Bangkok and there was an unfortunate 'parting of the ways' with one team member having to return to London; on the African Trail, a meeting had been arranged between the team and HRH Prince Charles which didn't take place; on the Oriental Path the Bikes had all been confiscated and there was a likelihood that the team might not be able to get into South Korea. All in all a 'bloody nightmare' and Steve who had begun to get involved again, felt he was unable to promote something with all these things going wrong. It was the last thing I needed to hear at a stage when I had so little support in the office but I put myself into 'calm mode' and dealt with each incident as it happened.

Belinda Harding rang. The tone of voice said it all. That dreaded phone call that something awful had happened to one of the riders. It was Thomas. He had been run down in Mexico by a truck and had been rushed to hospital. I rang Thomas in Mexico City where he was recovering and found him on a high, the effects, I suppose, of the pain killing drugs and the delayed shock. He was very bruised and had had to have 24 stitches in his head. I was so thankful to know that he would be alright. All I had to do was arrange for General Accident, our insurance sponsors, to cover his flight to San Diego where he would join up with the rest of the team — what a relief.

The Asian Highway team needed extremely sensitive attention; Pete Cogram had decided he wanted to leave. When the problem occurred I felt like an overloaded Amstrad, and had I been, there would have been a message on my screen saying 'RUN DISC MANAGER'! There simply wasn't room to take more on board than I already had to deal with. Whatever I did I wasn't going to be able to give this adequate attention however hard I tried. I got three other very fair minds to help me deal with it: Kim Walker, brother of Nick and solicitor to Four Corners, Ann-Marie Piper, a lawyer and Pete Cogram's power of attorney and Steve Armitage who went and met the team in Nepal.

Early morning meetings took place, powered by copious quantities of mugs of strong black coffee. There were obvious reasons for bias on the part of each individual but everyone tried to sort it out on the basis of what was best for the team, I.T. and Four Corners. Documents had been signed by each of the riders before departure which covered the eventuality of a rider leaving their team and this had to be looked into closely. First of all we wanted to see if an objective view might help the team find some way of salvaging the situation. In our optimism, suggestions of how they might continue as a team were sent. The ghastly thing is that because of time, these were sent by telex and because of expense they were abbreviated. The telex must have been an awful shock to receive and certainly didn't convey the depth of sympathy that was felt for the circumstances of the riders by us back at base. Because of the legal implications, much of it was drafted in cold 'legalise', but we prefaced it with the following: 'We have now had an opportunity to hear all of your reactions to the proposal contained in our telex of 27.2.87 and it is clear to us that it is necessary to revise the arrangements.

'The revised arrangements have been drawn up to reflect your wishes and what we consider will be in all your individual best interests and those of Four Corners and I.T. We are desperately concerned with the welfare and well-being of each of you and we are all doing our best to stand aside from the personality differences and to provide you all with a workable scheme for the duration of your route.'

Then followed a list of numbered points which suggested that Pete would continue the route but separately from the rest of the team; that he would continue to be covered by the Four Corners insurance, that for publicity purposes no mention of a split should be made, that Pete would continue as route photographer but that the others should also take photos and that we would try to arrange another person to go out as a replacement.

The telex ended with: 'Finally, we understand that some of you feel that little is being done for you in London. This is definitely not the case. We have all lost sleep, met regularly and are awaiting telephone bills to prove it. We have not found it easy gauging such a sensitive situation from long distance with such frustratingly difficult communications. The demands of our jobs, the other routes and Four Corners itself have not made things any easier. Please make allowances accordingly.'

To compound the situation, communications between London and the Third World are not the quickest. Responses took a long time coming from the team; *not* their fault, but nevertheless very frustrating.

With telephone conversations, time was obviously limited because of expense even though I'd decided we should allow as long as possible.

All in all it took close on four weeks to sort out and in the end we had to agree to make arrangements for Pete's return to London. In truth, the plan put forward was not terribly realistic, and hadn't been sent without some hope that feelings could be sorted out and they might all find some way of continuing as a team. Other teams had had difficulties and had overcome them, and it was by this example that we had pursued the idea. We didn't, I think, at first realise how difficult it must have been for the team in Bangkok being kept there against their will when they already thought the damage done was irreparable. I hadn't realised this because by now, with so much more work on, I hadn't got round to reading the Asian Highway diaries. During this episode, when I was forced to do so, I wished I had read them before as I would have detected the gravity of the problem earlier.

Fortunately, this is where Steve Armitage came in. As their Route Watcher, he had already had some contact with them through correspondence. As it happened he was going to Nepal for a month's holiday and was planning to meet the team anyway. This was an opportunity for him to go and just listen and reassure them of support from London, and that, be it inadequate, we were doing all we could for them.

As one crisis was being dealt with another seemed to be hatching elsewhere. On the African Trail the team were not aware that they were to meet with HRH Prince Charles. Their earlier arrival in Kenya coincided with the royal visit in early April 1987. Amongst many things HRH Prince Charles would be visiting I.T. projects and I.T. in London were also trying to arrange it so that the riders would meet him as well. However, between Dar es Salaam and Nairobi, communication was, to say the least, difficult. In short, a great opportunity was lost: Buckingham Palace only gave I.T. the go ahead to arrange something at the eleventh hour; we couldn't find the team in Kenya and so on.

Finally on the Oriental Path, there was some lightheartedness, with a telex being sent on April 1st: 'RHODA FRACTURED ARM IN RICKSHAW COLLISION. FLYING BACK HONG KONG/ LONDON. KEEN TO WORK FULL-TIME FOUR CORNERS. A SAD LOSS. LOVE CAFE CRAWLERS.'

A few days before a much more serious telex arrived however, telling me they had had their bikes confiscated and then I also learnt that they might not be able to get access to South Korea. Finally, I was told that this arrest could affect their access to Japan where the British Council had prepared a lot of publicity. My initial reaction to their situation had been anger since they weren't supposed to have cycled through closed areas in China. I couldn't believe how stupid they had been and wrote a letter — the words pouring out angrily onto the page. Here are the worst extracts: 'Firstly — thank you so much for all your kind letters.' (I hadn't received any!)

'Secondly — what the hell were you doing to get your bikes confiscated?! ... it's bloody infuriating when we covered this ground with you in the office. It appears you blatantly went ahead anyway into closed areas ... you know just how busy it is here without heaping more worry and problems on people back here ... You know, with this and the fact that no-one found out the most vital bit of information with regards to diplomatic relations between China and South Korea ... I shall have to take a closer look at your plans down the line. Are you absolutely sure you can manage all that you have planned to do? If not we'd better amend things double quick before publicity hots up. OK?!'

Whilst in the same letter there was reams more of news and views, which reflected the warmth I had for the team, the letter must have been quite horrid to receive at the other end. It was also a lot to do with the pressure and the isolation I was feeling now that all the riders had gone. At the end I reminded them individually, if somewhat antagonistically of the roles they were expected to fulfil, listing the tasks. We'd received virtually nothing other than Sebastian's photographs and it was nearly six weeks since their departure. This was the most angry letter I have ever written to anyone ever. When they read it the emotions I had felt writing that letter were mirrored by the team.

Aiden's reply began: 'Dear Mother Hen', and said '... I think it really is daft to send letters like that Miranda, it would pay to think more carefully at the time. I do have every sympathy with what still must be a chaotic situation in the office, I wouldn't be in your shoes for anything *BUT*, chaos or not, I don't see what you thought you were achieving.'

Sebastian explained about riding in the closed areas in greater detail: '... It was nothing more than a local issue which needn't have gone further than the Four Corners Office. We were certainly extremely careful not to involve the British Embassy when we could easily have called upon them for support. What can you do when the local Public Security office doesn't know that its own city is open to foreigners, albeit recently. At the time we were cycling between two 'open' cities, an area which we'd been referred to by some police in another province — who'd waved us away because it was militarily sensitive (but that's all they did) — they'd said that the Guizhov to Chongquing stretch was OK so we took their word for it. Cycling as a lurid (the clothes) team was perhaps a mistake, but it was only bad luck that got us a confrontation with a ghastly woman who was just out for a fight. She was a nasty bureaucrat and rather than just sending us to the train station decided that punishment was in order — confiscation . . . I still maintain that what we endeavoured to do was the best option. The alternative, proposed by Richard [Crane], was to leg it from hot-spot to hot-spot. We might have considered that approach to China, but you have to realise that CITS [China Internal Travel Services] are out to extort as much foreign currency from tourists as possible. They are not interested in showing foreigners real China. Money is their motive. Thus travelling expenses are horrendous, more so with bikes, which do not necessarily travel on the same train — prohibitively expensive, as there was, is, uncertainty about the support in Japan. Anyway, Chinese transport is exhausting, demoralising, and I wouldn't have put up with five weeks of trains especially encumbered with a bicycle. The same goes for the others. Before you can criticize that attitude you have to experience what it's like — which you haven't!'

And finally: 'With regard to our ignorance of diplomatic relations between China and South Korea we were perfectly aware of the difficulties of getting from one to the other. But officials tell you one thing and reality is quite another — we wanted to explore the latter option — that there might well have been boats from Shanghai to Seoul. The maps said there were. A Japanese said there were. A Chinese said there were — yet there weren't . . . a little misinformation.'

I appreciated being put in the picture so clearly. At the time, the lack of information in the telex made me feel justified in writing such a letter. In fact there was no justification and I should have waited to hear their version of events and trusted them more.

These circumstances merely served to exacerbate the situation where I.T. couldn't publicise something which almost seemed on the verge of collapse. I could understand their problem and I would have to get the project to a point where they felt confident enough to back us up. With faith that things could only get better and with the lovely people who were beginning to come on board, I kept battling on.

The Unsung Heroes

Helen Alexander, Kim Walker, Harriet Ware-Austin, Harold Carr, Annabel Park, Belinda Harding, Kate Nivison, Cathy Keogh, Richard Crane, Margaret Hansen, Hallam Murray, Astra Seibe, Simon Grosser, Sophie Griffiths, Steve Armitage, Theresa Bergns, Tony Redpath, Terrie

Natalie, John Luderman, Sarah Unger, Derek Ground, Sarah Clark, Kai Pauldon, Carey Downer, Richard Weyers, Sarah Shaw, Brian Hanson, Carol Redman, Paul Hinton, Alison Rendle, Anthony Brown, Catherine Blishen, Mark Webb, Nathalie Sfakianos, Aidan Foss, Amanda Harding, Jonathan Skipper, Martyn Baker . . . and many more made up the merry band of unsung heroes behind the scenes.

Thank goodness the stint of working virtually on my own didn't last. Whilst things might have been lonely in the day time, in the evenings it was positively loony. As the LDDC office workers were packing up to go home, these wonderful volunteers would pour into the office and the place would fill up with pannier bags strewn all over the place. Someone would be sent out to stock up on food and refreshments and people would get down to work, three to a desk, coffee flowing and empty food containers scattered everywhere. A happy scene and their enthusiasm was rejuvenating and their energy infectious.

These people, with their full-time jobs, were giving up weekends, and evenings to come all the way out to the Docklands to make this venture work. The levels of commitment varied in terms of time, but the passion for Four Corners seemed to span the very wide range of people who got themselves caught up in the whole thing.

Helen Alexander had been with Four Corners from the beginning of 1986. Once the riders had gone I viewed her as a 'partner' in Four Corners. Initially she had come on board as leader of the Oriental Path. She immediately became deeply involved, her motive being that she could no longer be 'a spectator' to the famine and poverty in the Third World. In her application form she had said that she wanted to give her intelligence to Four Corners — and when you've got as much as she has it rather understates what she has to give! Although she had to withdraw as leader of the Oriental Path, she continued to work back at base. She was a natural diplomat and hers was often the voice of reason and calm when all others seemed to be unable to see a situation clearly.

I was very sad when in November '86 she left for Brussels where her family had moved. She had been an immense strength and wonderful friend both to me and many of the riders to whom she wrote. Later, she once again volunteered her services and became our Co-ordinator in Brussels, organising things for when the Asian Highway and the Americas Route teams passed through Brussels on their way to Amsterdam. All of this she did without pay, and in the case of her work in Brussels and organising an audience with the Pope for the riders, she personally incurred substantial costs for which she wouldn't accept reimbursement.

Naturally, something like Four Corners was bound to attract lots of very special people. Cathy Keogh was another. Cathy, a close friend of one of the riders, Alex Sfakianos, came along to the family open day at the end of February and offered to do secretarial work for us. When we met up to discuss what role she could play, I found her to be ridiculously modest about her abilities. (This seemed to be a recurring trait of most females who in fact had masses of hidden talent.) After long discussion I asked her if she would be my P.A. and the Administrative Manager. She couldn't resist £50 a week for an 80 hour a week job!

She started full time at the end of April '87. One of her first tasks was to help me with the typing and distribution of a long term plan for each department; we did it one weekend and by late Sunday evening both of us were exhausted. This was sent out to all volunteers, parents and one or two advisors as well as to the riders and main bodies involved, for their comments. Much later that night, I was aching all over with fatigue and stretched myself out on the floor to rest. In the calm of recovering from the deluge of work Cathy turned round and rather incredulously said, 'Miranda, you're the only one that's thinking about this'. A thought which kept me awake at night, since if it were true, it was wholly inadequate. I desperately needed the contribution of other minds which of course, when the full-time riders had been around, had been forthcoming. I hoped that the plan we had just sent out would prompt others into adding their thoughts and maybe sharing the responsibility of running the thing. Cathy certainly eased the pressure from my point of view and continued to be more and more a key person and kept things wonderfully organised. On a personal level, she was wonderfully supportive for which I was extremely grateful.

Harriet Ware-Austin had been with us for some months. She was the Riders' Liaison Officer and as such, she was convinced that her role wasn't one of great importance. I think the riders would all be amazed to know that. Letters coming in from them constantly praised the amount of information she was feeding them. Harriet also kept all the family's and rider's contacts up to date, and helped organise volunteer and family gatherings. She did all this working half a week, the other half being spent earning just enough to pay the rent. She was a real people person. No-one could win so many people over as she did. She is also one of the funniest women I've met, with a humour and intelligence that came with ease and which she used to dissipate any friction or put things into perspective. She had a healthy disrespect for too much bureaucracy and organisation and was someone who was always neutral and really tuned into others. An essential in an organisation when things are moving at such a rapid pace.

Annabel Park, initially working in her evenings, arranged with her employers to go half-time on her job and spend the other half working voluntarily for Four Corners. She joined on this basis at the end of March, and continued to come in the evenings to delegate work to her Route Watchers. These were people who'd follow the progress of the riders, do forward planning sending publicity material out to contacts ahead of the routes and researching any route changes etc. Annabel concentrated her energies more on building up the support for the teams in Europe. A large area of responsibility.

Kate Nivison I have already mentioned. She joined just before the press launch and concentrated on regional publicity, getting the local press where the riders came from to follow their progress. This accounted for a substantial amount of the coverage that Four Corners got in this country. This she did on top of her teaching job, running a house and looking after a family, in fact, I think the latter had to fend for themselves during this period of her life. She did an immense amount for Four Corners in her unassuming, professional way.

Steve Armitage became involved at the end of February. I'd met him at a talk given by Richard Crane. He had run his own ceramics business and was now a carpenter, wanting to find a way of putting that to good use for I.T. at a later stage. At first he was a Route Watcher but it soon became obvious he had far more potential in him than that, though that is what he seemed perfectly happy with at the time. I invited him to consider the role of General Manager, but at the time of asking he wasn't in a position to accept the job and the consequent drop in salary. He did however, continue to give an immense amount of time and was responsible for getting the support in India, where there was a national day of cycling.

There were six months to go to the Grand Finale, and there was still no-one full-time on publicity. Though Steve could only manage a couple of days a week and the odd evening, at least he could edge this ahead when he returned from Nepal at the beginning of May until Margaret Hansen came onto the scene in July. Margaret Hansen working in the German Embassy in Cairo, had already generated considerable publicity in Egypt and Germany. She was a lovely presence in the office and brought so much to the Four Corners. I wrote to Andy praising his mother and describing her as 'a breath of fresh air'. She couldn't have been easier to get on with. We sat down together and we discussed what we wanted to achieve with publicity. I knew what I wanted done, but how best to achieve it was another matter. I asked Carrie Beeson a Director of a PR company if she would donate her services as a consultant to Margaret, which she kindly did. I also tried to give Margaret as much support as possible since her work load was staggering. Now that we had someone working full-time on the project, I hoped this might encourage the input from I.T. but it didn't happen. Nevertheless, with Margaret at the helm there was a good rapport amongst everyone in the publicity department.

Belinda Harding was another mum who came in to work on fund-raising. These mums were really brave to come into the chaotic and youthful environs of Four Corners. In Belinda's case it was an alien environment, and at first she wasn't at all familiar with word processors and photocopiers, but soon mastered them. She and her husband Frank and daughter Amanda had both been extremely supportive throughout Four Corners. In the final stages she was working alongside Annabel on Routes.

The list could go on and on giving countless examples of the team in Docklands that gradually built up to enormous proportions; the unsung heroes. In the case of those giving up their earnings potential of £1000s a year to live at subsistence level, their contribution was on a par with that of the riders. An inspiring bunch of people to be part of and for most of the time, there was a rare team spirit that would be hard to find in any other situation.

Volunteers were also gathering up and down the country organising local rides in towns and cities to coincide with the return of the World Bike Riders. It had been planned that this would be one of the main thrusts of the fund-raising. At the beginning of the year, Tony Redpath had spent countless evenings writing letters to all the obvious organisations to get some nationwide activity going. Sadly there was very little response — I guess because they were 'obvious' and thus used to constant approaches for support.

I put together some guidelines on how to organise local rides and what support could be given from base etc. Using these, we rang up all our UK contacts and asked them if they would like to organise something and then sent them the Guidelines. I couldn't believe how well people responded. I also rang up friends, Rifka in Brighton and Lulu in Bradford both of whom were to get two of the most successful of the rides going, neither of them cyclists themselves. Even my lovely sister Jane and brother Michael were to create their own epicentre of Four Corners' activity in Kettering — Jane had never ridden a bike, and had a wonderful time organising a ride that would take in several of the Northamptonshire pubs! John Morphy of Leicester had been organising a Four Corners' ride since the previous October. Others were to join in Steve Brody in Norwich, Mary Gilbert in Bristol, Paul Dawe in Cardiff, Mike and Liz Goldthorpe in Dewsbury, John Llewelyn in Oxford and more to come. The satisfaction of getting something like this going was so good that Lulu was to comment 'this beats sex any day'!

By July Richard Crane was to increase the number of rides with Sue Jesper in Derby and Sylvia Weil in Reading and others. He toured round the UK to visit the co-ordinating teams and encourage local press, radio and television coverage at the same time. He kept up the inspiration and Amanda Harding, Thomas's sister was to become his right hand whilst Tony Redpath now dealt with those planning to ride into London on the day.

So, up and down the country there were clutches of volunteers going through the same motions as we were: organising publicity, setting up entertainments and stalls, getting backing, recruiting helpers, route planning and getting people on their bikes for I.T.

Difficulties in the Docklands

We were now beginning to have more regular management meetings with all those playing a major role attending. Since the departure of the Oriental Path team these had been less frequent and were only attended by I.T. members of staff and myself, and quite often I would find myself having a management meeting all on my own! By this time Dirk Spiers, our original sponsorship man had dropped out, having his own business commitments to attend to. I desperately wanted to get a sponsorship company to deal with the whole area of sponsorship.

The problem with some sponsorship companies is that they want you to do all the ringing round of potential sponsors and then walk in, supposedly seal the deal and walk away with a huge fat commission. Since it was the ringing round that I needed doing, I decided to do without the middle man. One man suggested an incredibly elaborate scheme for the grand finale for which he reckoned on getting £500,000 backing — with less than four months till the end . . .?! When I checked him out and discovered he had a less than impressive track record and that his wasn't a registered sponsorship company, I chose not to use him. We were desperate and I was unpopular for taking this decision but by now I was rather suspicious and weary of these grand schemes and unfulfilled promises. Thank goodness there were more helping hands during the day which gave me freedom from the office to get out and do something about it.

Earlier in May arrangements for the meeting in Amsterdam of the World Bike Riders and the Amsterdam-to-London Bike Ride were to be given urgent attention. Helen had done some ground work the previous year and Dirk Spiers had made two trips to Amsterdam to get things in motion. From this side, discussions had been taking place with the ferry company Sealink who were to transport up to 1000 cyclists across the channel and back for the mass ride planned to celebrate the return of the World Bike Riders.

There was no time to waste and in Amsterdam in the space of 4 days I attended more than 20 meetings and presentations including; cycling organisations, the City Council, tourist organisations, environment and development organisations, public relations people, possible sponsors, the Ministry of Transport, the British Ambassador, the Dutch office of our accountants Spicer and Oppenheim, a firm of lawyers, a television producer of sports programmes and other possible volunteers.

I just could not believe the amount of cycles in Amsterdam. Railings were crusted with them and all the lamp posts had two or three bicycles wrapped around them. It was so funny to watch thousands of cyclists with completely anarchic road manners and two, occasionally three to a bike. It was surreal — I wrote in my report: 'Seeing is believing — EVERYONE cycles.' If only I had been able to visit before.

I would also have to look into accommodation, and start points, permission from the authorities, publicity . . . everything. It crossed my mind that, in the time given, this was an impossible task. Apart from the contribution that this sponsored ride was to make towards the £10,000,000 there was no way I could let the sixteen riders down, who were at that moment pedalling their way towards Amsterdam — a sobering thought. So much to achieve and on foreign soil as well — I braced myself and did what I could. Luckily most of the Dutch spoke good English.

Dirk had left instructions that people shouldn't do anything until television coverage had been guaranteed. That first day was desperately depressing realising that nothing had been organised. That evening I went all over town looking at the routes which Dirk had suggested. The best start point to begin the Amsterdam-to-London Bike Ride was an open space in the centre of Amsterdam, Museum Plein. A beginning at least.

On the publicity front celebrities might get the all important Dutch media coverage but Dutch people wouldn't be moved to join the cause just because of the celebrity involvement; they needed to believe in it. Media coverage was needed to let people know about us, so one was still needed to get the other. The television networks however operated in a particularly curious way. Each company represents a specific social and, or religious group. This at least meant you could target your market. But planning was hampered by the fact that each of the 10 companies are designated a certain amount of time on certain days and are not necessarily scheduled regularly. Sponsorship is also very complicated. Companies using the media to promote themselves, I was told, had recently been fined. There was so much to find out on all areas before I could suss out what kind of event it was possible to mount and thus what I was promoting.

By the end of the week after much toing and froing between Amsterdam and the Hague, I was on all fours and rounded the trip off with a lovely cup of tea with the British Ambassador, Sir John Margetson — a delightful gentleman and very supportive. I rushed to catch my flight grabbing a bunch of 'tulips from Amsterdam' for Cathy. British Midland Airways were serving up champagne free of charge. There would definitely be an Amsterdam-to-London ride; I had something to celebrate and the champagne went down a treat. When I told the airline staff about the troops back at Docklands, they gave me a bundle of small bottles of champagne to take back to the office.

I took them in the following morning. It was my birthday and Cathy also brought in champagne as well as orange juice and croissants for a birthday breakfast over the weekly management planning meeting! Cathy and myself spent our weekend in the office. I had to write up a very detailed and clear report of the trip, since I would have to hand this project to someone else to see it through to its conclusion. Notes on every meeting were typed up and letters to all those offering support were sent confirming plans, whilst plans for the next trip were made.

Soon after this 'Shirl the Whirl' (as she called herself), Shirley Parker was to enter the scene as Final Event Co-ordinator. I told Shirl about the £10,000,000 that I.T. needed. '£10,000,000! We could easily raise £20,000,000!' she said with her typical 'anything's possible' confidence. When I told her that we wouldn't be able to pay her and that she would have to finance herself and she still wasn't put off. Whilst her organisational skills as an executive secretary in an international advertising firm weren't a full qualification for Final Event Co-ordinator there would be appropriate support and advice on hand both from the organiser of the London to Brighton race John Potter, and the Docklands Corporation. She was to concentrate her attentions on the London end of activities and to be the Liaison with our Amsterdam contacts. But first, she would have to establish the Colchester-to-London Ride before handing responsibility of this over to someone else. Meanwhile, I would nudge things ahead at the London end until she could take over.

She began work just before my second trip to Amsterdam. In my absence she was to establish what was needed to get the Colchester-to-London Ride going so that she could begin work on the Finale as soon as possible. Time was against us. Before I left Steve Armitage spoke to me mentioning how worried he was about progress on the Final Event. I was as concerned as he was and said if I didn't get sufficient support in Amsterdam this time, then we would have to review the whole situation on my return.

This trip was similar in pace to the last one. Accommodation was Bunk No. 12 in Dormitory C, courtesy of the Amsterdam Y.H.A. The journey out had been on the overnight ferry with an armchair to sleep in courtesy of Sealink where I had been kept awake the whole night by loud drunks. My first meeting was conducted in Dutch with a translator. I could barely keep my eyes open.

At the end of this trip I came away with a promise of financial backing for a member of staff from General Accident Netherlands, with an indication of more support. Also, T.N.T. came up with £1500 and donated all our courier requirements throughout the U.S.A., Europe and the United Kingdom and support vehicles for the final event (totalling several £1000s in value). Lex Kraak at the Y.H.A. had offered office space. The Hague office of Burson Marsteller had agreed to handle our publicity; the City Council were positive about giving permission to use Museum Plein; the E.N.F.B. would be Routes Co-ordinators; the Cycle Union would organise marshalls; the tourist board gave half a dozen cycling holidays as prizes; the Y.H.A. were to give cheap rates on accommodation; the Amsterdam Spicer & Oppenheimer office would handle our finances and a legal advisor Philip Paterson offered his services. There was promise of more support which Shirley would have to finalise. Finally, I had another cup of tea with Sir John Margetson, inviting him along to meet the riders when they came into Amsterdam. Not an unproductive trip . . . but still not as good as I had hoped.

Returning, I found the atmosphere in the office had taken a nose-dive. Everyone kept telling me that Steve Armitage was deeply depressed and constantly saying the whole thing was chaotic and impossible. He sounded cheerful enough when I spoke to him on the phone, but later that day when he turned up at the office, his tone was to say the least, hostile. A meeting was demanded.

At the meeting I was told that certain offers of support that had been vital to the final event had been withdrawn in my absence. When this was explained I could understand Steve's concern.

In the light of this information the scale of the Final Event planned prior to my departure was beyond our means and a complete scaling down of the event was proposed. At the meeting I listened to what everyone had to say and at the end suggested that our thinking wasn't that different — that is until it was proposed to scale it right down to a beer tent at the end of the ride for the riders and their families and friends who could join them on a ride from Colchester. If things hadn't improved within a week then this was what was to happen. I said I would do a presentation to all volunteers of what shape the final event would take and a date was set for this.

In the intervening two weeks a small band of volunteers who not only withdrew their own support but persisted in maintaining bad feeling. Pressure was rearing its ugly head again, but it was a sad drain on the overall energy. I tried to blinker myself to getting the show on the road and not get involved in the developing personality clash. I was told of other meetings going on which I really 'ought to attend' but with time being so precious I felt any further grievances could be aired at the scheduled meeting of volunteers.

Against all the odds, at the end of this period it looked like we were going to have a final event that would encompass even more than I thought we might pull off. Shirl the Whirl with her persistence had got the Colchester-to-London more or less established. Meanwhile the London ride and London-to-Amsterdam ride were secured. We had all the necessary support for these and a few frills to boot.

The presentation went ahead to about 20 of the main volunteers and I sat down to listen to comments and answer questions. But the tone was disappointingly negative: communications weren't good enough; I was spending far too much time on sponsorship; I was spending too much time on getting celebrity support; the UK Rides weren't really happening and I was wasting my time on these; I wasn't spending enough time on the Final Event. My patience was running out.

'Well, we believe you're not spending enough time on ...' My patience finally snapped and I fought back, answering each of the criticisms. At the end of the meeting a vote was taken and all but one gave a vote of confidence. Pressure can make you lose track sometimes. I thought I had learnt to recognise it by now and to deal with problems it caused at an early stage before they became too disruptive, but this time I was a victim of it myself and the meeting resulted in a resignation.

It was three weeks since my second trip to Amsterdam and all this had used up a lot of precious time and energy. We now needed to get on. Cathy put a sign up in the office which read 'FOR GOD SAKE JUST GET ON WITH IT!'

Raising Awareness of I.T.

Although the routes were to have been planned around the projects that I.T. had worked on in 60 different countries around the world, for the reasons already mentioned, this proved to be unworkable. Another problem was that receiving guests is actually an expensive business. It takes up precious time and when 'small is beautiful' then time, for these small scale projects, is very precious. Then too, we had to consider that Westerners turning up on gleaming £800 bicycles might just be a touch insensitive. In the event we managed visits to just a few I.T. projects.

Even so, by going to countries that I.T. operated in, the teams often witnessed plenty of examples of local 'intermediate technology'. In Africa, the riders saw the simplest of technology with school children quite cheerfully doing their arithmetic in the earth, drawing figures using sticks. Extraordinary when you consider that children here are doing their's with the assistance of calculators and computers. In markets, vendors would be selling any number of things that they had made out of recycled items. A favourite was shoes and belts created out of old tyres. Another time, when Andy got a puncture, and hadn't got the right valve to pump it up and knew it would be impossible to mend without it, he watched incredulously as two locals tackled the problem in no time using rags to stop air escaping. It worked. This willingness to use whatever meagre resources existed is an attitude and way of life essential to their survival.

The others had similar experiences all along their route, particularly in Asia and South America. In China and Hong Kong the easily replenishable all-purpose bamboo was used for a vast range of purposes. Buildings would be seen covered in the stuff as it was used as scaffolding. And so it went on. In fact I.T. know they have a lot to learn from this incredible ingenuity which is why the process has always been a two-way operation with a sharing of knowledge.

Whilst Andy and the Publicity Officers on each route had initially done a tremendous amount of work trying to organise the raising of money in the countries passed through (with the exception of most of the Third World countries as this would seem inappropriate), the organisation of this proved too difficult, involving all sorts of legal spaghetti which we couldn't even begin to unravel without funding. Therefore the emphasis changed to raising awareness of I.T.'s work as they went along.

Various relevant organisations were approached for support, the obvious being national cycle associations, youth and environmental groups etc. The most forthcoming of these, naturally, were the cycle groups. The British Councils and British Embassy press offices were all contacted as well. The response varied, mostly depending on how Britain was promoting itself in each country and whether the arrival of riders clashed with other more pressing activities in their calendar. However, in places like South America, Mexico, Africa, Japan, Bangladesh, India and later Scandinavia and some European countries their support was absolutely invaluable. This involved hosting press conferences and lending other support which stretched to boosting team morale, and in some cases feeding and mothering them. Also, here in London, I.T.'s contacts in the Central Office of Information were extremely helpful, sending out regular updates around the world so that articles in the press would sometimes precede the arrival of the teams. Also, the teams made advance contact with the main media and followed this up on arrival in each country, with some back-up material being sent out from base. European countries, however were dealt with from London. These efforts created plenty of work with interviews and photo-calls becoming a regular occurrence for riders.

The Americas Route

Before they set off, no response had come back from those approached in Bolivia. This, as the other teams would also discover, didn't necessarily mean that things hadn't been organised in their honour. The Americas team's telex to notify the British Embassy of their late arrival was never received and so they discovered a BMX demonstration and other events in their honour had already taken place by the time they arrived! Articles about Four Corners had already been published in the press as well. Even after this odd beginning they still had lots of support in Bolivia and their departure was organised in Plaza San Francisco, the start point for all national races (though this was not a race). A starter line was in place, complete with chequered flag. There was quite a crowd of well wishers and Meryl gave a grand first Four Corners interview for the national television station, Canal 2 as journalists scribbled notes. They would be in all the National papers the following day.

'Adios! What a way to start the World Bike Ride, from a peaceful little square in a beautiful city, a few guards looking idly on, early on a Sunday morning on a day which celebrates the founding of America.'

In Peru they were greeted by a journalist for El Commercio, the biggest newspaper in Peru. Peru was very important for the team in that I.T. does considerable work there and their highly efficient Lima office organised accommodation, Press Conferences and visits for them. One area of the charity's work is that of micro-hydro electric systems. It would be virtually impossible for a national grid system to cover all rural areas of South America because of the mountainous terrain and the remote location of many villages. However, the Andes is the highest water catchment area in the world. This is created by high levels of rain and snowfall and the resulting fast flowing rivers make ideal conditions for micro-hydro systems. By harnessing the energy they can turn it into electricity, producing enough power for a cheese producing co-operative or a saw mill, and at night, lighting for a whole village.

The riders concentrated on I.T.'s other main area of work there: food processing. One project they visited was a company in Lima producing herbal teas: 'I.T. were asked to assist with the introduction of a mechanical drying system into Peru to replace the sun drying method previously used by the herb processing factory "Yerfil" . . . The result was that more efficient drying cabinets and a heat pump were produced with local help. It has been so successful that Yerfil no longer need assistance and the drying technology is being built locally for use in other parts of Peru and has even been adopted by other countries. That of course is what the work of I.T. is all about: creating viable and sustainable entities, independent of foreign help.' (Jo)

Perhaps to fully appreciate the benefit of the I.T. approach some background to this particular project is necessary. In the beginning experimentation with various drying systems took place until they found the required successful heater and cabinet combination. However, other problems existed. The herbs, mainly camomile, had been imported from abroad but home currency depreciation meant that dried herb producers had to look for domestic sources of the raw material. Peruvian farmers up until then hadn't viewed herbs as a viable cash crop so availability was a problem. Also, the product's main market (the middle classes of Lima) had progressed rapidly towards the herbal teas of Europe and America, thus demanding higher standards and specialist marketing.

Since this technology was aimed at the small processor, capital and time needed to deal with these areas were scarce resources. The savings made on technology alone weren't enough and I.T. assisted in researching and advising on these other problems. Now farmers are profitably substituting camomile for other crops. The dryer has proved so successful that it has been adopted by many other producers in Peru and other countries for other foodstuffs such as fruits and vegetables. Other benefits accrued to the processors and farmers and other related areas such as printers and packages. With Government backing interest in expanding the industrial development grows — so, the success continues long after I.T.'s initial input.

For the riders this visit served to drive home not only the purpose and worth of their ride, but the immense work that went into overcoming the problems and creating lasting solutions to poverty. Also it was greatly inspiring to witness the dedication and commitment of the field workers. The press were pretty impressed too: 'Their work does not become foreign aid islands unto themselves but bridges over which useful technology can reach and spread among developing countries' (*Lima Times*).

The team went on to visit another project just before leaving Peru, in a place called Lambayeque on the north coast. Here I.T. had with the Lambayeque Development Corporation assisted a local honey producing co-operative with the collecting and drying of pollen. Recent market swings in Europe and the U.S.A. have meant the health value of pollen has created a high demand for the product. I.T.'s assistance will help low-income, small-scale beekeepers produce this highly profitable product which, it is unlikely they would otherwise have been able to exploit.

In Ecuador the team visited the Universidad Tecnica in Ambato where Intermediate Technology is collaborating on food technology research, also related to pollen drying. As soon as they arrived they were being interviewed by local press and had to give a live interview in Spanish, which was broadcast to half the nation. After the more serious stuff about Four Corners, things took a lighter note: 'The interviewer asked who we missed most from home. The answer for two of us were our dogs!' (Jo)

This was the last of their project visits, but having seen I.T. working first-hand they were now fired with enthusiasm and well equipped to spread the word. Quito, the capital of Ecuador provided their first opportunity for this: 'We had superb support from the Cycling

Federation in Quito, who helped organise a day ride from the historic main plaza to the Equator. We ran around for days beforehand delivering information to the press and doing several impromptu interviews in Spanish, telling people about Four Corners and inviting cyclists to join us. On the day we had an escort of two police motorcycles, a police car, national press and TV, and 4 cyclists!! Still, with sirens blaring, lights flashing and a huge crowd of onlookers, we made an impressive news story on the next day's TV.' (Jo)

In Mexico, they joined a local campaign: 'We were very fortunate in Mexico to meet up with a cycling pressure group called 'Todos en Bicicleta'. We put in a guest appearance at a ride with 1,000 other cyclists along one of the main 'Avenidas'. This had been organised to draw attention to the terrible pollution in Mexico city. The smog is so bad that during the month before we arrived, 1,000 birds fell out of the sky!' (Meryl)

'... cycled down to Av, Insuigentes for 9.30, 18 kms away. Lots of people, lots of cyclists, a beautiful day, flags strung up and balloons along the way. They had cordoned off the two lanes either side of the grassed lane divider for the use of the cyclists ... There were other 'famous' personalities there – a world champion Mexican boxer, a singer called Lorenzo Antonio and a cyclist called Jose Manuel.' (Jo)

When the team had tried to organise publicity before they left, the country they found most difficult to crack was the USA. One day in London, Richard Kai wandered into the office. He was an ex-Harvard whizz kid employed by our sponsors the London Docklands Development Corporation. Being a keen cyclist, a mountain climber, athlete and traveller, he was immediately drawn to the world maps pinned up on the walls with routes and pins all over them. 'Oh, they're going through San Diego, that's where my parents live ... and all these other states are areas I know too and I know guys who live around here.' I don't think he realised what he was letting himself in for but Richard became a volunteer and when he returned to the States for a vacation his work continued with a round of visits at his own expense, to secure support for the riders. It was a very difficult thing to do, but one of the best things he did was to make contact with an organisation called Bike Aid.

'... In San Francisco we found out about Bike-Aid, a fund-raising venture of the Overseas Development Network (ODN), a student-based organisation. Bike-Aid annually sends groups of cyclists on five different routes across the States. On the way they help out in community projects, working with the homeless and on foodbanks. Each rider raises approximately $1 per mile in pledges and the funds raised go towards small-scale, appropriate and sustainable projects in the developing world. More importantly, Bike-Aid aims to generate awareness as to the problems facing poor people not only in the Third World but also in America itself.' (Jo)

The aims of Bike-Aid and Four Corners were so closely linked that the team joined ranks with them. In fact they became so involved with the running of the annual event that the team took six weeks' break from pedalling to get back behind a desk and once again get into 'work overload'. Alex wrote back at the time, describing it as 'sleep deprivation training'. They also hot footed it door to door in the wealthy 'silicon chip valley' in search of sponsors. On one occasion they were handed a cheque for $370; they too had to raise their $1 dollar per mile in order to participate in the event. Sixty per cent of the money raised by the team would go direct to Intermediate Technology.

When it came to participating in some of the bike routes across America, the team split into twos, Thomas and Meryl choosing the route from Portland and Jo and Alex the route from Seattle. They would meet up again in Chicago and then Washington for the last leg of the coast to coast to New York. Throughout the journey across the States, there was lots of television and press coverage and the English cyclists were often a focus of interest and thus were able to spread the word about Four Corners and the concept that we shared with Bike-Aid in a country where the average cat's daily protein intake is more than that of an average African.

The Asian Highway

It was a quiet start for the Asian Highway team from Melbourne, but as they pedalled on confidence built up, picking up several radio interviews and local press articles as they neared Sydney where they were interviewed live by ABC national news.

After cycling through Indonesia, they reached Jakarta just before Christmas, not the best time to organise a press conference. However, as they sat in a café an English couple came up to them and said they'd been featured in the *Jakarta Post*; it must have been arranged through the British Council.

From here they flew to Singapore where they met up with members of the Nature Society. They weren't sure what to expect ... but what a lovely surprise awaited them: 'In the middle of the table was a huge chocolate cake with 4 Corners and stuff on it and 'WELCOME TO SINGAPORE".' This was followed by a talk and slide show about Four

Corners and I.T. to a packed hall. The outcome of this was that they were invited onto a national radio chat show and had an article appear in *Tatler* magazine. An organised bike ride, their first, had also been arranged with members of Singapore's Nature Society joining them.

After 10 days they continued on to Malaysia where a press conference was organised at the British High Commission by diplomat, Ian Danson. On the day it was revealed that he himself was a keen supporter of the bicycle and made an impressive speech: 'Ian introduced us and explained the whole thing and then went into a brilliant lecture about why Malays should use the bicycle otherwise K.L. will end up like Bangkok.'

There was a good turnout which resulted in several press articles and an appearance on TV which gained them national recognition for the rest of the journey. I should think it made memorable viewing as well: 'We cycled up to the High Commission for our film session with the TV station. The crew was there in a jeep and Ian was running in every direction telling them *exactly* how they should go about filming us! The highly unsuitable location they chose was a stretch of dusty carriageway teeming with traffic — we were to proceed on our way and they to trundle along beside us with the cameras rolling. Unfortunately, very unfortunately, at the top of one particular hill Nick stopped abruptly to be interviewed and I, so intent on not doing the wrong thing, cycled smash crash into the back of Pete . . . This was *not* the best time for an interview — me shaking and Pete fuming and I don't think we were quite brilliant! Katharine was great. She was natural, smiling and talking sense. Nick said all there was left to say and when it came to me I went blank. I couldn't think of a thing to say that hadn't already been said and when I was asked what I'd liked best of all so far, all I could come up with was the damn food!' (Jane)

When they passed through Thailand they were able to make their first visit to see what I.T. got up to in the field. They met Dr Coovanatchi at Princess University in Sonkla. He explained to them that he was working with I.T. on a steam engine project which though fairly old technology, was extremely economic. It was being developed for rural Thailand for use as a water pump.

Their next stop at Dhaka in Bangladesh was a great success, gaining major publicity for I.T. when they visited The Centre for Rehabilitation of the Paralysed (C.R.P.) where I.T. has helped design an appropriate and affordable wheelchair. Throughout Bangladesh there are hundreds of thousands of physically disabled for whom there is little hope of any kind of future. The C.R.P. works with individuals who, mainly through accidents, have become paralysed. Initially helping them through the trauma, they go on to provide facilities for learning new skills for employment: weaving, carpentry, tailoring, block making, making fishing nets and so on. The main aim being that they should once again be able to return to their community and support themselves and their families.

Mobility is crucial to rehabilitation and access to employment, so whilst most of C.R.P.'s resources are geared towards rehabilitation and not the technical aspects of mobility this is where I.T. was helpful. Wheelchair designs that existed were unattractive, inappropriate, heavy, difficult and expensive. The latter was particularly important, because the earning power is removed from someone who suddenly becomes paralysed. The other areas also needed attention.

Being disabled in itself tends to make people a social outcast so attractiveness of the wheelchair becomes an important element of being accepted by the community. Also it needs to be appropriate to the individual's circumstances. If, for example, the norm is for people to be seated on the floor then this needs to be taken into account, as being placed high up sets you even more apart from your contemporaries. So, providing floor-level wheelchairs is what is needed.

Taking into account these and other problems, I.T. expanded the range of chairs available at C.R.P. from 3, to 5. The most successful of these was the tricycle wheelchair — much better for covering long distances and therefore more appropriate to generating income (one of these is being used in a kerosene delivery business). Designing a lighter wheelchair is obviously important for ease of mobility (the C.R.P. has its own basket ball team — brilliant!), but also designing it so it can be made locally and more cheaply was very important. I.T. have solved this by using bicycle components which are widely available, easily maintained and by not having to import, they are also less expensive.

I.T. didn't just present C.R.P. with the prototype but saw the whole thing through to its manufacture and supply. Central to their approach, is the effective production of tools, tools which will not 'displace labour or reduce the potential for skill development. They do however, ensure accuracy, reduce production time and hence costs . . .' (I.T. Transport Report). The wheelchairs are now being produced by C.R.P. in a converted double garage!

The riders were moved by the obvious benefit that the people at the centre were getting from them: 'We've just seen so many terribly disabled people as we've travelled that you are continually counting your blessings for having the physical well being to be able to do what we are doing now. For so many the only option is begging on the streets. Coming here and seeing people on their way to leading a normal life again is truly wonderful, though unfortunately, it's the only centre in the country.' (Kate)

'You think it's bad back home for people who are disabled and the problems they have to overcome, but here in Bangladesh where treatment and care is so scarce, the devastation this must bring to a family when the bread winner is stricken with paralysis is unthinkable.' (Jane)

The team continued onto Nepal where they visited projects in Kathmandu Valley using the same Micro Hydro as in Peru. In fact, I.T. have assisted in the installation of no less than 620 small water turbines in Nepal and in each case the machinery has been manufactured in the country. These are used for grinding corn, hulling rice, expelling oil from seed as well as providing electricity.

They also saw a roofing tiles project and were especially impressed with the efficient woodburning stove I.T. helped to design and develop: 'When we've been struggling up hills on our bikes, we've passed women carrying huge heavy bundles of wood on their backs. They often have to walk miles to collect it so it's obvious to us why this stove is so important, burning up to 50% less fuel than the traditional stove. Also, we've seen it being made by local blacksmiths and potters so it must be providing lots of employment too.' (Kate)

'What impressed me most is the fact that the project was being run by the Nepalese — not a Westerner in sight. We visited homes in which the stoves were being used very successfully, with that evening's supper bubbling away. Nepal has a mammoth deforestation problem so that the news the use of this stove was expanding was really encouraging.' (Jane)

This story is true of other parts of the developing world, especially Africa, where wood is extremely scarce. In fact, over 85% of the wood used in Third World countries is used for fuel. Over a BILLION people use wood as fuel at the expense of depleting resources. This is why the adoption of a simple technology like the wood burning stove is so exciting; it alleviates the hardship for those dependent on wood fuel and at the same time extends the time in which the wood depletion can be replenished.

India was another country where this stove had been taken up and there were many other projects to be visited here, including a mini-cement factory and weaving looms for cottage industry. India was to be very special in another way. In London, volunteer Steve Armitage had contacted his friend A. B. Bhardwaj, President of the Indian Ghandi in Action organisation asking him to back Four Corners. A. B. loved the idea and embraced it with heart rending enthusiasm: 'Our route through the Northern state of Uttar Pradesh was carefully planned to coincide with pre-arranged publicity events in the major towns. These were held at Ghandhi Ashrams.

'It took us about 3 weeks to make our way from the Nepalese/Indian border to our final destination in West Asia, Delhi. Almost every evening we gave talks and interviews and visited Intermediate Technology projects. [I.T. has been working with the Appropriate Technology Development Association in Lucknow for 20 years and it was ATDA who set up these visits.]

'It was an extraordinary time — cycling in high temperature, getting up and leaving by 5.30 am to escape the worst of the sun's power, and arriving at our destination each day to be greeted by enthusiastic Ghandians armed with enormous garlands of flowers.

'We have been linked up with the people of Ghandi-in-action in India thanks to their President A. B.

'These people feel our bike ride is in direct relation to their own view of the world. They see the ride as non-violent and productive, linking all countries of the world and breaking down national barriers. Tomorrow has been called a National Cycling Day in India (14th May).' (Kate)

'We cycled into Delhi through an arch of flowers and were welcomed by hundreds of excited Indians. We were shown to a podium and were garlanded with marigolds and roses. The scent from the flowers was overpowering and stained our shirts with orange pollen. There were endless speeches and a local blind school sang a song which had been specially written. Finally a brass band played a rousing tune as we cycled off to Delhi.' (Nick)

There followed a procession, as led by twelve marathon runners, as the team surrounded by hundreds of enthusiastic cyclists, pedalled through Delhi (minus Kate who at this time was terribly unwell in hospital).

'The following week was a non-stop programme of events including a meeting with the Minister of Defence, the Chief Executive of Delhi and with India's most respected Jain saint. We gave many talks, appeared in the national news and gave talks on the radio. All in all about 20 articles were written about us both in newspapers and magazines.

'To date we have had about 7 reception parties in India. Some more successful than others. At one we were given £25 by the minister of transport in Uttar Pradesh. We've had lots of coverage.' (Nick)

That there had been such a response in India was great news for those of us back at Docklands.

The African Trail

In Zimbabwe, after relaxing for the first few days with Bert and Mable, Willy's uncle and aunt, the team packed their panniers and pedalled the 70 km into Harare arriving at the Thomas Cook office at 11.30 where they met their publicity contact. 'Am I glad to see you!' She cried as they walked in hot and sweaty from their ride. 'You've got an interview with Colin Harvey of ZBC at 12.00. The driver is downstairs. Follow him up on your bikes — you might need them for a T.V. interview!'

They went straight back out into the boiling heat. When she had said 'up' she had meant it. The driver observed them through the stained glass windows of his air-conditioned car with a somewhat bemused look on his face as they pushed and panted their way up the hill, bikes fully laden and weighing a ton. When they reached the grounds of ZBC they all drank for about 10 minutes without a pause. Colin came out to greet them and chatted away until they felt relaxed enough to face the microphone. It was their first experience of it and Andy did most of the talking and explaining about I.T. and the ride.

The next day an official reception was held for them at the Harare Sports Club. It seemed that most of the media was distracted by a visit to the country by King Juan Carlos of Spain, so there wasn't a huge turnout. However, a couple of reporters turned up, one from The World Service and the other from ZBC — best to ease yourself into these things when you've not had the practise! There was little other publicity activity in Zimbabwe other than a photocall at the Zimbabwe ruins.

The rider's arrival at Lilongwe airport, Malawi was marred when customs demanded a £650 bond for the bikes but fortunately Norman Leigh from the British Council was on hand to sort things out and they were allowed in. The British Council had also organised an exhibition of I.T.'s work (helped by Gary Whitby from I.T.) and a press conference which attracted every newspaper and radio station in Malawi.

The following day they visited the Salima Carpentry Co-operative in Malawi. Here local carpenters were learning to make their own tools. This literally meant the difference between them being able to work or not. Tools, largely imported, are so expensive (costing 10 times the price they can be produced for at the co-operative), that the initial financial outlay for the carpenters would be too much for them to even begin to trade. The team were really looking forward to their visit, especially after having read the success story of Mr. Zinyongo ...

Mr. Zinyongo, a local carpenter of 12 years, working with a plane made from a machete, produced simple furniture and earned 1.25 kwech (40p) a day, nothing like enough to buy him a good imported plane at 150 kwecha (£60). He attended the carpentry co-operative and like fellow attenders, amazed the instructors by his eagerness to work 14-hour days and all weekend, not to mention the time he complained when the night-watchman refused him entry at 4 am to work on his project!

'Mr. Zinyongo had come on the course under the misapprehension that he would be given cash support to buy tools for his business. He left, though, with a fully-fashioned box of tools of his own making and a set of new skills with which he was certain he could carve out the future. Changed times for a man who had never had a woodworking bench and had worked crouched on the ground, using his foot as a vice.' (I.T.)

The team found lots of 'Mr. Zinyongo's' who were benefitting from the project and who were keen to show the riders what they had made. Andy commented 'very interesting indeed ... Also liked the idea of the co-operative working as separate tradesmen but using common resources to run the thing.' This visit created a good focus for media coverage of Intermediate Technology at work.

After a quiet entry into Tanzania, the riders were to find themselves whipped into a whirlwind of activity in the capital, Dar es Salaam. Here Dave Parsons of the International School had gone to great lengths to give them a tremendous welcome to the country. The Secretary to the president, Mr. Rupia, gave a long speech about the worth of what they were doing for the cause of 'peace and international unity' and then signalled for the beginning of a 10-kilometre circuit cycle ride around Dar es Salaam. They were joined by the National Cycling team and 220 kids on bikes, as well as crowds of non-cyclists to send them on their way. There was honking and ringing of bells, screaming, skidding and crashing and lots of people laughing, especially the team. This was not a sight that the people of Dar es Salaam were used to. There were a lot of bemused onlookers!

They'd spent quite a few days in Dar es Salaam oiling the publicity machinery. There was much pedalling round corners for the cameras and other entertaining of journalists to be done. But as much as they'd enjoyed their stay it was time to move on out of the city and escape to the great expanses of the Tanzanian countryside. When they went they were escorted out of the city with a member of the national cycling team.

Peace was enjoyed for a few days until a Land-Rover rolled up alongside a very weary Andy Hansen who was flaked out from a day's cycling in the sun. 'We've been expecting you for some days. Please follow me down to the International Hotel.' This was an official of the C.C.M. (the national ruling party). Andy followed. Thus began an unexpected itinerary of non-stop activity that rivalled any schedule that would be expected of Prince Charles. And as Andy put it 'HRH doesn't have to cycle to his engagements!'

From here until they were to reach the Tanzania/Kenyan border there was no let up. At first the team tactfully declined the offer of an official escort when they were presented with a band of beautifully uniformed policemen in full regalia of gold braids, epaulettes and white gloves. They thought after their first night of hospitality in the International Hotel that they were free to continue and pedalled off into the distance — only to be stopped and taken to a school where speeches were made and songs, especially composed for them, were sung. Further on, neatly uniformed children and women lined the road waving palm fronds, singing songs and chanting, the women dancing. This occurred every hour or so and as they came upon each group they would stop to shake hands and the rest would break ranks and rush forward. 'At one point we were followed for about a kilometre by dozens of jogging, singing girls. We couldn't pull away from all this unwarranted attention, so we were left to wonder at the amazing fitness of this fleet-footed choir . . .' (Andy)

On other days truck loads of cyclists would be awaiting them as well as police escorts with sirens sounding full blast and forcing all other traffic to move out of the way for them to pass — it was endless. A C.C.M. official would even surprise them as they were quietly relieving themselves behind a bush! After several days of this they were suffering 'thank you fatigue' as well as crushed hands from the constant handshaking and their faces were beginning to wear a fixed grin in response to all the greeting. At the end of it though, there was a rare treat in store as the C.C.M. arranged a very cheap expedition with porters and guides for them to climb Mt. Kilimanjaro, Africa's highest mountain.

The mystery as to why the C.C.M. had gone to such lengths to make them feel welcome was not answered. Was it the publicity they had received in Dar es Salaam? Or was it that letter Andy had sent full of typed errors and addressed in Andy's worst terrible handwriting to 'His Excellency, President Julias Nyerere'. This had caused Steve Bonnist to have one of his 'anxiety attacks' about creating the wrong image for Intermediate Technology. It was pretty appalling — but who knows, maybe it struck a chord with His Excellency? Anyway, whatever the reason, it was a welcome like no other experienced on Four Corners and left the team with lifelong memories of the people of Tanzania.

Kenya was busy: more interviews, more meetings with officials and their hosts. From Nairobi, Andy went ahead of the others to Cairo to do some advance groundwork on publicity, working with his parents who lived there and who had already got the ball rolling.

Egypt was very exciting. Most of the filming and interviewing took place along the Nile, in front of the Sphinx and amongst the Pyramids. On one occasion there was a photocall at a camel market at which Willy was called upon to 'kiss a bad tempered camel with halitosis' — on the muzzle. Not just Egyptian national and local media responded but the German also since this was Andy's mother country and his parents, diplomats working from the German Embassy had generated lots of interest from the German media in Cairo. A gruelling schedule but not without its compensations with visits to Luxor and the Pyramids and a chance for Willy to catch up on the gin and tonics at luxurious hotel accommodation!

The Oriental Path

In Hong Kong the teams had assistance in getting publicity through the Hong Kong and Shanghai Bank and the Hong Kong office of the Public Relations company, Burson Marsteller, where the press conference was held. Attendance at this was mainly by English speaking newspapers, magazines and television.

China was the one country on this route where Intermediate Technology had worked on micro-hydro systems. In the end due to travelling restrictions, it was not possible to visit these.

South Korea turned out to be very open to publicising Four Corners at extremely short notice. Literally the day after their arrival they were getting coverage just by ringing up the press and turning up. They linked up with the South Korean Cycle Federation and visited the Olympic Stadium. After that, word seemed to spread and they would be pedalling along and unexpectedly stopped by a press photographer who wanted to capture them underneath the canopies of cherry blossom.

Later down the road a van drew up along side and a television camera was thrust out of the window at them. The main publicity here though, was a half hour slot on a comedy show. They were miles from anywhere along a flat coastal road. The team had broken up and were several kilometres apart when Adria was waved down by a stranger. It was Korean Broadcasting System (KBS). At the side of the road they had two minibuses full of film crew. It was two hours before all members of the Oriental Path arrived.

All agreed to the filming as long as they could get the message across about what they were doing. The filming took place in a very beautiful valley, known as the Puryongsa Valley. Here awaited a 'famous' comedian sporting a red hat. The riders were filmed showing where they had been on a map and gave the names of places they were going but not speaking the lingo it was all a bit tricky. The comedian spoke rapidly in Korean with the odd word in English and the team had to pretend that they understood, nodded, giggled and smiled, whatever they thought appropriate and so it went on. This rates as one of the most unusual publicity encounters for any of the teams.

Finally, on the morning of their departure from South Korea, the 27th April, they were joined by the national Korean Roadracing Cycling team. Their calf muscles were something else! They provided good contrast for the cameras with these nimble bulbous muscled professionals on their small featherweight bicycles alongside four luggage-laden touring cyclists all packed for their flight to Japan.

In Japan, Japan Aid, headed by Toshi Hattori had set up a very strict itinerary with lots of talks and receptions in all the major towns they passed through. They were greeted with bouquets of flowers at Narita airport in Japan by Kazumi of Japan Aid and a member of staff from the British Council. Unfortunately the team only consisted of 3 members since Adria, an American citizen, had been turned back by Japanese officials who told her she would have to get a visa. In London they had been told this wasn't necessary; thankfully, she was able to join them in a couple of days.

Meanwhile the others found that they were totally in the hands of Japan Aid with regard to all the plans and itinerary. For starters they were whisked off in brand new big white minibuses with Four Corners logos on them — bikes would be too slow for the schedule they had to follow! Publicity wasn't just restricted to daylight hours either. One of the first things they had to do was ride back and forth in the dark for the cameras — it wasn't always easy to understand the point of why they had to do certain things, they entrusted all of that to the Japan Aid team. 'They are protective in the way they insist we travel inside their minibus because of disastrous traffic in Tokyo. The only times we've been riding our bikes is backwards and forwards in front of TV cameras.' (Rhoda)

At the press conference, the team were introduced to their 'campaign girl', a 15-year-old pop singer called Mari Mitzutani who had prepared a Four Corners song. Later the riders were to appear on the Japanese equivalent of Top of the Pops with her which went out live to 20 million people. There were to be about two dozen television appearances and countless press articles. The riders gained something of a celebrity status: once Sebastian was positively mobbed by school girls grabbing him and wanting to be photographed alongside him. He loved it!

Aidan was very good at getting the I.T. message across when talks were given at schools. It wasn't an easy task in Japan, a nation whose vocabulary doesn't contain an equivalent of the word 'charity' and where high tech is virtually worshipped. One comment by a student just about sums this up 'Why a bicycle, surely it would be easier travelling by car!'.

Language was an obvious barrier though Japan Aid provided interpreters for the whole trip. Occasionally the team was left wondering as to how they had been interpreted, especially when they were asked questions like: 'Does Four Corners object to killing Whales?' At the end of some talks there was a workshop which would create a forum for getting the people to think about what could be done in the developing world to reduce famine and poverty. Another time they were guests at a kindergarten where they were greeted by hundreds of tiny little voices singing and dancing and playing 'London Bridge is Falling Down'. After this the tots were let loose on the riders, climbing onto them for piggy back rides or stretching the riders long western noses in all directions.

Local cycle clubs would turn up perfectly clad in all the gear, complete with the Four Corners logo and would join them for the ride between towns and cities. There was little time to rest weary muscles at receptions with mayors and local government officials to whom messages from Four Corners and HRH Prince Charles were delivered. The Mayor of Nagasaki, Hitoshi Motoshima had his own message for the team: '. . . The highest technologies of the modern world are being poured into the development of weapons that will lead to the annihilation of mankind, and countries around the world burdened with local wars are buying weapons in astounding quantities. The resulting starvation, and, like a vicious circle, social unrest and apprehension lead to further conflict and war.'

Japan Aid worked extremely hard for Four Corners. When the entourage came to a halt somewhere, whilst the riders whizzed off to attend these various publicity appointments, the staff would be working in the hotels, making phone calls, having planning meetings, checking routes. All very efficient.

Team Dynamics

Would everyone make it back in September was the question many people asked. Apart from ill-health or accidents, the most likely reason for anyone returning home before the finale, would be if there was a major fall-out amongst team members. There would definitely be times when many had that 'I want to go home feeling'. Would they hold out?

My fingers, toes and anything else had been firmly crossed after pre-departure pressures had sparked rows and a few home truths had come out; a few seeds of distrust had been sown amongst some, but once they'd embarked on their routes only the teams could work them out.

Way back at the beginning of the venture I had had a lengthy discussion with a member of another charity cycle expedition which consisted of 13 cyclists riding from Bristol to India. Only one person had arrived in India and he thought it was due to lack of cohesion and the lack of delegation of tasks. I was determined that Four Corners should not suffer the same fate and to help guard against it I had drawn up an outline of team roles, which Jo had finely tuned. Although mentioned before, more detail is given below.

The Leader was to act as team co-ordinator and was responsible for ensuring that all the necessary pre-departure preparation, training and research was carried out. On route they were to have overall responsibility for decisions taken, and ensure that the other team members carried out their tasks; they were also to be the team representative.

The Logistics Officer's pre-departure responsibilities were to establish route requirements, food, clothing, bike equipment and camping gear, accommodation, medical requirements and organise any necessary team training such as languages, first aid and fitness. On route they were to send back regular route logistical reports, giving details about distances, dates and places visited as well as providing information on equipment provided by sponsors.

The Publicity Officer was in charge of researching any publicity opportunities along the routes such as places where linked events might be staged and make the necessary contacts. They also had to establish contact with the press in all the countries their team would be passing through. On route they were to liaise with all the contacts they had made, both those to do with events and the press. They were also in charge of keeping a record of press coverage and team progress.

The Route Photographer had to establish all photographic requirements and the needs of the press and sponsors. They also had to set up a photographic library system to ensure the thousands of photographs and slides they sent back were organised, and easily accessible for publicity and sponsor usage. On route they were to record and caption all of their work.

Whilst everyone developed working relationships and got to know each other before departure it was mostly in an atmosphere of riding high, with lots of other people around and lots of things happening. It would be a very different matter out in the field with just the other team members for company 24 hours a day, sometimes under very difficult conditions. Pressure of publicity on top of the exhaustion of cycling day after day after day was another potential cause of friction. And this was over and above the less pleasant aspects of human behaviour such as each others' moods, loud snoring, and nervous twitches! At the end of a tiring, puncture-full, corrugated-pedalling, excessively windy, sun-burning day disagreements came easily. Sulky silences would compound the exhaustion and bad tempers flared or just simmered on the verge of explosion with no more than growled monosyllabic exchanges.

I read the first few diaries that came back from the Americas Route team avidly. This was to keep me up to date generally with all things that were going on along the route, but I was also keen to keep an eye on team relations. The diaries would be the place that riders could let off steam about each other in confidence and it would be the first indication if things were not going too well on that front.

At first they showed good team spirit, though comments started to appear which indicated rifts. That was healthy enough, if not vital as an outlet to work out their own feelings about each other. Then they started occurring more frequently. I wrote to the team members individually and made a mention of this, suggesting that if the going got too tough they should simply split into twos to relieve the pressure and to switch around so that it didn't splinter the team into two pairs of two.

Reassuring letters came back with Alex's response putting it all into perspective:

'Whatever we say in diaries must be taken with a pinch of salt. Remember that in a close-knit and hard-working group it's often the best way to let off steam without disrupting things. So have no fear, we are working well together, having a very good time making our part of Four Corners work and getting stronger with every dispute. Hang on, that sounds like these are common occurrences, and they are not. But it has been difficult for us all, really getting to know each other, and learning how to come to terms with what we find. We are all four, pretty egocentric and determined in different ways, so the learning process has been interesting to say the least.'

By the time March had arrived, I had read sufficient accounts of frictions and fall outs for alarm bells to start ringing. I was sure that though these things were not happening all the time, they were obviously occupying a lot of thought space and energy, so that when a letter from one team member arrived saying that he felt he couldn't continue with the team, I felt I had to write to all the riders:

'Dear All,

'I WISH WE COULD HAVE A RIDERS MEETING because I don't know how this is going to sound in a letter. I don't want to seem like an old mother hen, which is probably exactly how I shall sound, however I do have to broach the subject of group dynamics and commitment.

'It is obvious that there are disagreements on route which could seriously jeopardise the team and FOUR CORNERS and it cannot be ignored from London. Though at the same time it should not dampen morale.

'The thing that worries me is that the lack of communication from us might be partly to blame and add to any tension that exists or arises. Letters are being sent weekly from the office and we have taken to adding a forwarding address for dates after you have passed. I am sure a number of these will simply get lost on route. More on this later.

'What really worries me is that any individual should be pressured into leaving the route because of personal disagreements. Everybody seems to have an immense amount of commitment to Intermediate Technology and should make their contribution.

'It seems as though every team is going to go through traumas on route, especially in the remoter areas where you are forced to share each other's company. This is when you are most likely to get locked into a situation and just not see a way out of it.

'From where I am sitting it seems that the very same team member whose neck you wanted to break, you later go and share some brilliant and rare experience with at another time and the bad bits fade into insignificance. If it gets that bad and seemingly irreparable, then a solution has to be found.

Leaving the team IS NOT a solution (unless you have lost your bolts completely!). To avoid losing your bolts try travelling in smaller groups i.e. 2/2, making sure that you maintain a meeting place with the team.

'I promise you that I will not give up back here until we've got there. The going does get pretty tough at times but when it gets too unbearable I shall take a day and indulge in some selfish pampering. Often when I just take myself outside of 4C for an evening or just have an early night it is so much easier to get on with things afresh and find a solution to what ever the problem was. I hope you can find a way of doing this whenever the need arises.

'I.T. was why I got involved and why all of you are in this. It is also why I stayed behind and though you may think it, that was no easy choice (I have to confess I go 'Orrible green when reading your letters and diaries) I'm not blowing my own trumpet. Just relating by my own experience to what you might go through when the going gets tough. Though the context is somewhat different, I hope I have an idea of what it might be like.

'Enough of my waffling. I'll just end by saying PLEASE hold out for the good times even when it gets really hard going, because they will come. When you come into Amsterdam in September all this stuff will be history.

'Though the context is somewhat different . . .' — well that was a bit of an understatement if ever there was one! In retrospect this must have sounded a bit condescending at the other end, but it was a hellishly difficult letter to write, especially with the time restrictions and having to make it a general letter for everyone in their different circumstances.

The **African Trail** wrote back with a hilarious reply: 'We are quite capable of handling any problems that may arise on our route — in fact I let down the air on Willy's tyres just the other day after he called me a pooh-pooh. Still, he got his own back — he bit me. Norman took my side and threw a pen at Willy, so Julia promptly wet herself with the excitement. As for Moira, her nose was buried so deep in her Filofax that she didn't even notice us stamping on her Walkman. So — that's how we handle inter-route intercourse. (P.S. please send spare pens, knickers and Walkman!)'

On a more serious note, they pointed out how important it was to have given this more thought in advance of the trip: 'We certainly found it very helpful that we discussed different cycling abilities/desires BEFORE we left. We decided on a policy of *NEVER* leaving one person alone at the back, both for safety and for psychological reasons. It's worked well. At different times we've helped Julia who has problems with hills, me with my dicky knee, Norm with heatstroke, Moira with a broken derailleur. Male Baboon Willy has not needed any supporting so far.

'So we're all feeling smug and pleased with ourselves. I must say though, that if Willy and Julia hadn't brought it up as a subject before we left we would have had problems.' (Andy)

Julia added in her letter: 'We have really been helped by having thrashed out the cycling mentality before we started and although there have been tensions, the cycling hasn't been one of them. I suppose it's something to do with the mental health of the team being more important than the individual, after all if one person's pissed off the others soon get the vibes. We also have separated into different groups from time to time.'

In fact, the Africa team seemed to have a fantastic rapport. They all had nicknames for each other and nurtured an image of themselves as the anarchic 'play girls and play boys of the organisation' with their yarns about lounging by the Hilton poolsides and downing gin and tonics. Really good for morale both for the team and back at the office. I'm not sure what Andy was called, but Julia the 'leader for life' also became known as the 'Duchess', Moira, 'Gismo Gadget' or 'Elephant Memory' (and an endless list of others!), Norman, well, Willy will have to explain this one! 'Norman has had his hair cut to about ¼″ all over — you'd die if you could see him. He has become really hard since his skinhead — he fixes us with his inscrutable Clint Eastwood stare and hence has earned the name "One-Eyed-Jack"! Another name was "Abnormal".

'By the way, since Willy has been insulting us all, I must give you the lowdown on him. He's had two names - "Babu" Taylor and "Male Baboon". "Babu" is a Shona term of respect for older men — it means grandfather. Willy likes it, but we prefer "Male Baboon" since he acts like one a lot of the time, running around naked and grunting. Honestly!' (Andy)

It was great to get all this rubbish in the sometimes stuffy and serious office, but also, it told us a lot about how the team was getting on. Moira, having come to Four Corners very late in the day at first felt a bit of an outsider. That seemed to dissipate itself pretty quickly. Obviously there were other frictions, but these seemed to have been kept in a healthy balance.

With all the teams it became evident that things like who was going to cook that night or who was paying for what could be cause for irritation or sometimes enormous ructures, and often represented much deeper held disagreements between team members. A good example of an unnecessary upset would be if one member of the team was left behind with a puncture and the others continued; not only that, but that the others continued and they had all the money, so the one left behind couldn't eat or drink. That was a really good one to get the sparks flying!

The Americas Route team had at the beginning, the most strenuous conditions to contend with. They had gone straight out to the Andes for some of the toughest cycling whilst the other teams at least had very good roads to begin their journey on, and this seemed to make quite a difference. There was also the problem of language. Few people they met in South America could speak English, and their levels of Spanish varied, all of them finding it hard to converse easily with anyone outside of the team. This threw them together even more, Other teams suffered patches of this, but none for so long. In fact, their team was to be on the road for the greatest length of time and when personality clashes occurred, it must have been daunting to know they would have to be endured for a whole year.

Once out on the route decisions took a lot longer to make because everyone had such differing views. Ten days after arrival Meryl was to comment 'We have split very quickly into the girls and the boys which I think is a bit of a shame'. This was before they had even got on the road. Meryl and Jo had been close for several months and so at this stage this was more related to that than any real split.

In December though, Jo was to record 'the worst of days', when everyone was 'incredibly selfish. No-one would do anything for anyone else if it meant being nice to them. If it wasn't for I.T. I'd be very tempted to split.' This was echoed by the others except for Thomas, though I suspect, even if he didn't vocalise or write it down somewhere, he must have been affected by it too. In fact, his youthful energy was often an antidote to friction, though at other times, when everyone else was tired and hungry, it also became wearing.

With the various illnesses everyone contracted, each person at some time took their turn at the back, due to feeling weak. Generally there was an unspoken rule that no one would be left behind. This applied to the cyclist with a slower pace than the others too - there was one memorable occasion when that slipped, the consequences of which were not happy — as Meryl recalls on one dark and bitterly cold night when she was left behind on a mountain pass in the freezing cold: 'I really lost confidence when we were overtaken by workmen walking up the road . . . I was in the midst of a blizzard — hailstones, wind, snow, bad muddy roads and feeling miserable.

'I went past a *pueblo* (village) and hoped the others would have waited but no. So I struggled on, past an amazing valley with big white pointed rocks, the only point of interest in an otherwise clean and snow swept landscape. Round every corner I thought I'd see them and was disappointed. The last straw was when I passed a shop and houses and was told they'd passed by. A few kilometres down hill and I saw a *pueblo*. But this time my hands were so cold I could barely cycle and my teeth were chattering. They were all outside the restaurant and I was so cross with them it was ridiculous. A little kid was trying to chat to me as I shivered, and tried to get into warm clothes, Thomas and Jo running about trying to revive me, me bursting into tears. Not a pleasant scene.'

Thomas, obviously fond of Meryl, was accorded the blame on this occasion. He felt very guilty and upset when he realised how serious something like this could be and how it had affected Meryl. 'The only way she had managed to get off her bike and walk in without collapsing was because she was so angry and upset that she had been forgotten, given-up. She had set up goals, at first 5 kilometres, and then 10, then the summit where she would meet us and finally collapse, but we had never been there.' Lesson learnt by Thomas and by all.

Thomas had especially bad luck with punctures and recorded this as one of his worst experiences; 'The manic paranoia between Cuzco and Nazca in Peru where I was getting so many punctures on these ridiculously bad roads, I was constantly aware of all the stones in the road, contemplating the "Clunk Clunk Clunk" as your deflated wheel chunks over the stones in the road. This was so important to me, that it made me continually nervous, therefore argumentative, intolerant and intolerable.'

Human nature being what it is, whilst other team members were at first sympathetic, they grew impatient with the delays caused by his punctures and this probably contributed to Thomas's paranoia. Another day though someone else would have the bad luck and then they'd feel persecuted too so it probably evened itself out. But this difficult stage at the beginning of the Americas Route definitely affected the team.

Relationships were definitely beginning to deteriorate. An incident that marked this was when Alex and Thomas, weary from punctures and ill health, decided to take a truck on ahead and the girls saw them pass by. There was almost an elation from the girls at being able to cycle together on their own: 'When Meryl came round the corner I tried to wipe the smile off my face but both of us started grinning like cheshire cats and she said "And then there were two!" They were beginning to need a break from each other and the team had naturally developed into boy/girl duets. Actually this suited Thomas's and Alex's cycling pace and the girls felt happier that they weren't holding the others back. After about a month of cycling most of the time in pairs, in Ecuador they came together again. After two days of cycling as a four however, it became official that a split was the best way to continue.

Thomas was very against this idea and wrote home to his family: 'It is quite grotesque that here we are trying to promote an organisation which tries to give people an opportunity to control their own lives and work as a community, and the four of us can't even get along together . . .'

The extraordinary thing is when they came together to celebrate Jo's birthday a few days later, they found they had missed each other. Meryl really missed Thomas and Jo had missed Alex's conversation, and in a discussion about team relations Jo found herself talking about all of Alex's good points. She also said that she didn't think anyone should be forced to leave the ride – they should only go of their own volition, adding 'There's no way that I would want to leave because the other three thought I should, not after all I've put in. I'd fight like stink unless I too wanted to leave.'

Days off were taken up with chores: shopping, washing, cooking, bike maintenance etc, and often these things were carried out together as a team. Absolutely vital when living on top of each other, was to find a way in which to have time alone. Hanging back or racing on ahead seemed to be a natural way of giving themselves some space. Everyone did this. Meryl said of Alex: 'When he gets going he just goes! He settles into a pace and gets smaller and smaller in front until he's out of sight.' Meryl created her own sanctuary by collecting wild flowers and plants. Jo enjoyed the solitude of the Santa Cruz Trail when she was able to go off on her own for a few days' trekking into the mountains and wilderness. Thomas meditated and so on. These activities helped each team member to retain his or her own identity and created the necessary space for time alone.

Mexico was to see everyone getting on a whole lot better. Alex wrote a lovely warm letter: 'Our group is thriving. It seems we are really coming to the right arrangement, and are getting on just fine. It's refreshing, fun and welcome. We all like it, and all want to make it better.' He went on to explain that his sister had written to him 'basically telling me to put my ego in a leakproof black bag, and just remember what we were doing it all for. Good advice.'

Good advice for everybody whether on a route or back in the office.

In Mexico Jo was to record 'We're all on a high' and in America: 'Meryl's the nearest thing I have to a sister.' So the pendulum would swing for them and the other teams.

I must stress, that in the main the teams not only got on but were extremely supportive and caring of one another. There was a great deal of sharing, reading of poetry which Alex apparently did beautifully, giving each other massages, helping each other to learn Spanish, doing yoga together and so on.

Thomas in one of his ecstatic up-dates (they were wonderful) informed me that the team had adopted the names 'Faw Paws', the reason for this being too complicated (and too daft) for here. Their individual nicknames were funny, though Jo protested against being called 'Ramba' until they changed it to Lady Ramba! I thought it was rather good myself. This was now regularly the kind of mood of their up-dates. It was a good sign that they had found a cohesion, which, hopefully would last them for the remainder of the journey.

Thomas and other riders were to write of how good it was to receive news from Four Corners. News from friends created a wonderful high and would be described by adjectives like 'sheer ecstacy'. This was an essential contribution that we could make towards team morale. It was very important to keep them in touch with progress, especially in view of their own involvement in building the whole show up, as well as trying to create a picture of what things would be like at the end.

'We love you, we think you're wonderful!' One of Thomas's letters began, and he continued: 'You cannot even begin to understand what a change has come over the four of us. The time away from each other in Ecuador and Guatemala, a change of attitude and the loss of pretence and bullshit between the four of us, and most of all the knowledge that people back home still think of us and that something not only concrete but wonderful in Four Corners has taken place.

'We were all completely bowled over by the press pack. It's quality and presentation.' (Thomas)

Equally the lack of letters and information would have a bad and demoralising effect. **The Asian Highway** team were to suffer particularly badly from this. It's difficult to say whether it was because we didn't send enough stuff or because it simply didn't reach them as was so often the case. I had to ensure that mail was sent out on a weekly basis in the end.

The Asian Highway team was never fully able to put the pre-departure rupture behind them which was terribly sad. The first time I became aware of it was when I.T. received a letter from Pete saying he was considering returning and asking if he might continue to help out with the project in some way. It seemed before departure that some fundamental differences had arisen that had been very hard to overcome so later when a crisis did occur, it was difficult to resolve. In fact he continued cycling apart from the team, usually very fast and ahead of them. Finally things came to a head when all the team reached Bangkok as already discussed.

This incident was to create a lasting scar in relations between me and the team. This was further compounded by the fact that they believed wholeheartedly that I blamed them for the situation. I wasn't in a position to blame anybody, and by not taking sides this was seen as blaming everyone. The fact that their commitment remained intact can only reflect well on them. Under the circumstances, that they all got as far as they did before it came to a crunch was remarkable. Jane, Nick and Kate continued for what was to be the most difficult part of the cycling and the busiest in terms of publicity for Intermediate Technology. It concerned me that with Pete gone, Jane would be a gooseberry with two people only married for seven months. However hard Kate and Nick might have tried to make up for this, there is no way that Jane couldn't have felt under some pressure. If is was difficult, she didn't let it show. On the contrary, she wrote home shining reports of how kind both Nick and Kate had been.

The Oriental Path had the least time in the field, but nevertheless seven months is plenty of time for tensions to develop, and like any other team, they weren't to be spared.

As a foursome they were very different. At first the team seemed to pair off in twos, Rhoda and Sebastian, and Adria and Aidan. This related to the way things had developed in London. Adria and Aidan had worked together in the office and developed a friendship around this. Aidan quite a bit older than Adria, carried a lot of ideas from his university days and this is perhaps where they parted company. Also, Adria found the hills tough and often took the rear position whilst Aidan lead out front, keen on maintaining a fast speed. These things were to put a strain on their closeness. For the team as a whole though, Aidan felt that more human contact between them would have been helpful: 'If we could have just got this right, an occasional hug, then this might have allowed problems to be seen in proportion . . .'

The other two were much more independent and shared cycling paces and travel objectives, and so often they would pair-up. They were both extremely good at their roles too — Sebastian as photographer sent some brilliant pictures back to base. Rhoda was the traveller of the team, always doing things to keep pannier weight to an absolute minimum, or saving space. Adria commented in her diary: 'Rhoda's been rolling a bog roll into ten little rolls. Space saving again. She's so fanatical about carrying as little weight as possible too that it wouldn't surprise me if she wasn't getting rid of the weight of the cardboard roll in the middle!' I may have complained about Rhoda's pre-departure contributions, she was to make up for it now; she has to go on record as being the best Logistics Officer of all the teams. Very clear reports came back. She was so conscientious about it. They all took their roles (and in Rhoda's case, rolls!) very seriously.

The pairs would sometimes switch round. Rhoda and Aidan would pound on ahead sometimes as though in a race! Adria's pace was slower and Sebastian took the rear now and again recognising that always occupying that position can be 'bitterly demoralising'.

They each seemed to have their own little idiosyncracies which they all noted. Rhoda, apparently had an obsession with hygiene. The first thing she would do on arrival at any hotel would be to get herself and her clothes washed. Nothing wrong with some good clean habits.

Adria became famous for being able to fall asleep just about anywhere, and for collapsing into fits of giggles. I suspect the latter had something to do with consumption of rice wine! She was also the most thoughtful member of the team, but then I'm biased. She wrote to me when she heard I'd had some very distressing family news and she also also remembered my birthday! Adria was meticulous about thank you letters, always listing those she had to do or crossing off those sent.

Aidan, according to other team members, seemed to have a fascination with the workings of his body, which is probably why he is so fantastically fit. It's not that surprising when you are so reliant on its performance. He was also the political commentator for the team which was very useful because this was a subject that a lot of people along the way were interested in, particularly in China.

Sebastian was terribly polite and always the one that remembered to say thank you to people. They were all great foodies but Adria commented that Sebastian got really impatient and irritable if he didn't get it and was joyful as a skylark if he did. He also had a soft spot for any pretty oriental girl with a coy smile!

Things which could cause great annoyance were consistently late departures and the amount of rests and stops that some members needed to have whilst others just wanted to get on to wherever it was they were going. Aidan explained how this had been dealt with: 'Our new cycling policy has been to go off at your own pace and meet up for meal stops. It doesn't always work out, but at least those annoying stops are avoided when the rest have to wait while one person takes off their jacket or adjusts something minor on their bike.'

Adria wrote to me: 'I've been missing home a lot lately. Not so much home, I suppose but friends and family, of course. On the surface of things the team gets along well but deeper down we all realise, I think, that we're an unlikely bunch and as you know us all quite well I think you can guess why. This is all very well from day to day but I find it difficult to express a problem — I know Aiden does too — which is kind of sad. We have a few laughs. We certainly are aware of how extremely lucky we are to be here at all, but in all honesty there's a lot of room for improvement in relationships between us. I'm convinced selfishness is spreading in the group.'

It made me think 'yes, there's four rather "unlikely bunches" of people out there and how extraordinary it is that they are all getting along'. It was a bit of a sad letter to receive but there weren't many like that. Nevertheless it reflected the underlying tension in the team. Tony Redpath, Adria's boyfriend joined the team in Scandinavia for three weeks and whilst that did wonders for Adria, the others felt a fresh person improved relations too. Another remedy for dissipating friction was skinny dipping in Norwegian fjiords! On a more serious note they found that their publicity work for I.T. also brought them closer as each occasion reminded them of all they had achieved together.

Sebastian wrote of 'group dynamics' and the 'day-to-day friction and humour': 'It's an education in itself travelling with other people. I never thought I'd learn so much so quickly about the three others. What surprises me most is how little thought I gave it in London — whether or not I'd get on. You accepted that as they were dedicated to what we were setting out to do, that in itself would iron out any differences. If only! Daily contact, and constant pressures of being on time, and fulfilling chores, and keeping up when cycling, etc, etc, create a lot of stress and the differences between us all become horribly apparent and the only opportunity you have to walk away is usually escape to sleep. Maybe that's why Adria's been sleeping so much. But as quickly as you can be depressed by the rest of the team so you can be lifted up into a state of farcical hysterics.'

I think this more or less captured many of the riders' feelings about their teams. I looked forward to seeing them all in September — fairly confident now that they would all pedal in together. And if they did then this would be one of the major achievements of Four Corners and the riders.

PART THREE

Countdown

By the beginning of July the office was buzzing with activity as preparations for the welcome home for the World Bike Riders got under way with just under three months to go before their return.

To coincide with their arrival there would be bike riders all over the U.K. and in London there would be the Island Ride, a 20-mile relay around the Isle of Dogs; a ride anyone could take part in. The die-hards could join the World Bike Riders at Amsterdam for a weekend ride of over 150 miles back to London. Finally, in Colchester more cyclists would join the World Bike Riders for breakfast followed by a 70-mile pedal to London; The Challenge Ride. So, there was a ride for everyone and to round it off there would be a concert in Millwall Park on the Isle of Dogs, with music representative of the countries Four Corners had passed through. The detail of all this still had to be worked on though.

Things were already way behind and with the three-week depression they had got even more behind. Moreover Shirley, our Grand Finale Co-ordinator was having financial problems. She had become vital to the project but there was no magic money in the kitty I could use and in the end some of it had to come from a sponsored parachute jump done by Cathy Keogh and Anthony Brown. That Cathy, who was being paid £50 a week didn't mind, speaks volumes for her commitment. We had to have a Final Event Co-ordinator or there would be no final event.

So, Shirley stayed, at first concentrating on getting the Challenge Ride firmly established before handing over responsibility for this to Harold Carr (Dad of World Bike Rider, Norman Carr out on the African Trail). Her next major task was to get the registration forms prepared and printed — not something she'd done before — but using her advertising contacts she arranged for the copy writing, design and the printing of these to be donated. She did a great job on this and at the end of July we took delivery of 30,000 glossy registration forms and a major distribution operation throughout London was done by volunteer despatch riders.

Meanwhile, Cathy and I were moving things ahead on the Island Ride and the concert. All the requirements were listed: stage, sound systems, security were to be secured by donation. Bands, entertainments and food stands were also to be asked to donate their services. Suppliers and contacts were listed and there was a great deal of activity on the telephone to get all this.

Steve Armitage continued with Four Corners, helping Shirley with the Challenge Ride. When poor Harold Carr dropped out after a few weeks because of ill health, Steve stepped in and saved the day with a loyal band of supporters, which allowed Shirley to go off to Amsterdam.

I remembered the vision I had had of thousands of cyclists joining the World Bike Riders after my first trip to Amsterdam, and warned Shirley not to get side tracked into this but to concentrate on getting U.K. cyclists there and back. 'We've got to concentrate on things in the U.K. Shirl, but I know you, you'll get out there and think you can get millions on bikes, and you probably will, but we haven't got time to risk it.' Everyone turned out of the office to see her off and wish her luck.

My publicity efforts were concentrated on getting coverage for the weeks before the arrival of the teams. By mid-July Margaret Hansen was working full-time and took over most of this and I just put a new press pack together. Steve Bonnist's original had only included my profile, so I did one on both Andy and myself as the co-founders although until the riders returned I was the person they would have to contact.

Meanwhile to get an advertising campaign together free of charge (there were no funds available), I rang David Miller, the Managing Director of Young and Rubicam. He sent along Accounts Director, Alisdair Delves to come and sort us out. He came up with a London-wide bill board campaign to run with a radio advertising campaign. "So, Miranda, what's the budget for this?" Alisdair asked me. 'There isn't one I'm afraid. I suggested to David that Young and Rubicam might use this in the advertising and marketing media for promotional purposes'. They wouldn't do it completely for free and for £500 Young and Rubicam handled the design side and co-ordinated the positioning of posters etc. Standard Chartered Bank funded this for us, whilst I got the printing and all the bill sticking donated. This was probably the first expedition with a bill board campaign!

I'd also been speaking to Midge Ure's Office as Midge was going to do a radio message for us. This was brilliant news! However, our advisors got it wrong on this occasion. The language of the scripted message they prepared had worried me and I had specifically asked that it not be presented cold. It was, and Midge was so offended that he refused to do any message at all. A lesson to trust your own judgement and I was very cross with myself for not handling this better — especially when it had obviously proved so offensive to Midge who usually was a keen supporter of I.T, and I knew that this really upset the charity.

We soon knew when Shirley was back from Amsterdam; 'They think we could get millions on their bikes all over the country! We've got to have an office Miranda with staff in it, they keep saying that I should go over there and be Co-ordinator'. I'm afraid I must have seemed like a real kill joy when I reminded her that her main job was to deal with the London Final Event. I loved Shirley's enthusiasm and energy, but I was afraid it was going to get misdirected. In her absence Harriet had announced she would be leaving to work overseas; Annabel's employers were uncertain about allowing her to continue on the part-time basis; Harold Carr had dropped out over illness, Amanda Harding was going to join the Americas Route and so on. I took her aside and explained we couldn't spare her. However General Accident were still keen to back a member of staff, so as a compromise I suggested that if we could find someone else, she should take them over to Amsterdam, show them the ropes and then return to finalise things on this side, maintaining her role as Amsterdam Liaison, but majoring on the London events.

Richard Weyers was handling the processing of registration forms — one of those wonderful people who just came in and get on with the job. His was no small task though and I was really pleased to be able to find a full-time assistant for him. His face lit up when he discovered she was a glamorous temp from Brook Street Bureau. At the same time two additional secretaries were seconded to us from Reed: Nicole Broderick for Margaret and Belinda, and Maria Phelan for me. Both of these girls were great. So, the sponsorship was paying off, albeit in kind, and I still had to work on the elusive cash sponsorship. It wasn't just for the concert, but there would be a hefty phone bill that could run into £1,000s; I might have to pick the tab up personally if I didn't get some money.

Shirley returned to Amsterdam having stayed longer than anticipated. There was little I could do other than wish her luck and get on with finding someone to do her work in London.

Things were definitely happening nationwide in this country.

Richard Crane working full time for I.T. now, was inspiring the U.K. co-ordinators with visits to give talks, telephoning and letters like this one: 'Countdown to the Grand Finale, just under 4 weeks to go! Things are hotting up in Docklands: Miranda moves in a blur of activity — soon we expect her to vanish in a puff of smoke!

'How are things going in the centres of fundraising activity? Those rides of yours are the crucial elements which crown all those thousands of miles of riding by the FOUR CORNERS World Bike Riders, and bring together in spirit the countless participants from all over the country. The national press are calling more and more frequently for the latest news . . .'

The local press covering the build up to these home rides was tremendous. Each of the rides, now numbering 25, was getting several articles and pictures and some were receiving radio and television coverage in conjunction with Richard's promotional tour.

In the last few weeks, another bright spark came on the scene: Richard 'cricket bat appeal' Spurgeon who initially helped Margaret. He then came up with the idea of running a Four Corners World Bike Ride Cricket Bat Appeal. He knew Gary Sobers and had arranged to meet him to get his signature on 20 children's cricket bats which had been donated. Shirley, he and Richard Weyers were to disappear from the office one morning to meet Gary Sobers and get the bats signed. Richard was convinced this was the route to £100,000s. I'd heard so many ideas (and had come up with a few myself in the past!) that with time running out I felt we simply had to get on with what we had in hand and not be distracted at this stage by new proposals. When I told him that if he wanted to do a cricket bat appeal he should go through the fundraising office at I.T., I wasn't very popular.

A strange thing was happening. New people were coming on board with bundles of energy, 90 per cent of whom were welcomed with open arms and put to good use. But in one or two cases, individuals were going off at tangents and doing their own thing. Trying to keep everyone on track was an enormous effort and there was little I could do if they were unsalaried. I was worried that things were getting out of control.

By mid August all the teams were well on their way home through Europe.

The Americas Route had arrived in Spain where the British Embassy had organised a press conference. The team's Spanish had gone a little rusty since they had been in the States since April, but Meryl managed the interviews and they had 'the best articles we've had yet', with half a page in the main daily national and others. They left Madrid with a police escort and all the staff turned out to see them off from the British Embassy. From here it was heads down and a race to keep to a tight schedule, with just three weeks to get to Amsterdam and more publicity stops on the way. The Pyrenees proved no obstacle after riding the Andes and Jo was to comment: 'The Pyrenees seemed nothing, there were three passes and we were up and over them within 10 hours of cycling'.

Around this time there were to be a series of hiccups. There was a support vehicle with them now and back in Madrid this had been broken into with three cameras and other belongings being stolen. Next, Meryl got lost in France. The rest of the team were in Spain still and eventually gave up the search. Alex was to end that day on the ground with blood pouring from his head — the result of a spirited water fight between he and Jo. Luckily it required no more than the first aid kit and with his head swathed in bandages he and the others continued the next day into France. Down the road in France they discovered Meryl safe and sound — and so onto Paris.

The Asian Highway team were having a quiet time of things in Europe and in Austria they cycled on cycle routes along the Danube and faded into the background somewhat amongst masses of other cycle tourists. In Heidelberg in West Germany they crossed cycle paths with the African Trail team and caught up on inter-route gossip before continuing onto Luxembourg where they were briefly reminded what it was like to be in the public eye again.

Meanwhile, Helen Alexander was awaiting the arrival of the Americas Route and the Asian Highway teams in Brussels where she had lined up lots of Belgian participation. Talks on the routes and Intermediate Technology and more publicity had been set up at the European Parliament which was attended by various government bodies and overseas development groups. The two teams were set to make quite a splash here.

The African Trail were to have the most eventful time in Europe. Team photographer, Moira had her camera stolen in Crete — which, photography being a passion, was as bad as one of the riders having their bike stolen (which was to happen to Alex in Amsterdam). In Athens the wonders of the Acropolis were somewhat overshadowed by those of the Pyramids and Julia wrote home 'I don't like this modern stuff'! Into Italy and into more publicity with filming in Rome by Visnews. A 'little' hiccup here though over an audience with the Pope.

This had been set up by Helen with the help of the European

Parliament and the UK Catholic Church hierarchy and great effort had gone into arranging it. News of the event had been sent to the team in advance but hadn't reached them. Unaware of this, we had continued with the arrangements so that when they did finally hear of it, just a couple of weeks before it was scheduled, they were 'incredulous' at not having been informed earlier. The team objected on the grounds of their principals and Julia wrote to explain: 'We heard via Andy that you are trying to arrange an audience for us with the Pope. We were rather taken aback that this was being arranged without any discussion with us especially as none of us want to meet him. We have many reasons for this. Apart from our religious feeling (we don't have any) we can see conflict between the Catholic Church, Third World Development and our concept of what Four Corners is all about. To briefly explain:

'Firstly, the Catholic Church is the richest organisation in the Third World — a fact which speaks for itself in the face of the extensive and terrible poverty which we and the other routes have seen on our trips so far.

'Secondly, the Catholic Church is frequently in conflict with popular movements for change (including with their own radical clergy).

'Thirdly, a large emphasis of Four Corners has been towards rural women yet the history of the Catholic Church's involvement in women's issues has been to suppress their development and keep them dependent.

'Fourthly, we have experienced again and again the destructive role of the church in Africa in its conflict with the existing social and cultural orders.'

While we respected these personal views, they omitted to acknowledge I.T.'s relationship with the Catholic Church, which is good. The Church, particularly through its UK-based and fairly radical development agencies CAFOD and CIIR has in fact been a vital supporter of I.T.'s work, not only on general and development projects over the past 20 years, but also especially recently on women's projects. In fact I.T. had collaborated with them on projects in Zimbabwe, Tanzania and Kenya — all on the African Trail.

It was unfortunate that the team had not received earlier information about the appointment with the Pope. It had been sent but had obviously not reached them; our contact points and post restantes weren't always reliable. It was a shame I.T. hadn't been able to put their point of view to the team; the view in London was that for the sake of the charity, they should have sacrificed their principles. It wasn't very easy to placate those who made the arrangements and indeed there was a suggestion I.T. should pull the plug on the whole venture! Helen was extremely upset having spent vast tracts of her time organising this. Also the national press from this country were going to cover it — so it felt like the plug had been pulled on essential publicity. Our contact in the European Parliament, Peter Lerhell had assisted and wasn't at all happy; he suggested 'disciplining' the team. When I finally spoke to Andy I passed on everyone's reaction and left it at that.

The Oriental Path found Denmark a complete contrast from the rigours of the Arctic Circle and snow-clad mountains. Rhoda was to write home 'Cycling in Denmark is like ice-skating after Norway'. The team were to find themselves once again at the centre of a publicity campaign, where Peter Elming and others of the national Danish cycle organisation had spent many months organising advance publicity. Every day was scheduled with organised rides cycling down 'skinny' lanes to get away from traffic, joined by lots of enthusiastic Danish cyclists. In cities along the route, festivals greeted them and in Copenhagen, there was a pop concert where much drinking of Danish lager was done and a speech given about the cause by Aiden was rounded off with 'Carry on drinking, carry on thinking'!

West Germany was a little more sober with very serious discussions on development attended by mayors and officials and a big party hosted by Richard Konig in Dusseldorf. With 'rarely any hills', this last ride before the Netherlands was smooth.

Dick and Nick Crane received a fun letter from Andy just before the final event:

'The African team have now reached Sienna. Most of the "Gin and Tonic route" lies behind us now, and we only have 2,000 or so km left till London. Phew! Thank God for that.

'I think that six months (maybe seven) is the longest a bicycle trip ought to last. After that it becomes difficult to stay fresh and enjoy new things.

'Africa was of course great — always something new and interesting, very friendly people, great scenery, cheap beer. Greece was also good, Norman remembered his required reading, and told us that the Metsovo pass was the highest road in Greece (Nick Crane *Cycling in Europe*). We duly sweated our way over it, chased all the way by a tremendous electrical storm. It caught us at the top, so we did the downhill in goggles and snorkel.

'Italy has provided nothing so exciting — it's all very beautiful but also very tame. Staying within budget has proved very difficult. We're still looking forward to the Alps and after that a fast ride to Docklands.

Thanks for all the work you are doing to promote "Four Corners".
'See you in Amsterdam.'
So the riders were nearly home.

On September 10th, with just 10 days to go, I called a Crisis meeting with Richard Crane, Cathy Keogh, Shirley Parker and Richard Spurgeon: all those dealing with the Final Event. We still hadn't got any money and not enough equipment or services were being donated to make the concert viable. With little time left we needed at least £4,000 for the concert. Cathy announced another crisis. Thousands of pounds worth of merchandise had been sent out to the U.K. organisers, on a sale or return basis. I hadn't realised this had gone so far, and of course sending it out sale or return meant that there was no cash available to pay the supplier — who was a friend of Cathy. 'So, how are we going to get round this?' I asked. Richard Spurgeon, Shirley and Cathy all suggested we cancel the concert, to reduce costs. This would limit the damage but leave no focus for the press and no attraction for people to come and buy the T-shirts. This plus the dreaded phone bill was a potentially miserable ending to the Four Corners. No, we had to be more imaginative than that. 'O.K., well I am going to personally have to accept full financial responsibility for this and find the money in the next couple of days,' I said recklessly.

Richard Spurgeon said he needed a day off and would take the following day. Cathy and Shirley wanted to follow suit but Dick supported me in the need to find our way out of the situation. I suggested we spent the following day on the telephone calling up all our contacts in the hope of finding cash sponsorship. This was agreed with a cut off point of Thursday 4 pm. Everyone round that table, bar Dick, thought I'd flipped. I was grateful for his support. In fairness to the others, I had put them under a lot of pressure and nerves were frayed.

The following day I arrived in the office prepared for an attack. By mid-day still none of the others had turned up. Marie was being fantastic and came up with lists and lists of contact numbers. I went through the whole lot, following phone calls with faxed proposals followed by phone calls. Everyone else in the office was wonderfully supportive: Belinda, Margaret, Annabel. Aiden Foss, one of the volunteers even offered to loan the money but that would have been too great a responsibility. At the end of the day I felt gutted, there'd been no let up, and it was a relief when office hours passed and there was no-one left to fax, telex or telephone. At this point Maria disappeared and returned bearing a plant for me. I was touched by the understanding and support of all those who had been around in the office.

A few leads came out of the day's work and someone who sounded like he was really going to try and help was the Managing Director of Burson–Marsteller, Terence Fane–Saunders. He was new to the company and knew little of Four Corners, but I asked if he could put our proposal out to his Account Executives.

Steve Bonnist and Helen Alexander came over to Docklands to take me out for a meal. After the day I had had, a quiet meal was lovely. Each of us agreed that there had to be a concert at the end. There were sufficient T-shirts to raise a profit of £4,500. If I could find a loan to cover this, I was prepared to accept responsibility for this and the remainder, which, with the phone bills would probably run into another £4,000 or £5,000.

Thursday came and I continued to chase people. Steve rang. He was prepared to loan Four Corners the essential £4,000 but it had to be approved by one or two executive members of I.T. I reminded him of the 4 pm deadline. I went across and quietly told Dick.

The other thing I'd been trying to find for the last two weeks was a concert organiser. In the end I found someone through my old pal Rhenna at Worlds End Studios. 'Yes, I know someone. He's called Dutch' she told me. 'I'll see if he can help.' That was a few days before. Now, with the deadline only hours away, I rang again to see if there was any news. 'Yes, he's free and interested. We've used him and he's very good, I'll tell him to come across then O.K.?'

Shirley, Cathy and Richard Spurgeon turned up just before the Thursday 4 pm deadline. Richard put his legs up on the table awaiting the 'verdict'. I had an irrational impulse to fire them all for disappearing when I needed them most but I realised once again that ugly thing called pressure was rearing its head and that I would regret it. Instead, when I.T. rang to confirm the £4,000, I said 'O.K. everyone, let's get this thing moving! The money's home and there's a guy called Dutch on his way over to come and take on the concert!' It was worth all the work just to see their faces — the satisfaction I felt was not an emotion I'm proud of, but then I'm only human too.

The Grand Finale

That evening, as the office welled up with volunteers, Carrie Beeson arrived with two large bottles of wine and crisps. Plastic cups were raised, and there was a relieved celebration that another problem (be it rather an important one!) had been overcome. Cathy was herself again and all geared up which was lovely to see. 'I've been an old bag to you' she said. She hadn't, she had just been worn out.

Dutch was an interesting and large presence in the office. He turned up wearing a floor length flowing black leather coat. He was over six feet tall, had a large impish face, messy layered fair hair, a loud American voice and a cellnet phone to hand. Cathy and Dutch were to be partners on the concert — a real Laurel and Hardy, Cathy being all of 4 feet 11 inches against this rounded giant.

By now the office was a mangle of bodies and telephone wires. There were several people to each desk whilst others were strewn or sitting cross legged on the floor. There were smart mums, tidy secretaries, scruffy students, trendies like Shirl, odd bods like Dutch and eccentrics like Dick. There were posters being pasted up, huge signs for rides being made, there were queues of volunteers at the photocopiers. And the racket! All the printers were going at once, word processors were being beaten into submission, phones ringing, people shouting across the room to each other, Dutch bellowing above everyone else interspersing his words with F... this and F... that! I should have taped it for the riders to hear later. I stopped for a moment to observe and absorb it all to be stored in my memory file. It was ridiculous and quite, quite wonderful.

Unhappily I had to try and quell this for the sakes of the L.D.D.C. staff. Their tolerance level was to say the least admirable, with the volunteers spilling well beyond the boundaries of space that we had been allocated. But the buzzing energy was rare and just brilliant — everyone working together — they couldn't be trying harder.

By now our bill board campaign had gone up around London. I had had last minute panics about the wording, which Young and Rubicam had assured me was 'generic'. Emblazoned on 80 bill boards around London was 'ON SEPTEMBER 20TH, JOIN HALF-A-MILLION PEOPLE ON A BIKE'. There would certainly be at least half-a-million people on a bike on September 20th, but in the United Kingdom, the World, the Universe — not just on the Isle of Dogs! It was late going up, but it attracted immediate attention. Around the U.K. other huge posters were going up in towns and cities where there were rides. The printing and sites for this were all donated by Eagle Star.

Well wishers were phoning in. Mary Wilson rang up and put Harold on the line — I could almost smell the pipe smoke at the other end of the phone; extraordinary to hear that incredibly familiar voice. Then Chris 'Superman' Reeves, rang from the States and was going to try and join us on some publicity. Then Joanna Lumley rang; she wouldn't be around to join us, but was all the same helping us with our publicity campaign.

In the Netherlands a company had been set up with the help of our sponsors Spicer and Oppenheim and a firm of Dutch solicitors that I had met on my first visit. Shirley and a Dutch volunteer, were made company directors; I just had to hope it was all in order.

Eight days to go and at the end of the day Shirley came to me looking very pensive. 'Miranda I think we'd better go and have a quiet chat.' She had taken on the Dutch volunteer in good faith and now our publicity people had rung to say they had been told that he had previously been involved in the embezzling of charity funds — articles were appearing in the press about it. 'Miranda, I don't believe what has happened, I feel such a fool.' She was obviously feeling very guilty. 'Well, let's see how we can sort this out' I said, pushing the calm button. 'Shirl, you are going to have to go out there and deal with these people face to face. Talk to our legal advisors first and follow whatever they say has to be done and keep me informed.' I was concerned that this could reflect badly on I.T.

The following day in the office, Shirl was writing lengthy instructions on what was to be done in her absence. That night, Cathy, Shirley and myself went for a quick drink before closing time. I was sad to see Shirley go. She would miss the build up this end and was going to have to deal with a sticky situation in the Netherlands. Also, with her gone, this would mean I would now not be able to be in Amsterdam to meet the riders, which I was very sad about. So many letters saying 'See you in Amsterdam'.

Everything was now moving at great speed. Shirley got things under control in Amsterdam fairly quickly. It transpired that the volunteer, a passionate and well-meaning character was also a little abrupt which had got a few backs up and resulted in the spreading of these bad rumours. Shirley would remain there to make sure everything continued to run smoothly. The office was hardly quiet without her, but her presence was missed. We hugged each other goodbye.

Days to go before the grand finale, and another crisis. I left the office to send a fax and returned and found everybody huddled together wearing extremely worried expressions. 'Oh, here's Miranda!' Cathy said in a tone which suggested, whatever it was, I was going to be able to sort it out. There was a Mr. Northcott on the phone, the chief Environmental Health Officer for the local borough. 'The concert's going to be cancelled — something to do with decibel levels, health and safety', Cathy explained. 'But we've dealt with all this' I said incredulously, 'I was assured all this had been taken care of.' I picked up the receiver.

No, Mr. Northcott hadn't been informed that a concert would be taking place. The notification for this was a minimum of 14 days. There were only six days to go! I put myself totally at this man's mercy and apologised profusely and sincerely — we arranged for Dutch and Cathy to go and meet him that afternoon to fill him in on all the details and assured him that we would do everything necessary to comply with the rules. He was on our side.

Cathy and Dutch went off to meet him and returned. By the next lunchtime they had to supply in writing a complete assurance that all requirements would be met, as well as a complete breakdown of the event, a list of all our contacts; names and addresses etc. There was more that had to be secured first too.

The next day Cathy and Dutch had everything lined up. You would not believe how much Cathy had managed to do over those last few weeks, but those last few days . . .! When she came to do her letter of assurance, there was just one hour left before it was to be delivered. She sat glued to the word processor with Dutch giving encouragement. Everybody, aware of how important this was, gave her a wide berth — the tension was amazing. Despite lots of activity going on in other areas of the office, it was remarkably quiet to allow her the utmost of concentration. If she got it wrong, the concert would be cancelled. The licence was delivered later that day . . . thanks to Cathy.

Meanwhile, I was trying to make sure that everything else was going to plan. Each morning there was a debriefing with those heading up the various areas. It was exciting. Articles had begun appearing in various magazines, including *Elle* and the *London Illustrated News*. Clippings were coming in from all over the country both from where the World Bike Riders came from and where there would be locally-organised rides, and in London the *Evening Standard* did a great picture story of a bobby being recruited on a bike! The quality press were beginning to pick it up as well with articles in the *Guardian,* the *Times* and the *Independent*. The latter was the first and had come out the previous Friday. There it was right next to the television page where everyone looked and it included a great picture of the Asian Highway team. Margaret was going great guns on publicity and on top of this there were various radio interviews lined up and very exciting, the following week there was to be television coverage on Blue Peter, London Weekend Television and the Terry Wogan Show! Everything was beginning to fall into place.

Four more days to go. On the sponsorship front, Burson–Marsteller had put us in touch with Flora Margarine. They were keen but the decision had to be approved at various levels. I lined up a printer that could over print Four Corners T-shirts with the Flora logo at the press of a button i.e. as soon as Flora came up with the money. These could then be couriered to the World Bike Riders as they entered the country on Sunday. To assist them in gauging the potential coverage the World Bike Riders would get following the event, I'd suggested we send them details of the coverage the Cranes got after their expeditions. I asked Steve Bonnist to fax this to them a.s.a.p. Flora would let us have their decision on receipt of this.

The next day I was to be on Blue Peter. That night, I left a list of things to be done in my absence; most crucial and top of the list was a reminder to Steve to send Flora details of the Crane's publicity. Before I went home I rang to speak to Julia and Willy who would also be on Blue Peter. It appeared they had been contacted by the B.B.C. about what would be expected of them. 'Funny' I said, 'no-one's done that with me. Maybe they're not expecting me'. I rang Dick who would also be on the show. 'Of course they're expecting you' he said. We left it that we'd see each other the next morning, and if he heard to the contrary, he'd contact me first thing.

So, the next morning, I psyched myself up for the day ahead and I made my way across the other side of town to Television Centre, going by tube, being too weary to even think of pedalling. First I had rung the office, making sure all my lists of instructions had been read and understood. I got to be the B.B.C. reception and was not surprised to learn that they weren't expecting me. I wasn't too happy that so much time had been wasted at this crucial hour and was eager to get straight back to the office but one of the secretaries came and met me. 'I don't know how this has happened, a man rang up and told us that you wouldn't be able to make it' she told me.

She didn't know his name. Whoever this person was, why hadn't I been told?! I was both furious and confused. 'Look, I've got to head back to the office . . .' I said, but she insisted that I came up to the studio to meet the producer. The studio was packed with school children and Four Corners people all wearing Four Corners T-shirts. I felt an idiot that I should have thought my presence would have been necessary, especially when I should have been sorting out the Flora sponsorship. I was so upset I just wanted to get away as fast as I could. I made polite noises and made my exit. Dick must have spotted me and came running out after me. I couldn't really take in what he was saying, and when he left I just burst into tears. My fuse had finally blown.

I cried because of the pressure of the Flora deal. I cried because it occurred to me that whoever it was, had rung the B.B.C. out of malice. I cried because someone had told me my name had been deliberately left out of an article about Four Corners. Could someone dislike me this much? In my period with Four Corners I had experienced occasions of extreme support but suddenly the bad experiences hit me with great force.

The problems that had occurred to date I had rationalised as they had cropped up as misunderstandings, the result of my own inadequacy at handling them, the odd ego getting out of control and not enough time to sort things out. Now they all crowded in on me — two years' worth — one after the other after the other. I thought back to the beginning. I thought of all the expectations that wouldn't be fulfilled if we didn't pull off the Grand Finale and all the people I would be letting down, not least of all I.T. In a fit of self pity I even thought how disappointed my old mum would be, sat there in front of the box later that afternoon, full of pride and looking out for her youngest on Blue Peter.

I felt wrought with grief that I might have engendered such hate and cried uncontrollable tears all the way back to the office. It seemed an endless journey, taking about 1½ hours. I just couldn't stop crying. I was no use any more. My whole body and mind was drained, aching, utterly exhausted beyond my imagination. All the frustration of the last 2½ years seemed to be hitting me all at once. I reached Docklands and wandered round until eventually I managed some semblance of composure and returned to the office.

Everything was under control. I had virtually delegated myself out of a job, having planned either to join the teams in Amsterdam or be doing publicity. Steve Bonnist was working at the office and when he saw me, suggested we take a walk. Perhaps he could explain what had happened. He came out with me to the side of Millwall Dock. 'I don't know anything about it' he told me. Well, that didn't matter anymore. Flora hadn't rung up, but everything else seemed lined up to happen. I told him 'Steve, I've done everything I can for Four Corners, and I think if I walk away now, then it wouldn't make the slightest bit of difference. I've decided to go home to Kettering, to Mum and Dad. Dick can do the Terry Wogan programme tomorrow night.' I had stopped crying, but I think Steve could see that I was in a delicate state and attemped to reassure me I was still very much needed.

Anyway we wandered back up to the office. When I got to my desk, Flora were on the phone. It is absolutely staggering how quickly, when the need demands, you can pick yourself up and dust yourself down and deal with a crisis. I had been certain I hadn't a gram of energy left.

Flora wanted to know if there was something wrong with our fax, they hadn't received any publicity details from us. I looked across at Steve Bonnist, and in a loud voice said 'You haven't received the details that Steve was going to send you, I'll get onto it right away!'. I'd never seen Steve move so fast! Before I'd even put the phone down he was half way through them and soon after, he was on his way down to the fax room to send it.

Everyone else, engrossed in their chores was quite unaware of my little trauma, though someone said to me 'You look TERRIBLE!!'

Margaret was busy connecting the riders up to do radio interviews from Amsterdam to their local home counties radio stations up and down the country. The atmosphere was electric again. And by 4 pm Flora rang to say they would be happy to support Four Corners and there was a cheque for £15,000 for me the next day! It was just too good to be true; I asked if she could put that in writing and send it on a fax. The fax came through:

'Dear Miranda
'To confirm our telephone conversation. Flora will be happy to sponsor the Four Corners event for £15,000.
'Best of luck.'

Talk about the eleventh hour!

Shortly after this, everybody, volunteers and some of the L.D.D.C. staff gathered round a miniscule television screen and watched Blue Peter with Dick and Nick Crane telling Great Britain to get on its bike. It was lovely watching Willy Taylor tell of his most frightening moments in Africa when he had heard lions roaring and hippopotomus noises!

Shortly after that was Radio One Newsbeat, with Thomas Harding doing a telephone interview from Amsterdam — Four Corners was going out nationwide.

The publicity meeting took place at the George that night, with Four Corners taking over one of the bars. Most of the national press had said they would be there on Sunday and both I.T.N. and B.B.C. television cameras were going to turn up. Everyone looked worn but spirits were high and hopeful.

Friday 18th September. It was the last working day and so if things needed doing then this was our last chance. The office was jam packed, each person had their own very tight schedule; the atmosphere was good but urgent too. There were still one or two frills to add to the concert and we rang round various companies and got them donated.

The cheque for £15,000 arrived from Flora and there was a brief pause whilst Maria Phelan photographed this historical moment; Dick Crane and a very jaded Miranda Spitteler clutching the cheque and beaming with disbelief.

I'd spent ages trying to drum up free advertising, now we could afford to dot it, but it was almost too late. I checked out where there were good slots on London Radio Stations to advertise the concert and I did the same with the national press to advertise the nationwide rides. Scripts and copy had to be written. Young and Rubicam dealt with this, Steve wouldn't agree with what they had written and so I had to smooth the way, being reminded that they were doing this f.o.c. The deadlines were stretched to the limits for us by the Independent and Capital Radio. I had to book a sound recording studio to do a tape for the radio slot — everyone was booked up. Time was running out but at the last minute one could squeeze us into a coffee break space and Dick Crane sped into the West End and dealt with this at a moment's notice. Capital Radio gave us their best rates, plus some free slots so that we would go out throughout the next day:

Saturday 19th September: it was vile weather; dark, dark grey and bucketing down with rain the whole day long. Despite that, down in Millwall Park, things were taking shape, the stage, scaffolding and railings were all up and I.T. were setting up their exhibition.

Back at the office, I was desperately trying to find a company that could print Flora banners that would be ready for display the following day. I'd told Flora I would do what I could to make sure they had banners at the concert. There aren't many companies operating on a Saturday but I found a company prepared to work throughout the night for us to get them done in time for the following morning.

It felt like the eve of something special; the atmosphere was so happy. There was a lovely feeling of everyone pulling together. The Bicycle Buskers, a band that I had asked to write a song for the riders, rang up. They were at their rehearsal studio and performed 'The Four Corners Song' down the phone; a very jolly reggae number with sax on the chorus. I put the loud speaker on the phone full blast so that everyone else on the office could hear and they all joined in the chorus in loud, happy out-of-tune voices.

The Colchester volunteers were in the office, sorting out packs of signs, refreshments and maps to take off to the various stop off points. Thousands of red, white and blue balloons, were being blown up, all with Four Corners logos on. Finally, very late that night photographs were taken of all the volunteers peeping out from mounds of balloons piled eight feet high. As the lights went out before we left, we could hear them popping and wondered how many would still be there in the morning.

Sunday 20th September: I would soon meet all the riders again. It felt strange after so long for this day to have finally arrived. Cathy had slept on my sofa the night before and we both got up at the crack of dawn, thankfully to clear blue skies. We arrived at Docklands at the same time as the World Bike Riders and hundreds of others were arriving on British soil at the coast. The balloons had survived and car loads of these were being delivered to volunteers who were tying them up in bunches all along the route of the Island Ride. Breakfast of piles of croissants and mugs of black coffee was devoured back at the office. In Colchester, the World Bike Riders would be sitting down to their breakfast at the Barracks with the Mayor and hundreds of cyclists.

After this it was go go go for cyclists and us at base. In the office, schedules were prepared and amended and Margaret Hansen together with Megan Jones, Anita and Steve from I.T. finalised press pack details. It was frantic. Then suddenly, we all stopped in our tracks — news came in of an accident. The World Bike Riders had been slip streaming, riding mudguard to mudguard, and had ended in a pile up. Julia of the African Trail team, having pedalled all those thousands of kilometres, suffered a cracked shoulder blade and had to complete the rest of the journey by car, with her arm in a sling.

By 1 pm the music was beginning in the Park with the Real Sounds of Africa. Shirley and Richard Spurgeon arrived at the office. Richard donned the Corporation mascot outfit — a crow suit — and leapt around the stage in between bands all afternoon; he clearly had a real talent for this! At 2 pm the first of the London cyclists doing the relay around the Isle of Dogs began, joined by two people on horses. The bands played on and at 3 pm news of the World Bike Riders progress was annouced — they were very close.

People were arriving on bikes having ridden in that day from Brighton, Kettering and Reading; those coming in from Cardiff had set off the previous day. The Town Cryer, Peter Moore, had arrived and was 'crying' and various celebrities arrived: Helen Shapiro, Tim Polly, Christina Dodwell and Nick Crane. Carmen Pryce arrived to co-host the concert with Richard Crane. Families and friends were excitedly gathering in the private enclosure behind the stage creating a nightmare for the security staff with their comings and goings. My brother Michael and sister Jane were there. It was lovely to have the family there. They'd brought fellow volunteer Clair, having organised their own Four Corners event in Northamptonshire that morning. There were several thousand people spread out across the park now and lots and lots of bicycles; it was one of the hottest days of the year.

4 pm arrived and so did the World Bike Riders. I rushed out to meet them via a backstage entrance — it felt weird. There was little time for hugs and camera men had followed me out — the riders had to pedal up and down for them. They looked very different people to the ones that had left; they were now blond, brown, extremely healthy and sparkling with some special kind of aura. I can ony imagine that I appeared the opposite to them! I don't think I was able to express how pleased I was to see them all. I was on automatic now. Everyone in the park was awaiting their arrival and I got on my bike and lead them round to the Park entrance. We made our way across the park, I was making Red Indian noises to clear a path and people peeled away to the side to let us through. The Chariots of Fire theme was booming and I should think for this moment we exceeded the maximum decibel levels. People were clapping and cheering and smiling — it went on and on. Once behind the stage, the bikes were relieved of the heavy panniers so each rider could take them up onto their shoulders as they walked on stage. A moving and quiet moment of reflection. There they all were. They'd made it! Suddenly Aidan whipped me up into his arms and ran back onto the stage with me; a sea of smiling faces eased forward towards the stage. T.V. cameras were running up and down just below us; Cathy brought on the bouquet of flowers and champagne, the latter was ceremoniously opened and shared with the audience and everyone joined in the Four Corners song.

There were lots of interviews with the press and photocalls and the hugs, kisses and joy was endless. Alex hugged the breath out of me and Steve Bonnist and I hugged each other too. A thousand balloons were released into the twilight as the last band, Loose Tubes played on and everyone, despite their various states of exhaustion danced in a delirium of happiness.

I thought that was the end, but little did I know what a lovely surprise there was for me around the corner. It appeared I had my very own Fairy God Person whose extreme kindness is worth extending the Four Corners story just that little bit further for. Maybe it will prove a wee breather from the hectic pace as well. Besides, it was yet a further example of the Four Corners spirit, and I should like whoever it was to know what pleasure they gave . . .

The Recovery

It was about 9.30 pm. I couldn't find my beautiful red mountain bike. Someone had stolen it from the concert enclosure which was a real shame, since it had seen me through the whole of Four Corners. Maybe there was some kind of message in this.

Michael, my brother was taking me home to my parents in Northamptonshire. We were driving out of Millwall Park when I spotted Andy. I stopped the car and leapt out and ran across and gave him a hug; the whole thing had come full circle from that original *Time Out* advertisement. I was just wearing my T-shirt and cycling shorts so we went back to my flat to grab a change of clothes. On the kitchen table there was a gorgeous scribbled note: '*Miranda* I just got back and I wanted to tell you how brilliant it all was and how fantastic you are for organising it all. You are a true *professional* and I feel so proud of you. I want you to know that there are few people with such conviction and courage as you have. You're a very special person and will always shine like a star.

'This week you must relax and switch off and gloat in the knowledge that whatever you do next cannot fail.

'Well well well done.

'Love Roger.'

Roger had been helping at the concert that day. He and his girlfriend Kate Benjamin had been staying with me towards the end of Four Corners and they had become valued friends. I was very touched and of course the words say a lot more about Roger and the person he is. That is what I mean when I spoke of the extreme support and love that came through Four Corners; the World Bike Riders were on the receiving end of this kind of thing too.

I got home after midnight. Mum was very excited. She'd seen Four Corners on the evening news and heard Radio Two and the World Service announce the return of the World Bike Riders. I was fed a huge supper and put to bed. The next morning I woke to hear my Mum on the phone to a friend 'We're so proud of her, I can't tell you . . .'. It was so nice of her but I felt a real fraud. It was over two years ago since it all began, I had had such high hopes and recalled our wish to double I.T.'s income of £2,000,000. I had made so many people believe so much was possible, and whilst there was much that was positive in the outcome, now the day after, I couldn't see it and felt a complete failure. Neither could I bring to mind the warnings I'd been given about post-event depression.

I was taken out for a celebratory dinner. My sister and brother had done brilliantly with their local ride in just a few weeks and I was feeling much more proud of their efforts than my own. All the family were chattering away but I couldn't enter into the spirit of things at all and I hardly spoke a word throughout the meal.

Back at the office Margaret, Cathy and Maria were holding the fort. Margaret had been chasing publicity. She must have been thrilled that all her hard work had paid off. There was a wonderful picture of Meryl in the *Times* in a tearful reunion with a close friend and there was other coverage in the *Guardian* and the *Mail*. Also she had organised radio interviews for the riders and they were whizzing round the country talking about their adventures and telling everyone how Flora had saved the day.

I returned three days later and that evening we had our last riders' meeting. Now they were back the fundraising was in their hands and the meeting was to plan the future and their fundraising and publicity efforts. There was also a post-mortem on how things could have been done better and how people at base could have done this and should have done that which was to be expected of course, though there was a feeling of exasperation from those around the table who didn't feel ready for criticism. It must have been very queer for the riders though, who were still very high after months of being the centre of attention; of having such a condensed life experience. Anyway, despite feeling low, I felt that we'd laid the foundations for a future Four Corners and just before the meeting adjourned, asked if anyone would be willing to help advise the next lot of riders. Whoops! It probably was a bit premature to mention this to them. 'You won't find sixteen saints like us again!' Julia said with everyone laughing.

If anyone of them was a saint, then it was Jo Doran. Without her support I think I would have been utterly disillusioned. She was the only one prepared to help me deal with the aftermath in the office at West India House. She spent the next three months planning and desperately attempting to get riders to go out and do fundraising talks.

Naturally, they were concentrating on picking up the threads of their own lives now. Debts had to be paid off, jobs found and flats hunted. They'd all given up a lot to take part in the event. Still it felt very strange to see them for a few fleeting moments when they came to collect all their photographs and press clippings from the office.

There was a party a week after the event with over half of the riders there. It was at my flat. The Bicycle Buskers appeared live in the corner of my front room and the Four Corners song was sung in unison. Volunteers were there too and the U.K. Co-ordinators came along from various parts of the country to meet those who had inspired their efforts. In fact the party was our way of saying thanks to them for all their inspiration and hard work. It was a very happy gathering.

This final part of Four Corners was odd; no target to work towards, no people around, just Jo and a range of secretaries Reed had supplied. There were hundreds and hundreds of thank you letters and chasing up of fundraising, but even eight hours a day was exhausting. Though the reduced hours and calm were much appreciated, I desperately needed a holiday but simply didn't have any money for it. In fact, having been on £50 a week for 2½ years I had debts to pay, with no immediate prospect of paying them off.

A few days after the party I returned home from work to Kate's greeting of 'Miranda, you've got an admirer!'. She handed me a mysterious package that she had found pushed through the door. 'MIRANDA' was written on it in bold red capitals. Someone had obviously hand delivered it. I opened it and pulled out a thick bunch of £10 notes . . . the two of us just looked at each other, our mouths and eyes wide open in astonishment. I counted it — £300! That's the amount that I had said to someone that I would need for a holiday, but I couldn't remember who! There was a note in the same pen in bold capitals on a scrap of paper. 'MIRANDA, HAPPY WELL-DESERVED HOLIDAY. MANY THANKS.' There was no signature. Who could it be?! I'll have to give this to I.T.!' I said. 'No you bloody well won't, you'll do as it says and take a holiday!' Kate told me in no uncertain terms 'That's for you' she added emphatically. I was deeply moved and spent the rest of the week going round saying 'people are just so wonderful' and wondering who on earth could have been that kind and generous. The World Bike Riders must have felt the same when they had been given hundreds of pounds (in one case £1,000) by individuals who wanted to help fund the subsistence costs of their trip. However, this person(s) wanted to remain anonymous.

It was difficult to take a holiday immediately, mainly because I felt guilty at leaving Jo. She hadn't had a break since her return. Anyway, a few weeks later she finally just told me to go. It was Friday morning 16th October. I would have to go somewhere I'd always wanted to go and I would have to let the whole thing just happen with the same spontaneity with which the money had been given. The following morning I booked a flight to Pisa in Italy. It was somewhere I'd wanted to go since I was 17 years old having read *Flowery Tuscany* by D. H. Lawrence, and more recently Laurie Lee's *Hills of Tuscany* in which he '... discovered Sienna hiding behind a bush ... all the green country rising and breaking round it ... '. That is where I would go to be replenished.

I packed my rucksack, and with a little phrase book arrived at Pisa the next day on Sunday afternoon with few plans other than to find my way to Sienna and find a place to stay when I got there. That was not to be, I missed my train by minutes and with the skies about to open, accepted an invitation to stay on the coast at Forte di Marmi. I'd decided to make few plans and to just allow things to happen, but then I thought it would be good to cycle through the Tuscany countryside doing a triangle of the ancient cities, Florence, Arezzo, Sienna. Florence was too enticing to cycle straight out of, and the bikes for rent were too heavy for such a journey so that plan went to the wall.

After three days of noise and pollution I went to a convent to ask if they could direct me to a monastery out in the country where I might escape the throngs of tourists and traffic. I was surprised to find the old nun had been expecting me! Earlier that day I had spoken to some Italians at lunch. The wife Anna Coleson was a 'Brumi'. When I asked for the bill I was told it had been paid! I had told them I was going to stay in a monastery and they had left a message at this one to invite me to go and stay with them but although amazingly kind I decided instead to pursue the peace and quiet of the convent. The nun couldn't speak a word of English and eyed me curiously over the top of her spectacles, chuckling at my terrible attempts at Italian, and finally suggested a convent that might take me in.

The following day I went to a closed convent of Saint Clarissa in a village between Sienna and Florence called San Casciano. We communicated through the bars which separated the sisters from the outside world, passing my phrase book back and forth. I was inspected by the Mother Superior who gave the okay for me to stay. They were somewhat perplexed as to what an English girl was doing alone in the sticks in Italy and not speaking the language. They sat me in the cool of the visitors room and gave me some milky coffee, cake and a bunch of grapes. These were delivered to me via a round wooden revolving cupboard to prevent direct contact. I decided that I should write a letter and explain how I came to be there; Four Corners, the magic money, and that I had come for a rest. I also added details about my family, since, if they could fit me into a family picture this would put them at ease. I did this in Italian (of sorts) with the use of my phrase book. It took ages and when I finished I placed the letter in the cupboard and pushed it round so the opening was back on their side of the bars. I then went off for a long walk.

When I returned that evening, there was a great flurry as three of the sisters appeared on the other side of the bars. One of them, Sister Gabriella was clutching my letter and Sister Maria had brought me supper. I think they thought that Four Corners was an act of God — maybe it was. They were wonderful, all smiles and enthusiasm and chattering; I couldn't understand a word but I thought that this was something of what the riders must have met with as they pedalled round the world. They also repeated all the English names of my five brothers and sisters and my niece and nephew. They must have learnt them by heart in my absence. They were a joy. It was like having two surrogate mothers fussing over me for the next couple of days.

I hadn't yet seen the Tuscany I had come to see. A lovely old Yorkshire couple I had met in Piazza Annunziata in Florence, Mr and Mrs Chapman, had told me I must go to a town called Greve in the heart of Chianti wine country. I made my way there by bus, up through luscious green country side and hills covered in vines heavy with grapes ripe for harvest. I sat next to an English girl on the bus called Belinda, and plotted with her, my return to Italy! Greve itself was lovely with its old cloistered Piazza. I immediately met some more English girls, Karen and Nadia who took me off to a bar and bought me a huge Ameretto. By coincidence they were living with a writer of Economic Philosophy, Edward Goodman, who had known Schumacher.

Accommodation was very expensive, but I'd managed to find somewhere to stay high up in the hills on Mont San Michele. Luckily I was still in Greve when I discovered in my pocket the key to the convent! I would have to return it straight away. San Casciano was miles away but I was told I could catch a bus leaving the town square at 2 o'clock. There was some time to wait so I sat in the empty square and read my book *Room with a View* by E. M. Forster.

After some time, I looked up from the pages and noticed a young man looking across the Piazza at me. I carried on reading. It was after 2 and no bus had arrived. I went across to the man and the girl he was with and asked them about the bus. It didn't stop in the square on Saturdays they said. I would have to get a bus to Florence for a connection. It would take ages. 'Oh no, I can't bear the thought of going to Florence again. Besides, I don't have time, someone is picking me up at 6 pm — they spoke a little English, but not enough to understand my rapid babble and I apologised for my rudeness.

The couple wandered off but returned to offer me a lift to San Casciano. I joined them and two others; his young brother Pietro and friend Federico who was at the wheel of a flash white volkswagon GTI. There followed a fast roller coaster ride round the twisting lanes and hills to the accompaniment of loud music — it was fun. The only Italian I had learnt was through writing the letter and so I told them in a mixture of English and phrase-book Italian my tale of how I came to be there. 'Magico eh?' I learnt that they were all architecture students. They waited for me outside the convent and took me all the way back as well. On the return journey, I was invited to tea by Michele, the young man, as where I had arranged to stay that night was within walking distance of his home. Together, we drove out of Greve to his house along a thin lane which wound round Mont San Michele — it was so beautiful — the Tuscany I had read about. We arrived at Michele's, a huge white-washed dilapidated green-shuttered rambling Tuscan farmhouse.

Inside Michele spread a map out on an old round table to show me how to reach the lodgings. 'Have you paid for this room?' he asked. I hadn't and he invited me to stay. I couldn't believe it. It seemed that wherever I went everything was being taken care of. Extraordinary. In fact, I had met with such hospitality that I was almost reluctant to accept yet more — but he had brought me to what appeared a rare and beautiful home. There was a strong sense of the generations that had lived there, including the current one. The square sitting room we were in with its dark, worn stone-tiled floor was furnished with lovely old shapes and was tinted with the warm hues of age. In the corner there was a sculpture of a mother giving birth to a child which added a slightly alternative air to the atmosphere.

I left him to study and went for a long walk through the woods. I felt I'd been brought to Paradise as I walked back and watched the sun setting over Chianti, silhouetting the surrounding mountains and hills. The villages and clutches of houses that had been prettily nestling in the afternoon light were fading as dusk fell. The light was heavenly, which in paintings I had thought an exaggeration, but here it was. I was joined by a couple of men who had been working on an old stone house. The three of us just stood in awe and chorused 'molto bello, molto molto bello . . .'. That's all I was capable of saying! They then took me to a spring and handed me a glass of delicious water.

Michele slowly ambled down the track to greet me. We wandered back to the house and on the way he said 'I would like to be able to spend some time with you but it is not possible because I have to study for exams.' I too wanted to get to know him, he was being so kind — he had such a lovely gentle face and manners that earlier that afternoon he had made me feel ashamed of my uptight city manners.

That evening, all of a sudden, I went down with a heavy cold, which left me with a pounding head; eyes and nose streaming. I'd not felt so ill since before Four Corners; I guess it was something to do with knowing that I couldn't get ill before, and now that I was relaxed, I could. I felt awful and was looked after for the next three days; hunting for fungi in the woods, collecting water from the spring, eating tasty Tuscan cooking, listening to music, sitting in the garden or . . . demonstrating the Hokey Cokey!

On the third day, I decided that I would most certainly have to leave because I was fast falling for Michele. Besides he was clearly a special person and I would rather preserve the friendship. I rang Nadia and Karen. They had told Edward about me and, though he himself would be away he had told them I could stay in his house and I was to join them the following evening.

The next day I woke feeling very much better. I couldn't quite pull myself away immediately and a large part of that sunny day was spent in Michele's company in a large airy room that had been the dovecot. It was high up at the top of the house and I just sat in an open arched window overlooking the Chianti Hills reading *The Prophet* by Kahlil Gibran, closing my eyes to absorb the last of the summer sun or simply staring out at the ravishing beauty. I'd been so starved of visual beauty over the last two years that I was just spellbound by it now. Michele continued with his studies.

As the afternoon wore on there was less studying and more talking — a process which required patience and understanding when you share so little of each other's language. It required a much greater sensitivity to expressions, intonation, gesticulations and eye contact too. Speech was slow and interspersed with leafing back and forth through a huge dog-eared family dictionary. This gentle pace felt wonderful after the high speed communications I'd been used to.

The discussion lead to what we wanted to do with our lives. Michele thought he might be an architect in the Third World. I told him about Four Corners, and how very difficult it was to do something you believed in, or to try and change things. He thought it was possible. His thinking, it seemed, had not yet been tainted by cynicism — I can't remember his exact words of broken English, but I can remember the feeling they conveyed; the way in which it stopped me in my tracks of pessimism; compelled me to listen; the hope that he gave me. My depression was lifting. I would have to find a way of cleansing myself of all the negative feeling that Four Corners had left me with.

Later that evening we shook hands and parted in Greve and I knew we would meet again . . .

Epilogue

Just before Christmas 1987, with the last load of boxes of office stuff packed into a waiting van, I closed the door on West India House for the last time. A quiet ending after all that had happened.

The last Four Corners bulletin had looked back at the beginning:–

'When Andy and I first began in May '85, there were no other fund-raising events known to ourselves of the scale we were planning. 'Live Aid' and 'Sport Aid' gave added inspiration as to what was possible ... The climate has changed dramatically since then and the competition has been fierce in the fund-raising market. This year there has hardly been a week without some major fund-raising event of some kind happening and it's brilliant that there is so much good will, but obviously the going has been much tougher than anticipated back in '85 ...'

Whilst packing up, I came across one of my Dad's letters in which he had proffered a few wise words of advice:–

'Every young person dreams dreams. Even your Ma and I did. Most big bubbles burst soonest. Some of the little ones last longer. But one lives on, cut down to size by the realities of existence. Whatever happens today the sun sets and tomorrow it will reappear. In the end Mum did not become Queen of England and I did not become the President of the US — Thank God!'

Maybe I should have heeded those words earlier than I did. However, even though our bubble seemed on the verge of bursting from time to time, it didn't, and the riders came home and there was much learnt. In fact, it had all been well worth it. Over 4,000 people got on their bikes on the 20th September, with the largest ride taking place in Leicester with 1,500 participants. Nearly £50,000 was donated to I.T. as a result of Four Corners with the UK Rides, 30 in all, bringing in the bulk of funds raised.

More than the fund-raising, I think the success of Four Corners was in generating so much publicity and goodwill for I.T. to millions of people around the world. Here in the UK exposure for the charity, obviously the most important, whilst not quite as extensive as envisaged, was substantial with both national and regional coverage in February before and after the final event. Once again, local events were extremely successful in this area, including radio and television coverage.

It was a struggle to get national media coverage though. Every telephone call Margaret made to the press was being met with the question of what celebrities we had taking part and in the end, we simply weren't able to get major celebrity participation. Also, we were trying to promote a charity event during a period of fund-raising fatigue and our message wasn't sensationalist enough for much of the media. It is a shame that coverage by the mass media could only be gained if the elements of starving children sensationalism were involved. In other countries however, it was more usual for the aims of Four Corners to be taken seriously. For another event, the dependency on press coverage should be achieved by a well-targeted, low-budget advertising campaign mounted well in advance in order to tap the potential participation of the millions of cyclists in this country. Unfortunately we simply didn't have the money for this.

Sadly the riders weren't able to exploit the most crucial period for publicity and fund-raising as was envisaged. They were to have given talks and slide presentations on their experience to schools and to other relevant groups up and down the country during the weeks following their return. Jo did the most and a few others did some. Maybe this should be budgetted for on another occasion whereby one person from each team is paid to spend around 3 to 4 months after the event organising and giving fund-raising talks, writing magazine articles and giving interviews of their experiences etc.

However, of those people it did touch, Four Corners inspired a passionate support for I.T. It had directly involved hundreds of people up and down this country, and world wide, thousands had helped. The response of those on the 20th September demonstrated this too with Sue Cussel up near Inverness, pregnant but still getting on her bike anyway. Then there was Tony Smith in Kettering who when his wheel buckled right at the beginning of the ride, completed the course by sharing a mate's bike alternately running and cycling every mile to complete the 20 mile route. And in Dewsbury Netty threatened to take her trousers off at the local pub if everyone didn't give her the money she needed to reach her target (maybe there's a novel fund-raising idea in there that

I.T. might like to take on board as a annual event!).

Someone whose views it changed completely and who became an eloquent advocate of I.T.'s work was my father. The local MP, the Rt. Hon. Roger Freeman presented me with a cheque for over £2,000 raised in Kettering and Dad was there extolling the virtues of I.T., giving clear examples of their work, adding, 'I know, I was in India, and these I.T. people have got it spot on'. The local journalist scribbled all this enthusiasm down. I smiled to myself at his change of stance. It was great that he had made the effort to inform himself so thoroughly and think beyond the 'condom' approach. I loved him for it and getting people to think like that was what Four Corners was all about.

I thought about continuing Four Corners as a regular event, since the ground work had been done and there was so much willingness by other organisers in the UK and other countries to build on what we had started — it seemed a crime to let all that go to waste. However, I decided that if it were to continue then it should be because others saw the immense potential it has to encompass and raise awareness of I.T. and other extremely urgent environmental issues.

I would strongly advise against the project being done again on a shoe string. The strains of doing something like Four Corners without cash backing are too immense and shouldn't be contemplated. Those involved at the outset should be kept to an absolute minimum. Two experienced people of kindred spirit and motivation, with a combination of a 'nothing's impossible' attitude, a deep commitment to the ideals and good levels of realism would be right, though hard to find! Responsibilities should be clarified from the outset. They should pin the concept down from the start and work out people and facility requirements, long term projections, budgets and produce a draft brochure and sponsorship proposal. The latter might be used to interest a professional sponsorship company to seek the financial backing necessary. It is a perfect vehicle for an international company to gain world-wide exposure and goodwill.

One of our mistakes was not to establish firmly what the I.T./Four Corners relationship was. We were an unpredictable animal and their support swung with our highs and lows. It was a first time for both of us and we obviously experienced difficulties. Naturally, with their extremely precious resources, they were not equipped to handle something of our size. Both of us had envisaged that Four Corners would get financial backing. In fact we added to the pressure that a small charity is already under, and by doing so added to pressure on individuals. However, much was learnt by both sides and certainly this has only added to the admiration that we have for their work. In fact, though this was by no means a direct aim of Four Corners, so much has been learnt by myself, the riders and some of the volunteers, that the true results of our involvement will only become apparent over many years. A course to have gained similar knowledge and experience would have run into £1000s and I think that there are many individuals who are eternally indebted to I.T. for providing the source of inspiration in the first place.

Volunteers were absolutely brilliant, and the first Four Corners could not have happened without their tremendous support and they will be vital to the success of another Four Corners. However, an event like this cannot be as dependent on volunteers as we were the first time round. Every pair of hands had to be put to good use and that could mean pushing a square shape into a round hole with people being put onto whatever had to be done without having the necessary skills to do it, myself included. As a result people were to tap their own potential beyond what they had thought themselves capable, which was a wonderful outcome. However, it makes for management nightmares with erratic time contribution, people going on holiday all at once and impossible communications; difficulties which could so easily kindle personality clashes.

Also, people's involvement in running the venture should bear relation to their input. If their time commitment only runs to a couple of days a week then their view of things cannot be sufficient to embrace the whole workings of the project and thus enable them to make a major input into how things are run. The latter can only be done by a full-time team heading up various areas of the project, working with volunteers whose ideas and input can be voiced at departmental meetings, the best of these ideas being incorporated into the overall plan via management meetings. This was how we attempted to operate, but with irregular turnout at meetings, it wasn't always successful. Also, the volunteers were put under unfair strain with much larger areas of responsibility than some of them could handle. Of course, my handling of the whole situation would have benefited from previous management experience.

I must add though, that female energy, stamina, courage, imagination and optimism should not be underestimated. I'm not suggesting for one moment that these aren't male qualities and I'm not necessarily speaking for myself, but the experience of Four Corners was that women had these things in abundance and it was just staggering at times. Women also have the good fortune to be able to let off steam more easily in the most natural way and I personally recommend taking yourself off and having a good cry when the going gets tough.

Done occasionally it's very cleansing and we should remember it's a human mechanism specifically for this very purpose.

I have rattled on about the difficulties encountered, perhaps too much in some areas, I hope not. However, these things will happen and far better that anyone contemplating anything like this doesn't go into it blindly. I hope this book goes some way to ensuring that the same mistakes aren't repeated, though, knowing what a fragile lot us human beings are, they will and new ones will arise. Future events can only be better though and the aims and joys of doing something like this are worth striving for. Perhaps Norman captured something of this when, on the shores of Lake Malawi, when he and Andy were playing chess in the last light of the setting sun, he said: 'You know, on this day, in this place, I honestly can't imagine anywhere else I'd rather be, or anything else I'd rather be doing. I wonder if I'll ever be able to say that again? Later when he recalled this, he added 'I've got Four Corners to thank for that experience.'

What really must continue is the UK Rides. Virtually all the Co-ordinators around the country said they would do them again if there was another Four Corners event. Whilst the efforts of the World Bike Riders served to provide great inspiration for these, Rifka and Liz in Brighton and Mary Gilbert in Bristol organised rides again this year. A lot of the local rides got off the ground using the guidelines that I have included in the appendix. Whether it be something that I.T. decides to co-ordinate, or whether people just 'get on their bikes' and decide to do it off their own backs, these are not that difficult and from all reports, a lot of fun was had in organising them ... and of course, cycling for I.T. is an ideal way to keep their coffers topped up — so keep the pedals turning and keep raising money for I.T.

As for the World Bike Riders, life goes on; Jo Doran I am full of admiration for as are many others. After the Four Corners office closed she took off on her own spending several months in Asia, which included learning more about I.T.'s work. She then went on to do an M.A. in Development Studies at the University of East Anglia. Meryl did a course in teaching English as a foreign language and now resides in Rome. Alex married Kim, whom he met in the USA whilst on Four Corners and has gone to live in America and is studying to become a physiotherapist. Thomas has gone on to Cambridge University, not to read engineering as planned, but anthropology. Nick and Kate Walker sensibly bought a home in Manchester before departure which is where they are now living, Nick as a landscape architect and Kate as a trainee mid-wife. Jane has returned to her job as an editor of technological publications and Pete Cogram has long since continued to do his photography. Julia Leeward has continued teaching and Willy Taylor is back in his old job as a maths lecturer. Andy Hansen spent a large part of 1987 utilising his experience on Four Corners to the benefit of Sport Aid as their Africa Co-ordinator. Norman Carr and Moira Poulton have become joint managers of Bike in Pimlico, (so you can expect expert advice and service if you go to them). Aidan, like Andy put his Four Corners experience to good use with Sport Aid. Rhoda went back to her original job of working with the Farnborough Airshow, though she has since returned to New Zealand. Adria decided not to return to the commercial world and has become a P.A. with V.S.O. and lucky is the person she works for. Sebastian Best, last but certainly not least (again!) is busily setting up his own photographic business and should you require your portrait picture taken or wedding photographs snapped then he comes highly recommended! And, on a lighter note, there are only 3 out of the whole bunch, who didn't start off with or find romance on the Four Corners!

As for myself, I shall be spending the next three years at University College London, who despite my only having 5 CSEs have given me a place to read anthropology and geography. There are three main reasons why I am doing this. Firstly, it would have been a great advantage to have had more knowledge of the development field whilst on Four Corners. Secondly, through I.T. I became very interested in the potential of the immense contribution of small communities in the Third World of maintaining a balanced ecology and lastly, the brain could do with some fine chiselling, perhaps to improve my critical powers and clarity of thought more than anything. This course will be of help in each of these areas and hopefully I will be able to continue in the development and environmental field in a useful capacity.

Finally, a quick return to Africa, where Julia and the team were faced with a barrage of questions from school children better versed in world issues than many back home. One child asked what Four Corners was contributing to world peace which the team were unable to answer at the time. However, there is a need for events like Four Corners and obviously others like Live Aid and Sport Aid (. . . and who is going to organise a world marathon street dance – very televisual?!) etc. Four Corners in particular captures the Small World theme, linking countries around the world and extending international unity and friendship at grass roots, contributing to an atmosphere in which war between nations is no longer an option. It would be great if that inspiring image of the Salt Tax March provided by the film 'Ghandi' could be transferred to Four Corners routes with thousands of people joining along the way on cycles. Maybe one day this will be realised. In fact, I'd like to see the wheels of Four Corners roll until the only interruptions in the routes are not caused by wars but just the world's seas.

In the meantime, there is much for us all to learn about working together to insure against the destruction of this beautiful planet of ours, but in attempting this, we would all do well do heed the words of Schumacher at the end of his book *Small is Beautiful*:-

> 'Everywhere people ask: "What can I actually do?" The answer is as simple as it is disconcerting: we can, each of us, work to put our own inner house in order. The guidance we need for this work cannot be found in science or technology, the value of which utterly depends on the ends they serve; but it can still be found in the traditional wisdom of mankind.'

This idea should be one that is embraced whether we intend organising a second Four Corners or just living life in general; on the other hand, I would say it is essential for anyone who contemplates this task to have his/her own house in order before they do so...

Appendix 1: Sponsors

A huge thank you is due to all our sponsors for their generosity, without their immense help the first Four Corners could not have happened:

London Docklands Developments Corporation (Main sponsor): supply of a fully equipped office and coverage of administrative expenses.

Flora Margarine: £15,000.

General Accident: comprehensive travel insurance for the riders plus final event insurance. Also £2,000 was donated by the G. A. Netherlands office for our Amsterdam activities.

TNT IPEC: courier services throughout U.S.A., Europe and U.K., £1,500, plus support vehicle.

Raleigh: 16 custom-built touring bicycles.

Biddle and Co.: legal services throughout existence of Four Corners.

Spicer and Oppenheim: accountancy and auditing services throughout existence of Four Corners.

Michael Peters and Partners: design of logo, marketing advice, artwork.

Kodak: supply and processing of all our film, both black and white and colour.

Bike: various equipment and accessories, logistical support, some building of bicycles.

Alpine Sports: 9 tents, 16 sleeping bags, 4 stoves, 16 sleeping mats.

BUPA: medical and fitness tests for all riders.

Young and Rubicam: consultancy services, support on advertising.

Reed Employment: secretarial support.

Bodyfit Clothing: specially designed cycle gear.

Burson–Marsteller: publicity consultants.

Garden House Press: printing.
Sprayway/Goretex: clothing.
Brook Street: secretarial support.
Thomas Cook: supported the African Trail with £2,000 plus publicity.

Other Commercial Sponsors: Nabisco, Barclays Bank, Sealink, Erpo, Wiggins Teape, Jockelson, Graphic Office Supplies, Olivetti, Carrati Sport, M. J. Horrigan Printers Ltd., Youth Hostel Association, Micronet, Peat Marwick McLintock, Sales and Marketing Initiatives, Accountancy Age, London Business School, Marriot Hotels, Presidential Nile Cruises, Youngs Cycles, Silya Line Ferries, Madison Cycles plc., Patagonia, Addition Ltd., Print Factory, Keith Johnson Photographic Limited, Lufthansa German Airlines, Standard Chartered Bank, Eagle Star Insurance, Master Press Printers, The Netherlands Board of Tourism, East and Central Business Machines, Northern and Shell, British Rail, British Telecom, August Martin, Mills and Allen, Lewis Machines, Ovendon Papers, Southern Publishing Company, Amstrad, B. C. A. Print and Design, Compass Colourprint, Metropolitan Security Services Limited, Falgate Ltd., Regional Poster Services, Premier Metropolis Printers, Capital Radio, Stanford Maps, Bencard, Johnson Progress, W. B. Pharmaceuticals, Mountain Equipment, Wexus International, Olympus Sports, Holland and Barratt, Spenco, Glaxo Laboratories, I. C. I. plc., Beecham Research, 3M Healthcare, Robinsons, The Welcome Foundation, Seton, Kirby-Warwick, Radio London, Duncan Flockast and Co., Smith Kline and French, Janssen Pharmaceuticals, Parke-Davis Research Lab., Boehringer Ingeheim, Rohan, C and A, K. Blythe (Optics) Ltd., Rothschild Bank, Brixton Cycles, Mountain Medicine Data Centre, P. Fixer Ltd., Robinsons, Ledesle Laboratories, Gold Cross, Merrel Dow Pharmaceuticals Ltd., Encounter Overland.

Our thanks also to the following organisations for their advice and support in the U.K. and along the routes: European Cyclists Federation, Friends of the Earth, Colchester Garrison, The London Cycle Campaign, Metropolitan Police, Band Aid, European Year of the Environment, Globetrotters, Royal Geographical Society, Cyclists Touring Club, United World Colleges, Council for World Citizenship, Commonwealth Linking Trust, Central Office of Information, British Councils, British High Commissions, British Embassies.

Equipment

Bikes: 16 lightweight touring bicycles were donated by Raleigh. These were tailor made for each rider by Gerald O'Donovan ('God' in the bicycle world) of the Raleigh Specialist Development Unit. They were assembled by BIKE in Pimlico.

Frames: Reynolds 531 'ST' tubing throughout. Double butted and LIGHT. The frames were individually sized ranging from 19″ (Rhoda) to 24.5″ (Andy). Sprayed in Raleigh Racing Team colours of pearl, red, blue and yellow. 'Braze-ons' include 2 x bottle cage bosses, gear cable guides, rear gear hangers, mudguards and courier bosses and cantilever brake bosses.

Wheels: Shimano off-road hubs with sealed bearings. Large Flange Shimano Deore XT hubs with solid axles. Designed for off-road use. Rims are Mavic Module 4, designed for tough conditions and to take wide tyres. Spokes will be 36, 4 cross. Tyres are specialized expedition and XK4 (Carrati Sports and BIKE supplied all the tyres for FOUR CORNERS).

Brakes: Shimano Deore XT Cantilevers with Shimano 600 brake levers.

Chainset: Shimano Biopace triple chainset with sealed bottom bracket. Biopace is a C. A. D. (computer-aided design) ellipitcal chainring, designed to maximise pedalling efficiency.

Freewheel: Shimano XT six speed block. Runs on sealed bearings. Designed for off-road use.

Changers: Shimano FD free changer with sealed pivots. Shimano 'Superplate' rear changer. Sealed pivots and a very long jockey cage are suited to wide ratios.

Saddles: What other than Brooks leather Professional.

Handlebars: Cinelli bars and stem.

Carriers: Blackburn alloy 'Low Riders' carriers at the front with 'Expedition' carriers for the rear.

Lights: Byka rechargeable dynamo system (supplied by Madison Cycles).

Tools and Spares: All provided by Bike Pimlico for the duration of the expedition.

Panniers: Karrimor Iberian front and rear panniers (provided by Karrimor at substantial discount).

Clothing: Bodyfit Cyclewear provided especially designed Four Corners cycle clothing and Sprayway/Goretex provided rainwear suits. Cycle and training shoes provided by Olympus Sports.

Camping Equipment: We found Alpine Sports to have one of the best ranges of camping equipment in London and they generously donated very high quality items such as: 3 x Phoenix 'Phreak' 2-man tents, 2 x Phoenix 'Phlighter' 1-man tents, 4 x North Face 'June Bug Alcove' 2-man tents; 16 x North Face 'Cats Meow' sleeping bags; 8 'Svea 123 climber' petrol stoves; 16 Karrimor 4-season vacuum expanded, closed-cell foam sleeping mats.

Other equipment taken includes maps, compasses, cycle repair kits, tools, 35 mm cameras, 4 Red Cross first aid kits, gifts (postcards, cigarettes, badges).

Innoculations/Health: You need to check these well in advance as some countries require a course of injections over a period of time. The following innoculations were recommended by the London School of Hygiene and Tropical Medicine which is where many of them went to get their jabs. Other went to the British Airways innoculation Centre in Regent Street, London, though you should be able to get these through your doctor.

Americas Route: Yellow fever, tetanus, cholera, polio, typhoid, rabies, hepatitus, malaria.

Asian Highway: Cholera, typhoid, rabies and malaria.

African Trail: Tetanus, cholera, yellow fever, typhoid, hepatitus, rabies.

Oriental Path: (to follow).

A wide range of medication and tablets were taken as recommended by our expedition medical advisor, Doctor John Lewellyn. This included 27,400 anti-malaria prophylactic tablets provided by Kirby-Warwick.

Each team took a supply of multi-vitamin tablets with them as well.

Appendix 2: Guidelines on Intellectual Property

In early 1986 when the project really seemed to be taking off with major sponsorship coming in and there was interest from film companies in covering the event, it appeared that there might be substantial income to be made by I.T. through 'intellectual property' (videos, book, articles, interviews, film etc). To ensure that there would be no overlap of interests between the charity and the riders, i.e. who was paid what, Riders Guidelines were drawn up. This was done over weeks and weeks of meetings with Riders, I.T. and Kim Walker, a solicitor from Biddle and Co., the firm of City Solicitors who were donating their services to us. These legal documents were signed by the riders before their departure and the charity Intermediate Technology. Certainly a lot of expeditions of whatever size are safeguarding themselves against any legal problems following their expeditions by drawing up similar documents.

Intermediate Technology
The Four Corners World Bike Ride ("the Project")

Guidelines on Intellectual Property

Introduction

This memorandum sets out, in Section B (Obligations), the way it is proposed to deal with the ownership of the various categories of "intellectual property" (categorised in paragraph 2 below) arising from the project, and the rights of ITDG and the Riders to exploit it.

Section A (Objectives) sets out the objectives of the Project and the guidelines; it is in the spirit of these that the obligations in Section B are to be read and understood.

The memorandum may appear rather "heavy" and legalistic. It must be appreciated, however, that the intellectual property which is the subject matter of this memorandum is crucial to the success of the Project, since it is through its exploitation that money and profile will be raised for ITDG. ITDG has a duty as a charity to ensure that the best possible use is made of this potentially valuable intellectual property, without being unfair to the Riders. Hence the need for this rather lengthy document.

A. OBJECTIVES

1. *General*
The main objectives of the Project are to raise *money* and *profile* for the concept of Intermediate Technology and in particular the charity Intermediate Technology Development Group ("ITDG").

Therefore the efforts of all participants in the Project need to be geared to those twin objectives.

Although it is hoped to raise funds for ITDG through sponsorship (firms and cyclists) and schools, it is also hoped to raise considerable money and profile in the period **after** the Riders have returned to the United Kingdom in about October 1987.

To do this successfully, ITDG and its subsidiary, Four Corners World Bike Ride Limited, will need to kindle the interest of the public in Intermediate Technology, the huge range of people and places the Riders will encounter and the experiences they will have during their travels from the four corners of the world.

2. *Methods*
It will therefore be essential to exploit the experiences of the Riders by making use of the following kinds of material which will arise out of the Project:

Category I
Written Word: Articles and features in newspapers, magazines, journals etc. Books about the Project.

Category II
Talks: Interviews (T.V., radio, newspapers). Talks, presentations etc. to live audiences.

Category III
Audio Medium: Audio tape.

Category IV
Visual Media: Film, video, photographs/slides.

3. *Reasons for this memorandum*
The main reason for this memorandum is to provide just and workable guidelines for all riders in the Four Corners World Bike Rider team (referred to in this memorandum as "Participants" or "Riders") in the area of exploitation of all the categories of media outlines above.

The memorandum will also operate as a legal document to the extent that it sets out who is to have the legal ownership of the copyright and other associated rights in the written, photographic and audio media set out above. ITDG and each Participant will be signing a letter indicating agreement with the contents of this memorandum and transferring (or granting exclusive rights in) the copyright in the media to ITDG on the conditions and for the periods of time specified below. *The contents of this memorandum will be legally binding on ITDG and each Participant.*

4. *The need for guidelines*
Guidelines are required because, in order to meet the main objectives, it is vital throughout the Project to have a co-ordinated and unified approach to the various media; in order to achieve that it is necessary to ensure that individual, unco-ordinated media initiatives do not arise out of misunderstanding or conflict of interest.

5. *Conflict of interest*
While it is apparent that all participants are highly motivated by the objectives of the Project, it is also understandable that certain of them will want to use the Project as some way of promoting their careers (e.g. the photographers in the team) or as a way of earning cash to survive in the period following the return to the U.K. until he/she gets employed or self-employed. The potential for conflict of interest between the Project and the individual Participants is therefore obvious.

6. *Specifics*
The approach below is conditioned by the following considerations:

1. Which components of intellectual property will bring in the highest return to ITDG in terms of profile and cash?

2. That the intellectual property would not exist unless the Four Corners Management Team had worked and planned for over a year to raise the support and cash to bring about the Project.

3. That the successful use of the intellectual property will not be possible without the benefit of ITDG's support and the support of commercial sponsors, P.R. firms etc.

4. The Participants may have an understandable wish to use some of the intellectual property arising from the Project either to promote their careers or

to raise cash to survive in the short term.

5. That the period following the return of the Riders is the key period in which to raise cash and profile for ITDG.

B. OBLIGATIONS

The obligations of Participants and ITDG are as follows:

1. General Obligations

Compliance with the spirit of this memorandum

1.1 It is agreed that, since it is not possible to cover in a written document the multitude of situations which may arise in relation to intellectual property, the Participants and ITDG will comply with the spirit and not just the letter of this memorandum.

Notification of ITDG Press Officer and Participants

1.2 The Participants will notify the ITDG Press Officer as far as possible in advance before making any use (other than domestic or private use) in any part of the world of any material (including the giving of talks etc.) referred to in this memorandum and relating ITDG or the Project and will comply fully with all reasonable requirements of the ITDG Press Officer as to alterations, editing etc. to be made to such material or the re-scheduling of the publication of material or the giving of talks. ITDG will where possible notify each Participant of all articles or other written material relating to the Project of which it is aware in which that Participant is to be referred to personally.

1.3 These obligations will subsist until 1st October 1990. The obligation to notify ITDG is to prevent ITDG's reputation or effectiveness being harmed through detrimental use being made (accidentally or deliberately) of material arising out of the Project.

Full accountability and accessibility of material

1.4 The Participants will account fully to ITDG for all fees and donations received directly or indirectly through participation in the Project. The right to such fees and donations is dealt with under each category heading below.

Full participation

1.6 Every Participant will participate fully in the spirit of the Project and will do his/her utmost to achieve the objectives of the Project outlined in the first part of this memorandum.

Specific Obligations

Category 1 (Written word)

2. *Diaries

Log

2.1 Each group of Riders will keep a log-type diary recording accurately the statistical and geographical details of the Ride such as distance travelled per day, place reached at the end of each day and route followed.

Personal diaries
2.2 Each Rider will also keep a personal diary (whether in the form of a conventional book-type diary or in the form of letter (e.g. to the ITDG Press Officer) recording his/her experiences en route and impressions of the Rider, fellow Riders, the places visited and people encountered. Each of the Riders will do his/her best to ensure that the contents of the diary are the kind which will be of interest to the public.

Availability of diaries
2.3 Both the log-type diary and the personal diaries will be made available to ITDG regularly in accordance with the procedures agreed in advance with the ITDG Press Officer. This is subject to paragraph 10 below (Privacy and Confidentiality).

Rights to diaries
2.4 Each Rider will grant to ITDG exclusive rights in his/her diary for a period beginning on the date of his/her departure from the U.K. and ending on 1st October 1988. After that date, rights in the contents of the diaries will revert to the Riders, subject to ITDG retaining a non-exclusive right to the contents after that date. The period to 1st October 1988 coincides with the period during which it is expected that ITDG wil be producing one or more books on the Project and, by obtaining exclusive rights, ITDG will be entitled to use extracts from the diaries in such book(s) and for other purposes connected with ITDG. Each Rider must recognise that, by granting exclusive rights, he/she will be unable to use extracts from the diaries for his/her own purposes without the express agreement of ITDG's Press Officer. The prohibition is only on quoting the diaries or extracts from them; there is of course nothing to stop the Riders writing or talking about their experience on the Ride, provided the rest of this memorandum is complied with.

3.2 All articles written by Participants (or with their co-operation) with a view to publication following the return of the Riders to the U.K. but before 1st October 1988 in the national or regional press (e.g. the Yorkshire Post or the London Standard) or in magazines, journals etc. with a national or regional circulation will be provided in advance to the ITDG Press Officer who will have the right, following consultation with the author of the article in question, to edit the article, if agreement cannot be reached on the substance of the article, the ITDG Press Officer will have the right to require that it will not be submitted for publication.

3.3 Articles written following the return of the Riders to the U.K. but before 1st October 1988 by Participants (or with their co-operation) for publication in the "local" or "provincial" press will be submitted prior to publication to the ITDG Press Officer for his information. The decision of the ITDG Press Officer as to whether press etc. is "local" or "provincial" or not will be conclusive.

3.4 These obligations in paragraphs 3.1 and 3.2 will not affect the general obligations of the Participants to make full notification to the ITDG Press Officer in accordance with paragraph 1.2 above.

Remuneration

3.5 Each Participant will be entitled to receive up to the first £100 (excluding payments of expenses to the Participants) of all fees (which includes any syndication fees) arising out of articles for which he is responsible. All donations to the Project or ITDG will be payable to ITDG. The right to any fees over £100 will be negotiated with ITDG. Where more than one Participant is responsible for any article, the split of £100 between the Participants will be a matter for negotiations between them.

Meaning of "press" and "articles"

3.5 In this paragraph 3, "press" includes journals, magazines and other periodicals and "articles" includes interviews which result in articles in the

Ownership

3.6 All rights in any article will belong to ITDG until 1st October 1988 when ITDG will grant a non-exclusive right to the author to use all or part of the article for his/her own proper purposes. Notwithstanding this, it is expressly agreed that every Participant will notify the ITDG Press Officer in advance of any negotiations before 1st October 1988 with any section of the press relating to the rights in articles and ITDG will have an absolute right to prohibit a Participant from dealing in such rights.

4. ***Books**

Publication

4.1 In order to maximise the impact of the official books which ITDG intends to arrange following the return of the Riders to the U.K.:

(a) no Participant may engage before 1st April 1988 in discussions or negotiations on contracts with publishers for the publication of a book relating to the Project or ITDG without the express written consent of the ITDG Press Officer; and

(b) no book written by a Participant or with his co-operation (for example, with the assistance of a "ghost-writer") and relating to the Project of ITDG may be publicised or published before the date two years after the publication of the first book arranged by ITDG or 1st October 1992 (whichever is the earlier) without the prior written consent of the ITDG Press Officer.

Ownership of copyright

4.2 Subject to any prior rights of the publisher, the copyright of any book the publication of which is arranged by ITDG will belong to ITDG. Notwithstanding anything else in this memorandum but subject to paragraph 10 below (privacy and confidentiality), any Participant who is the owner of any material mentioned in this memorandum and relating to the Project and/or ITDG will grant ITDG the right to reproduce such material (e.g. extracts from diaries, photographs etc.) in any such book.

Category II (Talks)

5. ***Interviews, talks and appearances on television and radio**

Requirement for approval

5.1 All proposals to give interviews, talks and appearances for broadcast on T.V. or radio will be notified as far as possible in advance to the ITDG Press Officer. Where such interviews, talks and appearances are proposed to be broadcast before 1st October 1988, the ITDG Press Officer will have the right, following consultation with the Participant in question, to require that the interview, talk or appearance should not take place or should take place at a different time or in a different locality.

5.2 The obligation in paragraph 5.1 will not affect the general obligations of the Participants to make full notification to the ITDG Press Officer in accordance with paragraph 1.2 above.

Remuneration

5.3 Fees (including any syndication fees) arising out of interviews, talks or appearances for broadcast will be payable first to each Participant involved in such interview etc. (subject to a maximum of £100 per Participant (excluding expenses). The balance (if any) will be split by negotiation between ITDG and the Participant(s). All payments for expenses will be payable to the Participants and all donations to the Project or ITDG will be payable to ITDG.

6. ***Talks to live audiences**

Requirements to inform ITDG

6.1 The ITDG Press Officer is to be informed in advance of any talks proposed to be given.

6.2 He will have the right to require that such talks be not given or be re-scheduled or given elsewhere where in his reasonable opinion it would conflict detrimentally with another existing event connected with the Project. All fees and remuneration for such talks shall be payable to the Participant(s) concerned (subject to a limit of £100 (excluding expenses) per Participant, above which the balance will be payable to ITDG) and all donations from the audience will be payable to ITDG.

Appearance fees

6.3 If any "appearance fees" are received by a Participant before 1st October 1988, the first £100 may be retained by him/her and any balance will be subject to negotiation with ITDG. After 1st October 1988, all appearance fees will be receivable by the Participant.

Category III (Audio Medium)

7. ***Audio recording tape**

7.1 All rights in any audio tape relating to the project or ITDG will belong exclusively to ITDG for a period until 1st October 1988. ITDG shall be entitled to permit the maker of the tape to take copies for his/her own private use.

7.2 All income received directly or indirectly in connection with the audio tape will be payable to ITDG.

73. After 1st October 1988, physical possession of all tapes will revert to the maker of the tape, subject to ITDG's right to retain and use a copy for its own purposes.

Category IV (Visual Media)

8. ***Films and video**

Ownership

8.1 All rights in any films and video tape arising directly or indirectly out of the Project will belong wholly and exclusively to ITDG which may at any time permit a Participant to take a copy for his/her own private use.

8.2 All income received directly or indirectly through the use of such film or video tape shall be payable to ITDG.

9. ***Still photographs/transparencies etc**

Copyright

9.1 Copyright in photographs belongs automatically in law to the person who owns the material on which a photograph is processed. Usually this will be the negative. If an instant camera is used, then the owner of the roll of film would be the owner of the copyright in the photograph. The owner of the copyright is *not* necessarily the person who takes the photograph.

9.2 Where the owner of the copyright is a Participant, he/she will transfer copyright in all still photographs, negatives and transparencies relating to the Project or ITDG ("photographic material") to ITDG until 1st April 1988. Until that date, no photographic material may be used for any purpose (except private, domestic purposes unconnected with ITDG or the Project) without the express written consent of the ITDG Press Officer. For the avoidance of doubt, it is agreed that Participants may arrange to have film developed abroad during the ride, provided all photographic material is returned to ITDG in accordance with paragraph 9 and complied with. For example, no photograph developed abroad may be published in local newspapers without the consent of the ITDG Press Officer, but such photographs may be used for private, domestic purposes unconnected with ITDG or the Project.

Income

9.3 Any income from the use of photographic material arising before 1st April 1988 will be payable to ITDG (subject to the rights of Participants giving talks (see paragraph 3 above) to receive fees in accordance with those paragraphs). In the case of income arising before 1st October 1988 from exhibitions mounted by a Participant, income shall be payable first to the Participant(s) involved, subject to a limit of £100 per Participant. Any balance will be split between the Participant(s) concerned and ITDG by negotiation. All donations to be the Project or ITDG will be payable to ITDG.

Compliance with agreed procedures

9.4 Each Participant will comply with the procedures agreed with the ITDG Press Officer regarding the logging and marking of films and their despatch to the U.K.

Copies

9.5 ITDG may at its discretion sell a copy of any photographic material at cost to any Participant or make available to any Participant original negatives or transparencies for copying prior to 1st April 1988 on the strict understanding that such photographic material may only be used for personal, domestic unconnected with ITDG or the Project unless (before 1st April 1988), the written consent of the Photographer (as defined in paragraph 9.6 below) is obtained.

Transfer of Copyright

9.6 On 1st April 1988, the copyright of all photographic material will revert or be transferred to the originator of such photographic material ("the Photographer") without prejudice to any other rights of ITDG contained in this memorandum (e.g. to publish photographic material in a book). Following the date, photographic material will be held as follows:

(a) ITDG will be granted a non-exclusive licence (with a right to sub-licence) by the copyright owner to use all photographic material for its own proper purposes.

(b) ITDG will make duplicates and black and white prints of the photographic material it wishes to retain and return the originals to the Photographer.

(c) ITDG will transfer the physical possession of all photographic material it has no further use for to the Photographer or a person nominated by him.

(d) Provided the Photographer in question agrees and the rest of this memorandum is complied with, any Participant will (upon giving reasonable notice to ITDG) have full and free access at any time to any of the photographic material retained by ITDG.

**Miscellaneous*

10. Privacy and Confidentiality

10.1 If, in the genuine and honest opinion of the Participant concerned, an entry in his/her diary or a photograph taken by him/her or relating to him/her is so private or confidential in its nature as to be unsuitable for use other than private or domestic purposes, the Participant concerned will arrange for such diary entry either to be clearly marked "private and confidential" or to be placed in a sealed envelope and clearly marked "private and confidential — not be opened except by (Name or Rider or other)" and addressed "c/o ITDG Press Officer". ITDG agrees to comply with any such instructions. Similar arrangements will be made (e.g. by marking the photograph log book) to notify ITDG of the private and confidential nature of the photograph.

10.2 No diary marked "private and confidential" may be read other than by the ITDG Press Officer and the Four Corners Co-ordinator without prior written consent of the Participant responsible for the diary. This does not apply to the log-type diary to be produced by each group of riders, nor to private and confidential material in sealed envelopes (in which case ITDG will comply with all instructions marked on the envelope regarding restrictions on access).

10.3 ITDG agrees to procure that all such private and confidential diary entries or photographs are not published in any way without the express written consent of the Participant concerned.

11. Use of material

ITDG agrees that it will not use any material arising out of the Project for any purposes whatsoever except to further the objectives of the Project as outlined in this memorandum.

12. Defamation

Nothing in this memorandum is to be construed as expressly or impliedly authorising the publication of defamatory material.

13. Consent

Where in this memorandum the consent, approval or authorisation of the ITDG Press Officer or of the ITDG or any Participant is required, such consent, approval or authorisation will not be unreasonably withheld.

14. Keeping of records

ITDG agrees to keep full and accurate written records of amounts, sources and other relevant details of all money received through the exploitation of the material referred to in this memorandum. ITDG agrees to grant to any Participant the right to inspect such records, upon him/her giving ITDG reasonable notice of his/her intention to do so.

15. Disputes or grievances

Any dispute or grievances between any of the parties referred to in this memorandum which relates to any of the matters set out in this memorandum will be referred (unless otherwise agreed by those in dispute/aggrieved) to the board of directors for the time being of Four Corners World Bike Ride Limited who shall appoint a panel of two of their number to adjudicate in the dispute or settle the grievance. Such panel shall give a fair hearing to the parties in dispute/aggrieved and the decision of the panel shall be final and binding on all concerned, except that the parties shall not be prevented from disputing such decision in a court of law.

16. Headings

The headings in this memorandum are for ease of reference only and are not intended to affect its construction.

17. Governing Law

The memorandum will be governed by and construed in accordance with the laws of England.

ENDS

These guidelines proved absolutely invaluable when one of the riders had to return home during the course of the ride. However, it was following the event that they were most used. I.T. and riders, were to fully exploit the ride for publicity purposes, and subsequently there would be substantial 'intellectual property'. Whilst substantial however, it was not of the scale envisaged by both parties, and as such both charity and the rides in the main, got on with other things.

Hopefully this book will do something to raise awareness of I.T. and, whilst I have received a fee for writing it, anything that is received in royalties beyond this figure, will go directly to ITDG.

Appendix 3: Fundraising in the U.K.

The following guidelines got many of the U.K. bike rides off the ground and should contain plenty of ideas for any would-be fundraisers or sponsored bike ride organisers doing things locally.

FOUR CORNERS (GREAT BRITAIN)

Co-ordination Team Guidelines

Four Corners Great Britain

Introduction

On May 25th last year, all over Great Britain people took to the streets and ran for Africa. This year it is the turn of the cycle and for everyone to 'Get on their bikes' for Intermediate Technology, a charity helping the Third World help itself, not just in Africa, but in all FOUR CORNERS of the Earth.

To this end, four teams of cyclists have been riding from Four Corners of the world since September 1986 to complete their journeys, totalling 30,000 miles! This massive ride, taking in areas where Intermediate Technology operates, is a demonstration of their immense commitment to *long term* help for the Third World. Intermediate Technology's approach has been hailed as the best way of combating famine and poverty and for this excellent cause, we want everyone to support the World Bike Riders and get on their bikes!

Objectives of FOUR CORNERS

- TO PROMOTE THE WORK OF INTERMEDIATE TECHNOLOGY AND THE IDEAS THAT LIE BEHIND THE CHARITY
- TO HELP RAISE £10 MILLION FOR THEIR WORK IN LONG TERM DEVELOPMENT IN THE THIRD WORLD

As a British-based charity, the main area of raising funds and public awareness will take place in this country. Therefore, it is vital that we have local organised committees and teams of people working to these ends.

How Money Will Be Raised

Money will be raised through:

- locally organised sponsored bike rides taking place up and down the country
- sale of T-shirts and Sweatshirts
- donations from the general public

How Public Awareness Will be Raised

Public awareness will be raised through the publicity generated at national level by the four teams of cyclists riding in from the four corners of the earth. This will mount up as they are joined by thousands of cyclists as they get close to completing their rides, a staggering 30,000 miles! On the weekend of 18th September, the 'Amsterdam to London Ride' will create a crescendo as all four teams come together for the final leg of the journey to London. There has been a fantastic response in Holland and with 11 million cyclists in that country, this promises to be a huge challenge to Great Britain where there are a mere 20 million bicycles — such potential! I hope you won't miss out on 20th September when everyone gets on their bike to support FOUR CORNERS in its effort to HELP THE THIRD WORLD HELP ITSELF.

The United Kingdom Rides

Here in the U.K. there has been a very enthusiastic response from cyclists wanting to participate in sponsored rides in Sunday 20th in what will be the greatest day of cycling ever! There will be a choice of three rides:

- The local ROUND TOWN RIDE of approximately 25 miles
- The BIG RIDE to London to greet the four teams as they complete their awesome journeys
- The AMSTERDAM TO LONDON RIDE taking all weekend and with only limited spaces

More detailed information about the logistics of organising a ride will be given in the next set of guidelines.

These first set of guidelines are to outline ways in which you can support FOUR CORNERS in your area. Not everyone can ride 30,000 miles, but just about anyone who owns a bike can manage 25 miles. We need local organisers to set up and publicise sponsored rides locally, getting as great a participation as possible (in their thousands if you think you can manage it!). Whatever the scale of activities you plan, I hope these guidelines are of assistance in helping you make it a great success for an extremely worthwhile cause. Best of luck!

The People Needed

Setting up a Co-ordinating Team in Your Area

WE NEED YOU!

You will need people to make FOUR CORNERS as successful as possible for INTERMEDIATE TECHNOLOGY. In fact, you will need as much help as

you can get but first you will need to set up a Co-ordinating Team for your city/ town of at least four people each with specific tasks covering:
— Overall Co-ordination
— Route Planning
— Administration
— Publicity
(Part 2 covers more specific tasks within these areas)

Further to this, you will need to get lots of volunteers to cover more general areas such as sticking up posters and stuffing envelopes.

Recruitment Drive
We will of course put you in touch with people from your area who have written to us direct. When I was trying to find World Bike Riders, however, I had great fun stopping people on their bicycles and asking them if they would like to ride round the world! So why not amble up to people on bicycles in your area and pop the question "Would you like to become involved in the biggest bike ride the world has ever seen?!". You might get some funny reactions, but I got some of the keenest people through this method! A more conventional approach is to put up posters (see enclosed) in newsagents, bicycle shops, cafes, colleges etc, which can be very successful too. You should be able to get your local paper to do an article stressing the need for local assistance.

Introductory Meeting
This is only a suggestion that worked very well for us. I noted names and addresses of all those interested and invited them to an Introductory Meeting. This is much easier than telling people over and over again what FOUR CORNERS is and what you want them to do. Maybe this could be organised using a local college hall or depending on the size of the gathering, it could be very informal and friendly round the kitchen table! Whatever, it does save time informing everyone of what you are up to and gets all the questions answered all in one. It also gives up an opportunity to ensure that everyone is well aware of the commitment needed and no-one who is serious about an involvement will mind how often this is stressed.

Delegation of Tasks
I have found myself at times snowed under with everything from route planning to typing to doing press releases and not doing any of it well. It is much better when people are putting their energy into what they are good at and carrying out specific tasks. You will probably also find yourself doing all sorts of things out of necessity. It is better though to find people with relevant skills, someone who can do all the typing, who has access to photocopying and office facilities, someone who is good at organising the local rides etc. Seek local expertise and advice — people are only too willing to help.

Local Support

Company Sponsorship
Look at what needs you might have and list these. For example, a major requirement will be photocopying and printing. Approach the local printers

and offer them advertising on any material they produce. In fact, this is something you can try and incorporate into any local news articles, asking local companies for their support, whether it be to cover the costs of mail or a few telephone calls. In fact, we all paid for this out of our own pockets before we got the office in Docklands, but, nevertheless, it's worth trying to get this covered if you can.

Other Support

To get further participation in the final rides to raise funds for Intermediate Technology, ask anyone and everyone, making approaches to:

— Local cycling organisations
— Friends of the Earth Groups
— Youth Hostel Associations
— Local Youth Groups
— Universities, colleges and schools
— Local Fire Brigade
— Local Police Force
— Nurses and Doctors and local hospitals
— Companies who can organise whole teams with the sponsorship of the work force

Publicity

The Rides

Publicity is absolutely vital to the success of FOUR CORNERS. Here in London we will concentrate on nationwide publicity. But the local co-ordination teams will be responsible for generating local publicity letting people know about local rides, where they will begin and what time. Press briefings will be sent from London, with details about the charity and FOUR CORNERS, and local information should be built into these. Let as many people know about Intermediate Technology and raising money for them as possible. Ways in which you can do this are:

— Put up posters in cycle shops, cafes, schools, colleges, youth clubs, churches, newsagents, libraries, Post Offices etc.
— Contact the local papers, radio and television and tell them all about FOUR CORNERS in your area

Fundraising

Further details on collection, accounting and delivery of funds will be included in the second set of guidelines. In the meantime you might put up a countdown map of the world placed strategically with collection boxes, showing the riders progress. Good places for these would be schools (get them to have a fundraising target), shopping centres, pubs etc.

Intermediate Technology

Intermediate Technology is the inspiration and heart of FOUR CORNERS and it is very important that you spread the message of their work and ideas.

Their resources are extremely low (hence the need for an event like FOUR CORNERS!) so they will only be able to supply a minimum of literature. However, their annual report should give sufficient background to enable you to speak confidently about their work.

Should you have further questions or need more information on Intermediate Technology, contact Steve Bonnist, the Press Officer at Intermediate Technology Development Group.

For collection boxes contact Francis Carroll, Fundraising Manager.

PART 2

Roles of the Co-ordinating Team

It is important to give people specific tasks relevant to their individual skills and qualities. However, in view of the limitations of lack of money and time to recruit precisely the right people, you may find yourself developing new skills all the time.

Co-ordinator

Someone must have overall responsibility for FOUR CORNERS in his/her county/city/town. However, with regard to very major decisions, these will need to be taken with London.

They will be in charge of management of all functions with the aim of achieving maximum fundraising and publicity for FOUR CORNERS and INTERMEDIATE TECHNOLOGY in their area.

They will need to:

— plan and schedule priorities
— establish a permanent base and contact address
— form the Co-ordinating Team
— set and delegate tasks
— ensure the effective flow of communications between London and their base
— ensure there are enough people to carry out the tasks
— be responsible for the channelling of funds back to Intermediate Technology
— liaise with organisers in other towns/villages in your region

Secretary

It is a great strength to have an organised support system, someone who is responsible for:

— typing
— filing
— arranging team meetings (weekly/fortnightly)
— writing up action notes of meetings

Routes Planner

It would be useful if this person had a knowledge of long distance cycling as they oversee all to do with route planning. We may be able to recommend the best cycling routes in your area. Their tasks will involve:

— planning the route to London to be timed to arrive in London on Sunday September 20th
— planning the 25 mile circular route around the city/town
— organising the marshalling of rides/events and supplying refreshment points (encourage the support of W.I. and scouts for this)
— getting out on the road and checking the routes
— securing permission and assistance from the police and relevant authorities for the ride to take place
— organise BMX displays to coincide with the ride if possible

Publicity and Fundraising Officer

The publicity is obviously vital to the success of the fundraising and spreading a greater awareness of the work of INTERMEDIATE TECHNOLOGY. He/she would need to be well briefed on both the charity and FOUR CORNERS. They would be responsible for handling the following:

— getting coverage in local press, radio and television
— writing press releases on local activities
— appropriate insertion of information into promotional material for local purposes
— distribution of publicity material; leaflets, posters and sponsorship forms etc
— encouraging local companies to display FOUR CORNERS material, maps of the routes etc and do collections
— merchandise distribution
— encouraging local companies to have teams on the ride
— contacting local organisations, schools, women's groups, scouts, churches etc to ask them to participate in the fundraising

U.K. Co-ordinators Guidelines Two

When Dick Crane came on board promoting Four Corners around the U.K. he and I produced the second set of guidelines. I've not included the full set since they are lengthy and tend to duplicate information that has already been given. The previous summer Dick had worked on another fundraising bike ride for I.T. 'Life Ride', so he had plenty of first hand experience of the logistics of organising rides. He's ploughed lots of information back into these guidelines which you will find below. Also, there's some more 'official stuff' on publicity.

Going Concrete

By the end of the second week you should have "gone concrete" so that you can type out a single A4 sheet of information about the ride telling anyone everything they need to know:

1. The contact name and address and telephone number for all further information (this will probably be your home address and telephone number, sometimes employers are happy for you to use your work number. Whatever you choose, it must be constant all the time up until the 20th September and preferably for several weeks after that. (People file the number away and pull it out when something jolts the memory.)

2. The date is Sunday 20th September — the time at which your ride should start (we suggest 2 pm to coincide with the beginning of the main ride in London, so all the rides are happening simultaneously).

3. Headquarters address at FOUR CORNERS, West India House, Millwall Dock, London E14 9TJ. Head Organiser Miranda Spitteler.

4. The route, especially the start and finish points (see below)

5. Names of principal local sponsors

6. If possible, names of a local celebrity, the Mayor, MP or Chairman of a local large company who will join in the ride or will be at the start.

Deciding on the Route(s)

Planning a route is often considered, like the search for the Holy Grail, to be a major undertaking of infinite duration. But in reality it is a case of arriving quickly and smoothly at a reasonable compromise. No doubt your home area, like all areas of Britain, has countless places of interest; be they beauty spots, historic houses, monuments or relics of bygone ages or steep hills. Your job is not to find a route which includes all of them, but to be able to cycle past a few. Whilst chatting about the ride with other locals, you will discover that whatever route you have chosen you will be passing many places of interest new to you. Remember that the success of your ride depends on the fun the riders themselves bring such as fancy dress or a picnic en route.

You might think of getting one of your local big parks (through local authority) to give permission for a kids ride. This could be a few circuits around the park amounting to about 15 miles. This is a good option because it will be safer for youngsters; there being no cars, and this will be popular with the police.

It is important to decide fairly quickly on the specific route to be taken and the start and finish points because until you have that you will find you have difficulty persuading your press, sponsors and supporters that you really mean business. As soon as you have fixed your route, you can send out the info to your local press and get them to print a copy of the route and entry details (more on this under press and publicity).

A few thoughts about the route:

1. Start somewhere well-known and easy-of-access where there is plenty of spare space for car-parking and for people to wander around and sit about having picnics. Make sure you've seen similar-sized gatherings of people there before because if that is the case then the authorities or owners will almost certainly give you permission also.

2. Finish somewhere well-known, if at all possible in the same place as the start.

3. After the start, get out as directly as possible to open countryside.

4. Try to include in the route: one steep hill (so people have a good excuse to get off and walk!), or more local scenic spots for lovely view and stopping to eat sandwiches, at least one historic place, a pretty village and how about for contrast, a nice big factory or industrial area.

5. We're trying to get everyone to organise marathon-distance rides, i.e. 26.2 miles. The exact distance doesn't matter too much, or if you feel a different distance would fit better locally then — go for it!

6. If at all possible it would be nice to arrange the route into a square shape — four corners — get it?!!

7. Try to keep off main roads, i.e. A class roads and dual carriageways. Roundabouts can be quite dangerous for big groups of cyclists because car drivers like to go around them fast. Routes with traffic lights are much better. Even the tiniest lanes are good for cyclists, do however try to keep off dirt tracks because many cyclists think these damage or dirty their bikes. Do not do too many turns in quick succession or else all your cyclists will get lost.

Permission — Police and Local Council

Before you tell the press about your FOUR CORNERS ride you must start the ball rolling on red tape. Go to your local police station or ring them up to ask who you go to to get permission for a big bike ride on your route (see other info above). The first people you see will probably tell you it can't be done — but don't be put off because eventually, maybe 3 or 4 weeks, they'll either give you permission for that route more-or-less as you proposed so that it accords with the highways code and doesn't cause an obstruction to other road users.

If your first proposal is absolutely impossible, you'll usually find they'll help you fix a better route. Once you've got this sorted out, you let the local press know about the "NEW IMPROVED FOUR CORNERS ROUTE — MODIFIED FOR YOUR SAFETY AND CONVENIENCE!".

The rules regarding who's allowed to organise what where and how vary from place to place. Events which are not very big (e.g. cyclists keeping to the Highway Code and not riding more than two abreast) usually don't need special permission but it is always best to inform your local services as soon as possible. You ask their advice — they are always very helpful — you don't give them a fait-a-compli.

Variations of Rides/Events

You might like to organise other sorts of FOUR CORNERS rides or events. For instance, Liz Davis in Carlisle is organising a Cycle Treasure Hunt, Mike and

Jane in Kettering are arranging a Scottish Fancy Dress Ride, Chris Henley in Basingstoke is putting on a FOUR CORNERS tea party and John Morphy in Leicester is doing a Four Corners of Leicester Bike Ride, with four 10 mile routes meeting up in the middle. Of course, many towns and cities have riders doing a ride to London for the Grand Finale at London Docklands, or joining in with Amsterdam–Colchester–London rides. Further details on the Grand Finale will be winging your way soon.

Well, that's about it on the rides side, except for the enclosed CTC Guidelines which should fill any gaps we've missed out.

Things to do Nearer 20th September

— Ask the ice-cream vendors if they'd like to come along with their vans on 20th September. Maybe try charging a small fee. Ditto hamburgers, tea, etc.
— Get your materials together for an I.T. display stall (optional and contact I.T. headquarters).
— Get use of a local large hall or find somebody to provide a marquee, to cover the unlikely eventuality of rain.
— Get the local bike shop(s) to put up displays and be available for bike maintenance on the day.
— Ask a couple of pubs on the route if they want to accept masses of cyclists. If they agree then put up banners: "FOUR CORNERS official PUB STOP".
— Persuade a local store(s) to give you a couple of prizes which can be used for various competitions on the day. An idea which always works well is to have a "Most Impressive Team" competition — the team which gives the best impression of fun and teamwork. You can then get each pub to put in a team, you get works teams, school teams and groups of neighbours. Getting different teams into a sense of competition is a great way of getting many more people to join in. Different teams have different ways of doing it: some dress in a set of smart suits, other all wear thematic fancy dress, you might get a six-man dragon or best of all you'll find a team all wearing FOUR CORNERS tee-shirts, with FOUR CORNERS shorts and a FOUR CORNERS banner.
— Marshalls will be needed for all the cross roads and turnings along the route.
— Photocopy maps of the area and highlight the route. This can be available at the 'checking in' desk.

Press & Publicity

The local newspaper won't ring you — you ring them. Make friends with a reporter, ask for him/her by name, promise to give them updates every week or so. If you are not getting a FOUR CORNERS mention every two weeks during July and August, every week in September, then switch to another reporter. Always suggest a fresh photo opportunity, e.g. shaking hands with the local mayor, visiting a school, a special profile of a local rider. The same applies to local radio, and on a longer timescale to T.V.

Whenever you contact the local press, indeed whenever you contact anyone, remember that you're contacting them apologetically to ask if they want to know, you tell them positively and friendly: "Our FOUR CORNERS ride on 20th September is getting really big now. We've got 120 riders signed up, the Round Table are organising marshalls and now we'd like you to provide special refreshment stalls. Our local newspaper is doing a feature, etc. etc.".

Always ask for the local press to slip your contact address in at the end of the article so that local riders can write for more info and to sign up. If you don't ask for the address to be put in it will not be put in.

Do not ever rely on articles in the local press to bring in riders or volunteers (unless of course you are Margaret Thatcher or Prince Charles). People join in because they are impacted from at least two directions: the first time they read in the papers or hear from friends about their local FOUR CORNERS ride sets the seed but nothing happens until they receive similar information from a different source a few days later. You must continue to put the ideas around by word of mouth.

Local media are often quite good at making appeals for volunteers to help the organisers of charity events. This is also of course good general publicity. The first time you ask try to get a general appeal put out, then if they're not prepared to run it several weeks in succession, try asking them to put out a special appeal for a volunteer to work on something specific like, typing, doing artwork, painting a banner or marshalling on 20th September.

Some people have been able to get the local news group to become closely involved as sponsors of the event — they get exclusive coverage and interviews in return for printing info sheets for riders and having their name on banners, etc.).

There's loads more itemised information on this in the more 'official' stuff below, but all I want to drive home is that you should deal with this side of things with as much enthusiasm as you can muster so those lovely press people will enjoy covering your story and come back for more ... read on for more about how to go about it:

The Publicity Machinery

Publicity will back up all your hard work, generating local interest in FOUR CORNERS. One of the best ways to gain publicity for FOUR CORNERS nationally is through local coverage, especially when it centres on a local event. (Did you know more people read their local papers than they read the nationals.) To help make your FOUR CORNERS ride a success on September 20th, you must put energy into local publicity and this must start NOW.

One of the key figures in your co-ordinating committee will be your publicity officer as outlined in the earlier guidelines. Try and appoint someone who is familiar with writing, e.g. someone who has an 'O' level in English!

Follow our guidelines and just ask us any questions you need answered.

Who to Contact

1. Newspaper
   - make a list of every local paper, including free ones
   - find out their deadlines and send a press release including relevant local details
   - get the name of the reporter so that future updates are sent to the same person
   - keep them up-to-date with new news
   - don't neglect those that don't publish first time round, keep going back
   - telephone your best contacts with any latest news
   - always make a follow up call to press releases
2. Local Radio/T.V.

A similar approach can be made here as for the press — but other points should be noted:

- make sure it's the same person who deals with initial contact and continuous follow-up
- be well briefed. All information must be positive and accurate. You may be on air 'live' and it is vital that key information get across clearly
- when answering questions, make sure you keep to the point. Your first sentence should sum up the answer to the question that has actually been asked, then if the interviewer looks happy for you to continue, bring in subsiduary points. Keep saying 'FOUR CORNERS', 'Sunday 20th September' and the time and place of the start
- check out the local hospital radio — they are usually desperate for interesting stories and you can often get a long interview — good practise for talking about Intermediate Technology and FOUR CORNERS and a way to gain confidence prior to local radio and television.

Writing Press Releases

We enclose a 'typical' press release and you could model your local press release on this, drawing on as much local detail as possible, such as the personalities involved in organising the local event and later those that will be cycling on the day.

At key times we will supply you with press releases from H.Q. that should be sent out with your own accompanying update.

Finally, on approaching the press, it is vital that you are prepared and that you work in as professional a way as possible. However, sometimes being really honest with those you are dealing with, saying you are new to this game and asking them for the best way in which to go about publicising FOUR CORNERS, can pay off — you will be the best judge of whether this approach is appropriate by how comfortable you feel in doing it.

For yet further information, there is the enclosed 'Contact Media' sheet (the latter was supplied by the Cyclists Touring Club, Godalming, Surrey and was excellent).

Photographs
We have a limited supply of black and white shots of the teams which can be despatched on request to the local newspaper (but see the last line of this paragraph). However, the local press are far more likely to be interested in you and your local event so try and create a picture for them. Make it interesting. It would be fun to get all the co-ordinating team involved in this. Give it a local flavour, i.e. in Scotland, you could get a shot of yourselves in your FOUR CORNERS T-shirts wearing a kilt riding bikes swinging your sporans gaily! Or, how about if you are from the seaside getting down to the pier off on the beach. Always donn your FOUR CORNERS T-shirts and get on your bike in the most imaginitive way for the occasion, (write to Dick for more details on imaginitive riding positions!). Newspapers, almost without exception send their own photographer round to photograph you.

Distribution of Publicity Material
Each Co-ordinator will be supplied with publicity material, but you will need to make sure this has your contact address on it. (Maybe you could persuade a local printer to print up some sticky labels for free with their company name in small print on each label in return.)

The following list of suggested venues for placing publicity material in your locality whether it be for volunteers or cyclists:
Shops, newsagents, pubs, local companies, post offices, schools, colleges, cafe pin boards, whole food shops, community centres, youth clubs, UHA (hostels and local groups), Sports clubs, (athletics, sports, tennis etc.) swimming baths, churches, cycle clubs (racing and touring) . . . I am sure you can think of lots more.